*Books by Ira Berkow*

OSCAR ROBERTSON: The Golden Year
BEYOND THE DREAM: Occasional Heroes of Sports
MAXWELL STREET: Survival in a Bazaar
THE DuSABLE PANTHERS

*In Collaboration:*

ROCKIN' STEADY: A Guide to Basketball
   and Cool (with Walt Frazier)
CAREW (with Rod Carew)

# Carew

*by Rod Carew*

*with Ira Berkow*

SIMON AND SCHUSTER
NEW YORK

Copyright © 1979 by Rod Carew and Ira Berkow
All rights reserved
including the right of reproduction
in whole or in part in any form
Published by Simon and Schuster
A Division of Gulf & Western Corporation
Simon & Schuster Building
Rockefeller Center
1230 Avenue of the Americas
New York, New York 10020

Illustrations appear between pages 64 and 65 and
pages 96 and 97.

Designed by Irving Perkins
Manufactured in the United States of America
    2   3   4   5   6   7   8   9   10


Library of Congress Cataloging in Publication Data

Carew, Rod, date.
   Carew.

      1. Carew, Rod, date.      2. Baseball players—
United States—Biography.   3. Minnesota Twins (Baseball
club)   I. Berkow, Ira, joint author.
GV865.C315A32      796.357'092'4 [B]      78-23278

ISBN 0-671-24236-9

*For my mother*
R.C.

# Foreword

WHEN ROY CAMPANELLA was being inducted into baseball's Hall of Fame, he said in his speech, "To be a good ballplayer, you've gotta have a lot of little boy in you. When you see Willie Mays and Ted Williams jumping and hopping around the bases after hitting a home run, and the carrying on around home plate, you realize they have to be little boys."

I believe what Campanella said is true, but not just for athletes. High achievers in any field, it seems to me, respond with the fresh enthusiasm of youth. I understand that Picasso, for example, is supposed to have been a devilish prankster, and Hemingway was a ham.

Ballplayers may be more obviously childlike than people in most other professions. We run around in caps and knickers. There's a lot of locker-room bantering. But the game itself—I still love to play it as much today as I did when I was growing up in the Canal Zone in Panama.

There is a special sensation in getting good wood on the ball and driving a double down the left-field line as the crowd in the big ball park rises to its feet and cheers. But I also remember how much fun I had as a skinny barefoot kid hitting a tennis ball with a broomstick on a quiet, dusty street in Gamboa.

To hit well—to do anything consistently well—you must love it. Hitting was the most important thing in my life growing up. That was all I dreamed about. I won a Ted Williams Model bat as Most Valuable Player in my Little League, and I actually took that bat to bed with me at night. When I was a minor-leaguer, I'd stand in front of the mirror in my room and swing the bat for hours. Someone told me that Williams did it, too, and once actually whacked a bed-post and broke down the bed. Williams exclaimed, "What power!" Well, I never broke down a bed. But I have knocked over a few lampshades, which may point up one difference between Ted and me—he was more of a long-ball hitter.

Anyhow, my wish to play in the major leagues came true; not only that, but I went on to hit as well as I could ever have hoped. In the summer of 1977—when my batting average was over .400—*Time* magazine did a cover story on me entitled "Baseball's Best Hitter." I don't know if that description is true, but I don't think anyone ever worked harder to earn the title.

The rewards for me have been terrific: a measure of fame, a degree of fortune and a tremendous amount of satisfaction.

But playing baseball has not been an endless procession of joys and successes for me. I was moody, intense, lonely, insecure, quick to anger. Several times in the minor leagues and the major leagues I was ready to jump the club and quit. Cooler and more mature heads than mine prevailed. I'm glad they did.

Although we are often set up on a pedestal by the public and made to seem like gods, professional ballplayers are also sometimes treated harshly. Those cheers which run goose bumps up and down your arms can turn to boos in an instant. I've had people throw bottles at me, curse me, threaten my life. I'm not unique in this regard. I think it is hard for many people to realize that a guy in the public eye, a celebrated athlete, is also a human being and capable of the same kinds of mistakes and foolishness as a college professor or a garbage collector.

I think it's important that people know the human side of public figures, especially ballplayers, because it is my experience that athletes have a tremendous impact on young people in our society. Sure, we're men playing a boys' game. But it has been said, and I agree, that someone like Pete Rose has more influence over American kids than any English teacher; a Tom Seaver is better known than any of our poets, and a Henry Aaron more admired than our scientists. It may be tooting my own horn, but I believe that somewhere in there among the ballplayers you might add the name of Rod Carew.

I remember in the winter of 1977 I was invited as a special guest to a Christmas party at the Hennepin County Home for Juveniles in Hopkins, Minnesota, not far from my home in Golden Valley. They were supposed to be tough street kids, but they seemed really excited to see me. "That's the champ!" "Hey, my main man!" I slapped palms with some of them. Others, though, stood back a little and checked me out. They checked out my blue blazer, the ring on my finger, the shine on my shoes—they checked out the way I was *looking* at them.

We sat around and talked. One of the kids told me how nice it was that I would take the time to visit their place. I asked why. "'Cause all you guys come from rich backgrounds," he said.

I looked at him for a moment. "A lot of ballplayers—a lot of people who have achieved something—got started with nothing,'' I said. "And I'm not ashamed to admit that I think my childhood was in some ways like yours.''

He was surprised, and I went on to explain. I don't know what significance, if any, some details of my background had for that kid, but I'm glad I told him. I'm glad he has just that much more information for dealing with the world.

In the following pages, I've tried to be candid about my life as a ballplayer and as a man. Some readers may wonder why I chose to speak so freely about my private feelings, and my personal life, and the friction I've had with some teammates and managers. Well, I thought that if it was worthwhile enough to tell my story at all, then I ought to tell it as honestly and fully as I could.

ROD CAREW
February, 1979

# Chapter I

AT ABOUT 7 o'clock in the evening of October 1, 1945, my parents, Olga and Eric Carew, boarded a Panama Railroad train and found seats in the car marked COLORED. Men going to a prizefight in Panama City filled much of the train. My parents weren't part of the sporting crowd. They were traveling from their home in Gatun, the Canal Zone, to Gorgas Hospital, about forty miles away, in Ancón. My mother was expecting. She preferred Gorgas, the largest hospital in Panama, to the neighborhood medical centers where facilities were poor and, she would later tell me, "everybody was dying so much." The train began to bump along. As soon as it did, my mother started feeling funny. A nurse named Margaret Allen, on her way to work at Gorgas, was in the car and suggested she lie down. My mother said, "I don't think I can wait." She couldn't. A few minutes later, Mrs. Allen delivered the baby. A conductor ran to the white section to see if a doctor was aboard. Dr. Rodney Cline came hurrying down the aisle. He finished the job, and my mother named me for the doctor: Rodney Cline Carew.

As I understand it, when word spread that a baby had been born on the train, a cheer went up from the sports fans on board. I wish I could remember hearing it, because it took many years before I did anything to merit a reception like that again.

Margaret Allen, a total stranger to my mother, became my godmother and by another strange set of circumstances would be important to my coming to the United States.

For some reason, my family and close friends in Panama always called me "Cline," while to everyone else I've been "Rod" or "Rodney." The first time my mother met my wife, Marilynn, she began talking about Cline, and Marilynn had no idea whom she meant. Marilynn thought they were carrying on two different conversations. When Marilynn asked her something about Rod, my mother answered something about Cline.

There is similar confusion about Panama, or at least some people's misconception of it. I've been asked, "What's it like to grow up in a grass hut in a jungle?" Well, I didn't grow up in a grass hut. I didn't grow up in a jungle.

The first years of my life were spent in Gatun, a little town of 2,000 people, beside the Panama Canal. When I was 8 we moved to Gamboa, a few miles south on the Canal. Gamboa's population was about 4,000. That was my home until I went to live in New York City at age 15.

In both Gatun and Gamboa we lived in wooden apartment buildings just a few minutes' walk from the Canal. The towns are so similar in my mind that when I talk about one I could just as easily mean the other. All through the day I could hear whistles and heavy foghorns from the vessels going through the locks. The Canal was dug right through the mountains and straight across the forty-two miles of the Isthmus of Panama from the Atlantic Ocean to the Pacific. Ships from all over the world sailed every day virtually right by my window. The Canal is a shortcut between oceans for these ships. Before the Canal was completed in 1914, those cargo and naval vessels had to go all the way down and around the southern tip of South America to get from one ocean to the other. Now they save weeks of travel by shortcutting through Central America.

People in Gatun and Gamboa would go up on a hill and watch the boats coming through the locks. It's a thrilling sight. We would watch the ships negotiate a bend in the Canal. Sometimes it looked as if these big ships would swing around in two motions, like some giant reptile. First the front end would appear, and then the tail. Their colorful national flags would be flying. The gates would rise up and drop. The sailors on deck would wave, and we'd wave back.

My grandfather worked on a tugboat in the Canal. My brother, Dickie, and I would take him his lunch, and then he might take us for a little spin in the tugboat. That was great. I remember bouncing up and down in the boat with the water spraying in my face. I'd have a little bag of mangoes and bananas with me, and the three of us—Grandpa, Dickie and I—would share it.

I lived with my father, mother, brother and two sisters (my oldest sister lived with my grandparents) in a second-floor five-room apartment. My parents had one room, and we four kids slept in one bedroom with two beds. We didn't have much in the home. The furniture was simple, what they call "native furniture"—just tables and chairs. My mother kept an altar of St. Jude in my bedroom. On the china closet was a small "striking" clock that chimed every hour. That was all we had in the way of ornaments.

The street I remember best was the one in Gamboa, where I lived from ages 8 to 15. The street had no name. In the black section of town, streets weren't named. Our

twelve-unit apartment building had a number, though—
number 282. The section of town we lived in was called the
Dust Bowl, because the buildings in the area had been
newly constructed by the Panama Canal Company, and all
the construction had created a lot of dust. So our address
was 282 Dust Bowl.

The streets were clean and pleasant and tarred. The
houses were generally gray, and the roofs sloped to keep
the water from the heavy tropical rains from accumulating.
What's unusual about the houses there is that they're built
on pillars. Under the buildings cars are parked, and women
do their wash in tubs there.

Only when I moved to New York did I appreciate how
spacious and pleasant the streets were there. Garbage
wasn't piled up, and people weren't all on top of one another and irritable. People spent a lot of time in the street,
sitting in front of their houses. Kids played; adults talked
and played dominoes. I remember at World Series time
everybody would plug in their radios and come down and
sit on boxes and play dominoes and listen to the game.
People couldn't wait to get out of church on Sunday and
come back to hear the game. During the week, men working on the Canal always returned at lunch hour to listen to
the Series.

Some men put up a big blackboard on the sidewalk, and
they'd write the lineups on it and keep score by innings.
Radios would be blasting, and you could hear the crowd
cheering in the ball park. On our street, there'd be a lot of
chatter. Then someone like Jackie Robinson or Roy Campanella—one of the black players—came up, and all the
people around me grew quiet. Then if the black player got
a hit—pandemonium! Everybody was jumping and clap-
ping. Then Jackie would steal a base and the place went
wild again! There I was, just a little kid, running around in
shorts and bare feet, taking it all in. Let me tell you, it sent
shivers up and down my spine.

Jackie Robinson was a hero down there. Even neighbors who knew nothing about baseball idolized him. This was the early 1950s. Only a few years before, Jackie had become the first black in major-league baseball; there still weren't very many others. My neighborhood was all black, so it was natural for the black players to be favorites.

The Canal Zone was segregated. When the Canal was built, starting in the late 1800s, a lot of whites from the southern states in America came down as organizers and laborers. They brought some of their racial attitudes with them. Workers were also recruited from the black populations of the West Indies—my grandparents included. From the start, there was discrimination. Living quarters, schools and even toilet facilities were separate. In the pay scale, a white truck driver might earn three times as much as a black truck driver doing the same kind of work. However, my grandfather told me that there was no discrimination in death: pneumonia, malaria, yellow fever and careless dynamite explosions took thousands and thousands of lives, white and black. When the Canal was finished, the people who had built it stayed on and worked the locks, the tugs, whatever jobs needed to be done. They were also set up in housing. The Canal Zone, which takes in about five miles on either side of the Canal, is under the jurisdiction of the U.S. Government, though the people living there are technically Panamanian citizens. (All that will change soon under the terms of the recent U.S.–Panama agreement.) To this day, white people live in one section, blacks in another. The commissary was where most of the people in Gamboa did their shopping. A partition divided it in half, and the whites shopped on one side, the blacks on the other. About a mile away was the town theater. Seating there was also segregated. Blacks sat in a roped-off area on the side.

I can't remember ever being called a racial name in Panama. But we knew enough to stay out of the white areas. When I was growing up, none of this bothered me. I ac-

cepted it as a way of life. We were in our own little sur-
roundings and we were happy. We weren't even envious of
the swimming pool the white kids had—the only swimming
pool in town—which my friends and I, being black, were
barred from. The sign on the swimming-pool fence read, NO
TRESPASSING; we knew that meant us. During the day we
might stand for a while at the fence and watch. Then we'd
go to the Canal to swim. Most of our parents hated our
swimming in the Canal, because there were so many
drownings there. The water gets rough when ships pass
through.

One day when I was about 13 we swam pretty far out to
the buoys. We decided to race back. I got caught in an
undertow and grew tired trying to swim out of it. I developed a cramp. I went down and was gulping water. I was
drowning! My brother, Dickie, who is two years older than
I, was swimming nearby. He shouted, "What's wrong with
you?" "I got a cramp," I said. He swam over. "Relax,
relax," he said. He said he'd dive under me. "You dog-
stroke and I'll dog-stroke," he told me. "Don't panic—
because if you kick me while I'm getting under you, it's all
over." I said, "Okay, okay." Slowly, we made it in.

That scare convinced me; I never swam in the Canal
again.

Although I didn't live in the jungle, there is a jungle in
Panama, and it wasn't far from our house. Sometimes we'd
walk the few miles to it and pick mangoes off the trees. The
jungle was beautiful. There were trees thick with hanging
vines, and there was a heavy underbrush. We'd see all
kinds of birds and flowers and monkeys and sometimes an
iguana and, in the distance, a jaguar. But the animals didn't
want to tangle with us any more than we did with them. We
worried about snakes, though. One time a big brown boa
constrictor dropped out of a tree and right onto a friend
walking in front of me. The snake wrapped itself around
him. Boas aren't venomous; they kill by crushing you. We

tried to fight the snake off with sticks. Another kid ran and got a policeman (we were at the edge of the jungle). The policeman came with a broomstick and pried the snake off. Believe me, it was a long time before I visited the jungle again.

But I really didn't care very much if I didn't go to the jungle, or didn't swim. For me, all other interests paled in comparison with baseball. From the time I began playing it, or versions of it, it was the most consuming thing in my life. All I wanted was to play baseball. When I was 5 and 6 and 7 years old, the kids in the neighborhood would use broomsticks for bats. We'd paint the broomsticks and make them look pretty. I painted mine black with yellow trimming. Then kids would put a name on it, the name of their favorite player. Everyone wrote down Jackie Robinson. I wrote it in orange.

We used tennis balls for baseballs and paper bags for gloves. We'd play in the streets. When there was no one around, I'd throw the ball against the steps of our apartment house. Catching it and throwing it and catching it. I could do it all day long. I wouldn't stop playing until the sun went down. I dreamed I was playing in the World Series before that crowd I heard on the radio.

As I grew older, I began playing baseball in the big open field near my home. With real bats and balls and gloves. I began playing with older boys. I was small and thin, and at first they let me in only when they were short some players. I brought a bat once that my mother had given me for Christmas. She worked for a white family, and they had given her the bat. Well, we were playing and then a few older guys showed up and they kicked me out of the game. I got mad. I took my bat home. They chased me all the way back.

Funny thing, but as far back as I can remember, I could hit a baseball. I would always say to myself, You can't get me out, I'm the best hitter. And I remember people watch-

ing us play and saying, "Damn, that boy Carew can sure do
it." When I was small, I could even hit for distance. I don't
know how or why, I just could. The commissary building
was behind the open field, and at the far end of the commissary outdoor movies were shown at about 6 o'clock in the
evening. I once hit a ball over the commissary and into the
movie crowd. The guy I hit it off of was named Wendell,
and he lives in Oakland today. I saw him one day when the
Twins were playing there. He came to the ball park and
called out to me. It was good to see him after all those
years. Wendell reminded me about that ball I had hit off
him.

He said, "Rod, what's happened to you?"

I said, "What do you mean?"

"Well, you've gone from a power hitter to a line-drive
hitter."

"Wendell," I said, "I guess the caliber of pitching has
changed." And we laughed.

Throughout these early years the man who meant the
most to me was Joseph French, my uncle. He had been a
Caribbean decathlon champion in the late 1930s. He was
now the gym teacher in my grade school. And what an
imposing man: six-three, broad-shouldered, powerful-look-
ing, with a big voice that told you he meant business. He
was a disciplinarian. No one got away with anything with
Mr. French. He encouraged me, and I know he told people
that I was "a natural." He started me in the Little League
in Gamboa. He saw that I got a uniform even though I
couldn't afford to buy one. I painted the outfield fences and
the seats and fixed up the field—the whole works—to pay
him back.

I couldn't wait to play. God, it was something. Uniforms,
a nice field and people in the stands cheering you. I played
shortstop and second and pitched. But I hit so well right
from the start that some people claimed I was older than 12
and it wasn't fair for me to be in the league. They couldn't

believe someone my age could hit so far. I wound up with a .667 batting average.

Mr. French began taking me to play against older boys and even men in the interior, the name we use for the rest of Panama—the Panama away from the Canal Zone. I kept hitting. I had complete confidence with a bat in my hands. The stiffer the competition, the greater the challenge.

When one game ended, I'd travel to play in another. And if there wasn't a game, I'd be dragging someone to pitch batting practice to me, or hit me ground balls. It didn't matter if it was 105 degrees in the shade, which it sometimes was.

When I was on the baseball field I felt I was king. I could outdo any of my friends on the ball field. This was so important to me because, growing up, it was the only place I felt at ease with the other kids.

I didn't have any really close friends when I was small. My home life was never happy, and that affected everything else in my life. I wasn't happy at home because of my father. I got along well with my three sisters and my brother, and I was Mother's pet. But I never felt my father liked me. He never gave me a thing, and he never taught me a thing. The memories that stick out about my father are of him whipping me and grounding me all the time. I didn't really have much to look forward to except baseball. My father knew that, and for no reason at all he would ground me. We lived near the park, and I could see the kids playing from the window. I used to sit there and cry. I used to think the only reason my father grounded me was that he knew how much I loved baseball.

When I was on the field, I was so thankful to be there that I never wanted to leave. Other kids might bring a sandwich with them. I wasn't interested in that when I was on the field. I was interested in nothing but playing. It was my private domain.

When I got on the field, I forgot about my father. I could

block him out. Sometimes I'd lose track of the time. And if I wasn't home when I was supposed to be I thought, Oh, I won't be allowed to leave the house for a week.

My father's name is Eric; my mother is Olga. The kids in our family happened to call our parents by their first names.

We lived in fear of Eric. He was a lean man, about six feet three, with a thin mustache. I'd look out the window and I could tell just by the way he came up the sidewalk whether we were in for trouble or not. If he was walking easily, then things might be okay. If he was swaggering and wore a frown, he was in a foul mood. He was that way especially when he was drinking. He had a high-pitched voice. He'd come into the house cussing. Loudly. So loudly the whole neighborhood heard the screaming and cussing. It was horrible. He always had a kind of glassy look in his eyes, whether he had had a drink or not. I will never forget the look of hatred on his face for me. He would call me "Sissy," and he'd say, "I'm gonna whup you till you whistle." I believed he wanted to really hurt me, and he did. Eric himself had a loud whistle that you could hear all over the block. He'd put two fingers in his mouth and really let go. He whistled when he wanted us home. We usually heard it and got home with the speed of light. If we didn't, we'd get whacked. If we did, we might still get whacked. He used a knotted cord from a pressing iron to whip me, and sometimes the welts he raised were bad. In gym class at school, we'd have to take our shirts off. This was mortifying to me because of the way my back might look. Mr. French, the gym teacher, understood this and often allowed me to keep my shirt on. I was the only boy who did. That was nearly as embarrassing as having the shirt off. When you're a kid, you want to be like everyone else. Anything that's different is embarrassing.

He sometimes hit my mother with blows meant for Dickie or me. She'd jump in front of us and take the blows for us. She was unbelievable. She never raised her voice.

She stood there and would begin to sing gospel songs. It infuriated him. He'd be screaming, and she'd be singing "Nearer, My God, to Thee" or "Amazing Grace."

Eventually my mother left him, but for years she had the impression that when you get married you're together with that person for the rest of your life, no matter what.

Why was he the way he was? Sometimes I wondered if he had flipped. Maybe the drinking. Maybe he felt trapped by the responsibility of having five kids and didn't know how to relieve his tension any other way. My mother says that in the first several years of their marriage, he was a fine, "nice" man. He was good-looking, and he had a beautiful smile. But for some reason, at about the time I came along, he changed.

I was embarrassed at how poor we were. Eric worked as a painter on the Canal. He'd paint bridges, buoys, ships and so on. He had money, but he never left much of it at home. Luckily, the rent was taken directly from his paycheck by the Canal Zone Company. What we lived on was what my mother earned as a domestic in Panama City for a white family named Fortner. She was paid a dollar a day. They were nice people and gave us gifts, and sometimes they'd give my mother a bonus. My mother also played the lottery, like most other people in Panama. She called me her good-luck charm. Every Sunday she woke me up and sent me to buy her lottery ticket. It was amazing the number of times we won. It seemed like every Sunday, though it couldn't have been because we had so little. I remember wearing shoes that were so ripped up I had to walk alongside the walls of the school hall so that the other kids wouldn't see my soles flapping.

Sometimes we hardly had enough to eat. We lived on rice and peas. Sometimes Eric would come home with chicken or pastries, and he'd eat them himself. We didn't sit around watching him. We went about our business. But we sure knew what he was doing. I remember days when I was so hungry I went to a neighbor and borrowed sugar and made myself a drink—sugar and water. That was all I'd have.

It got to the point at which my mother had just one nice dress and wore it to church on Sunday. But she went to church only every other Sunday because she felt embarrassed to have to wear the same dress *every* Sunday.

Eric has said that he grew up with a father who was a strict disciplinarian. It is a tradition in Latin homes that you respect your parents. But parents, to get this respect, must give the feeling that they love their kids. I never got this from Eric.

There were days, and weeks, when he didn't show up at home. No explanation. That was heaven to us. The most important thing in my mother's life now was keeping the children together. Her mother had told her, "No matter what, Olga, always keep your family together." Every so often we went to stay at my grandmother's house in Gatun. For example, when my father came home once and got angry and threw everyone out of the house and locked the doors—we went to Grandmother's.

On Friday nights my mother would give the kids ten cents apiece to go to a movie. My father didn't want us going to the movie. He wanted to punish us. My mother said, "They're good kids; they're going." He'd stalk out of the house like a lion. When we got to the theater, he was there waiting and sent us home. When we told Olga, she marched us right back to the theater. "The kids can at least go to a movie one night a week," she said.

One time he said, "They're my kids too, and I can discipline them."

Olga said, "They're not yours—not the way you treat them." He resented her saying that. He'd tell her she'd always loved the kids more than she loved him. She denied that; she said that he had forced her to change when he began to whip the kids. And the more my mother stood up to Eric, the more we ignored him.

But he was my father. I wished he could be like other fathers. I'd look at kids I went to school with and see their fathers teaching them things or taking them to a ball game. My father never took me anywhere. Never came to a Little League game. Never showed me anything. I don't remember ever getting a Christmas gift from my father.

My mother, meanwhile—well, she was the world for me. She would buy a pair of shoes or a shirt and she'd say, "Take care of this. We don't know when we'll be able to get another one." So I cleaned my shoes every night, and I ironed my shirts and pants.

Sometimes my mother would come to us and say, "Well, I've worn my shoes down to slippers. So nobody ain't gettin' nothin' today but me. I'm gettin' a pair of shoes that I need." I recall that the shoes she bought cost $1.99 a pair.

I remember when I had just one pair of shoes. I had no sneakers. When we had gym class and would play soccer, I took off my shoes because I had to preserve them, and played in my bare feet. I'd kick the ball with my bare toes, and I'd run over the rocks with my bare feet. I hated the whole thing.

To this day, I'm careful with my clothes, with everything I own. When I come in from infield practice, for example, I have a towel on the bench and I brush off my baseball shoes. It was interesting when I came to the Twins' spring training camp in my rookie year of 1967. There was a story in either the Minneapolis or the St. Paul paper about me, saying I wasn't the typical rookie who is flashy and immediately goes out and buys a big car and lots of clothes and has a gold tooth. What the writer meant was that I wasn't the typical *black* rookie, or what he wanted to believe was the typical black rookie. I received a $5,000 bonus to sign with the Twins. I put most of it into the bank. The rest I gave to Olga. She had taught us to be careful with our possessions and our money.

My mother wasn't above whipping us either. But when

she did, it was different. We knew it was for a good reason, for something we had done wrong.

She watched over us like a mother eagle. She told us to stay out of the white neighborhood, because black kids found there would be picked up by the police. She'd say, "When the law touch you, they're forever touching. So don't let them start."

And she didn't want us swimming in the Canal. One time she was home ironing and something inside told her Dickie was swimming in the Canal. She dropped everything and started running to the Canal. She said she was so worried she felt as if she were running backward. Dickie was there, and she whipped the daylights out of him.

I'd come home late sometimes and she'd get nervous. I walked into the house once with Mr. French, her brother-in-law. It was past dinner. And she took the strap to me. Not badly—just some "little whops," as she called them.

Mr. French said, "Leave the boy alone, Olga; he was with me, playing ball."

"I don't care," she said. "He knows I worry."

My mother, though, always encouraged me to play ball—*after* my chores were done.

I never got into the kind of trouble some other kids get into—petty thievery, playing hooky, that kind of thing. I was sociable enough, and played ball with the other kids, of course, but I always wanted to go my own way. I didn't like their talking about my home life, or razzing me about it. I shrank from talking with anybody. I was afraid the subject would come up. So I was happy to be by myself, or with my brother.

In school, I had an aptitude for art. I guess there is a streak of that in my family, since my father works with paints. And I was a pretty fair student. So I was never a problem along those lines either.

When I was 10 years old, my mother bought me a bicycle. Every boy in the neighborhood had a bicycle except

Dickie and me. We wanted bikes too. She finally bought them on credit. I remember that the first time I ever really went anywhere with the bicycle was to run away from home. This was after a whipping from my father. I got on my bicycle and just pedaled and pedaled along the highway for miles. The wind was hitting my face, and the tears were coming down. I finally stopped by a hill and found a tree, climbed up and stayed in the tree for a couple of hours and cried. I decided after a while that I'd better get home—since there was really no place to run to. Whenever I was unhappy after that, I rode my bike out to that spot and climbed into that tree.

It seemed like an endless flight. I kept hoping that one day I could be going to something better.


I WAS always getting sick. The least little thing, and I'd get a fever. This displeased my father. He called me a weakling. Or he'd call me a sissy. Especially when I told him I didn't like girls. I'm 10, 11 years old. Now, what boy that age is going to admit he likes girls? My father said, "Don't like girls! Only sissies don't like girls." To prove my manhood, I was determined not to cry in front of him. When he hit me, I'd bite my lip so I wouldn't cry. I bit it so hard I almost bit a hole in my lip. Even though I didn't admit it, and even though I did block him out of my mind when I was playing, I was playing for his approval, nonetheless. I knew he knew I was a good ballplayer. Everyone in the neighborhood began talking about it. So one time he wanted to get into the act. It was the one and only time he ever came around when I was playing—he came to get me *out* of the game. He was shouting to Mr. French.

"He's living under my roof," said Eric. "I pay the rent. He comes home when I want him to."

"But the kid wants to play, Eric. There's no harm. And besides, the game's almost over."

I sat there quietly, staring toward the field. Eric finally stormed off, and I finished the game.

One time, I even played softball against Eric. He was a good fast-pitch softball pitcher. But by the time I was 12 or 13 I was a better player than he was. I wanted to do well against him. Did I! When I came to bat, I heard the other guys hollering, "Show the old man you can hit, Cline." I got three hits off him. When I got to first base, I wanted to steal on him. It's not easy to steal in fast-pitch softball. But I stole. And I scored. I was just breezin' around. Oh, it felt good. And guys got on him and kidded him about my play.

He never acknowledged that I was good. Never gave me a compliment. God, I think I would have kissed his feet if he had only said—just one time—"You're a nice player, son." But I didn't exist as far as he was concerned.

I came down with rheumatic fever when I was 11, and I almost died. For nearly three months I was kept in an isolation ward, and then I was moved to a ward with other kids. I had wild nightmares. I saw airplanes flying at me, and I heard bombs and people shooting at me, and someone was always chasing me. And I'd get up and run down the hall and run out of the hospital. I was delirious with the fever. They'd bring me back, and then a net was put over my bed to keep me down. I remember they used to pack me in ice in a tub to break the fever. Oh, I hated that. And I remember I used to wonder, God, am I losing my mind? I used to think, I'm going nuts. I was terrified.

When my mom came to visit, I'd ask her, "What's wrong with me?" She'd say, "You're sick. They're trying to find out what's wrong. Everything will be all right." That comforted me. "Everything will be all right." She has always said that, and it has usually comforted me.

I couldn't figure out what was happening to me. I knew I couldn't go out and play ball like the other kids. The doctors came and pounded around my chest and back. I didn't know why. I didn't know what this sickness meant.

My mother was working about forty miles away, and she used to stay at the Fortners' house Monday through Friday, but when I got sick she took the long train ride to the hospital almost every day for six months. She'd bring comic books and candy. She'd always pat my head and check how warm I was. If I was sweating, she'd wipe my forehead. She'd sit down and doze off in the chair. I had watched the door all day waiting for her to walk in with her shopping bag in her hand and with something in it for me. The few times she didn't come, I'd cry until I fell asleep. I felt totally deserted. In those six months, Eric never visited me.

The only thing I can remember about getting better was that they moved me from the isolation ward.

I remember leaving the hospital. In the hallway, my mother pointed to a tall man with blond hair. She said, "That's the doctor who saved your life. Go over and thank him." I was shy, but I went to him and hugged him around his leg. I looked up and said, "Thanks for saving my life," and then I ran back to my mother.

I couldn't wait to get back to playing baseball. My brother likes to tell the story of when I arrived home. He says when he saw me I looked "white as a sheet, excuse the expression." I was weak, after half a year in a hospital. And I saw he had his baseball glove and he was leaving the house. "Where you going?" I asked. He said, "Parallel Park." We had four parks in different parts of town—Parallel, Dust Bowl, Front Street and Church Square. I said, "I'm going too." My mother told me not to leave the house. But I had to get out. I had to play. Dickie said he didn't want to be responsible for my going outside. I said, "Look, let's don't go together. That way you're not responsible." He said okay. He stopped by to pick up some friends, and I was already at the park when he arrived. It was so good to feel that bat in my hands again.

Now, at Parallel Park there is a hill that begins to rise just beyond second base. During the course of the game I hit a ball that bounced up the hill, and as I was coming around second base I saw I'd have a close play at third. As I came in, the throw hit me smack in the back of the head. I went down. I heard Dickie holler out, "Oh, no, he's dead!" I got up right away and raced toward home plate and scored. Everyone came over and wanted to know how I was. I was fine. I was great. I was playing ball again.

For the rest of the day, Dickie was looking at me kind of funny. When we got home, he asked how I was. "Nothin' wrong with me," I said. Later he would tell me that it had ruined his day. He had kept waiting for an aftereffect. He had thought I was going to faint on him and that we'd be found out.

But seeing the reaction of amazement from the kids, that I could take a blow on the head like that, began to give me some confidence that I was no weakling, despite my illnesses.

Maybe that developing attitude had something to do with the one and only fight I can remember getting into in my school days.

There was a kid named Butch in my class. A big kid, kind of a bully. A lot of kids were afraid of him. And he was always razzing me. Sometimes he'd shove me around. I'd just walk away. One time, though, he pushed me hard and I got mad. I said, "One day we're going to have it out." I don't know why I said it, but a lot of kids heard it. So I was on the spot. For the rest of the day kids would come by and say, "Hear you and Butch gonna fight after school." I thought, Gee, I didn't make any definite arrangements. I just said to Butch, *One day* we're going to have it out. Well, word got around like wildfire, so I couldn't back out. The kids were anticipating the big fight. They couldn't wait to get out of school and see it. The school I went to, an all-black school, was a wooden two-story building on pillars. The area under the schoolhouse was used for kids at recess when it rained. Now we were supposed to meet under the school for the fight.

As soon as the bell rang, the kids all gathered around Butch and me. We decided—I guess *they* decided—to find some spot away from the school so that teachers couldn't break it up. A big group of kids followed Butch and me. We got in between some buildings and the kids formed a circle. Everybody kept yelling, "Give 'em some room." The only room I wanted was room to run. But we squared off, and he threw a punch and knocked me down. My mouth was bleeding. I was scared. Jeez, what am I in for? He hit me again. And then something happened. I just felt blind rage. I went at him and started throwing punches, and I knocked him down. He got up and I knocked him down again. The kids were all jumping up and yelling and screaming, "Hit 'im again, hit 'im again!" I knocked him down again, and now his mouth was bleeding. His clothes had been all cleaned and pressed and now he was dirty. Then the safety patrol came and broke it up.

After that, I felt I had really accomplished something. I was about 12 now, and I felt proud that I hadn't backed down from this guy. Not that the kids had given me a choice—but in my mind, after the results, I gave myself credit for not backing down.

The next day Butch and I got called into the principal's office and got our hands whipped. The principal had a thick leather belt and he just went *whack, whack, whack*. Feeling a belt was nothing new to me. And besides, I had a new stature in school. My hands hurt a little, but it was really nothing. After that, Butch and I became pretty good friends. Not really close, but we walked to school together, and we talked.

Actually, in fifteen years in Panama, the only close friend I had was Carlos Long. I admired him because even when he was very young, his father used to take him under cars and the two of them would work on fixing them. His dad was a mechanic. I envied their closeness. His family was poor too. Carlos and I became good friends and we did a lot together—went to movies, went to school together, and I used to ride his bike before I had mine. He was the only kid who would let me use his bike. The others were all very touchy about their bikes.

At home, I loved to sit by the radio in our kitchen and listen to the baseball games in the United States. They came in very clear on the Armed Services station. I'd keep score. And I'd hear that crowd and tell my mother that one day I'd be playing in front of crowds like that. I wasn't sure how I was going to do it, since I figured you had to get to the United States one way or another. But I had no idea how I was ever going to do that.

# Chapter II

THE STATES seemed like the most distant place in the world. I had seen a lot of movies about New York and California and the big buildings and the fast life, and I seemed so small and poor and so far away from it all. But some people from my hometown had moved up north to the States. One of them was my godmother, Mrs. Allen. I had never met her until she came back for a visit one time and she wanted to see me. We talked, and she asked if I'd ever want to come to the States. "Yes," I said, "I sure would." She said maybe she could help. But she didn't say how. I was 14 years old then, and I was playing in the senior leagues and had played on the Paraiso High School team and done well. Now, I had heard that scouts from the big leagues sometimes came around and watched games and sent reports back north. I had never seen one of these scouts. I wasn't sure if they existed. But if they did, I knew

I had to be awfully lucky. First, to have one at a game I played, and second, to play well enough that particular day to impress the guy. Whoever he was.

By now, to leave Panama was also my mother's dream. She had decided that the best thing for the family would be to get away from Eric. She also realized that the opportunities for her children were limited in Panama. I knew a lot of kids who graduated from high school and then sat around doing nothing because so few jobs were available. Others—smart kids, too—had menial jobs.

About a year after Mrs. Allen and I spoke about the States, she called my mother at work at the Fortners'. Mrs. Allen said that the papers for her to come had been cleared. She said, "All you need is the $300 the American Consulate requires of immigrants to get into the country, and the $162.50 plane fare." My mother was excited and grateful, but her heart sank. She didn't have the money. She went home and wondered where she could raise the $300 and the plane ticket. As it turned out, my uncle Clyde Scott then in the Air Force in Hawaii mailed her the money.

Leaving the family worried Olga. She never wanted us kids separated from her, but this was the only chance to get us to the United States. She planned to earn enough money to send for the four of us as soon as possible. (My eldest sister, Sheridan, or Sugar, was married and living in Panama City.) Deanna, or Nannie, would cook for Dickie, me and the youngest, Dorine, and my father, when he was around. Actually, we all were pretty self-sufficient and all of the kids could cook. I wasn't your basic four-star French chef, but I could boil up some rice when the occasion demanded.

In New York City, my mother worked in a purse factory as a floor lady. Her salary was only $32 a week. She lived in an inexpensive room and saved almost all of her earnings. After a few months, she had enough to send for one of us. Mrs. Allen said, "Send for two. One of them will be

Rod. I'm his godmother and I haven't done anything for this boy since I christened him, so I'll pay for him to come.'' Then they put the names of my sisters and brother in a hat and shook it up, and it came out Dickie three times. So Dickie and I were sent for.

There was a lot of excitement. We ran around getting our papers fixed and our pictures taken for the visas. Everyone knew we were going to the States, and all the kids—well, they were happy and sad and, I'm sure, envious. Everyone would like to go to a beautiful place like America, but not everyone could afford it. Mr. French helped us with the papers. He knew people who worked on passports and folders and anything else we needed; he'd call ahead for us.

My dad took Dickie and me to get our final papers for emigration. He also bought each of us a tie. I couldn't believe it. I was also fearful. I hoped he wouldn't get into one of his moods and change his mind at the last minute and say, ''You guys aren't going.'' I never knew what to expect from him.

I was so happy to be leaving. God, I was finally getting away—away from Eric. At this time, there were no plans for him to go to America.

On June 30, 1961, Dickie and I went to the airport. I was feeling like a millionaire. My mother had bought me a suit, the first suit I had ever had on. And I had never been on a plane before. Can you imagine? As the plane headed toward the clouds, I really felt I was on my way to heaven.

When we approached New York, it was nighttime. It was the most amazing thing I had ever seen. All those lights! For miles! Dickie and I had our noses pushed against the window.

We were anxious to see Olga. We looked all over the airport but didn't see her. She was supposed to meet us— but no one was there. We were two lost kids. We had Mrs. Allen's phone number and called her. Mrs. Allen said that there had been a mixup because our plane had landed early.

My mom and uncle were on their way to the airport, but she told us not to wait. We got a cab, gave the driver her address and were on our way.

When we pulled off the highway and into the area where she lived, in Washington Heights, in Upper Manhattan, the first thing I saw was a guy going through a garbage can for food. I had never seen anything like that. I had never seen anyone eating out of the garbage, except dogs. That wasn't the America I had seen in movie clips.

It was a wonderful reunion when my mother and Uncle Clyde showed up from the airport. My mother had rented a small apartment at 145th Street and Eighth Avenue. It was mostly a black and Spanish neighborhood, with a lot of bodegas and liquor stores. The difference between that neighborhood and the one in Panama was incredible. First of all, there were so many people. Then there were the papers and garbage scattered in the streets. It was summertime, so people were sitting on stoops, and I saw men on the street drinking wine and whiskey. I saw guys on park benches sleeping, with empty bottles on the ground beside them. None of this was in the movies of America I had seen in Panama.

I enjoyed the subway, though. I loved the way the doors opened and closed and the people rushed in and out as in a precision drill. My brother wasn't as interested in going around the city, so I went alone. I didn't mind that. I was used to being alone. I went all over town, to Radio City Music Hall, the Empire State Building, the Statue of Liberty. I saw shiny tiles and clean streets and nice stores and elegantly dressed people. But when I returned home, I returned to a completely different world.

Being so protective, my mother was very much concerned about us.

We learned that you couldn't leave your doors open in New York the way we did in Panama. And the weirdest things went on. One time some guys raided the neighborhood police station to free some friends locked up there. It was like a jailbreak out of the Old West. I'd never seen so many policemen running around the block.

Olga warned us about being out after dark. And she built up a fear in us about the muggings and violence and getting into trouble. And about the dope. None of us had really seen dope addicts before. In the first building we lived in, we had to share a bathroom, which was one flight down. Sometimes you'd go in there and you'd see someone sleeping in the bathtub. The first or second day we were there, my mother came upstairs and said to Dickie and me, ''Come downstairs with me.'' We didn't know what this was about. She showed us a guy in the tub sleeping. There was a needle on the floor, and alongside it were pieces of bloodstained cotton.

She said, ''See that? If you boys—if you ever do something like that, I'll die.'' She opened her eyes wide. That meant she was serious. She used to try to intimidate us by opening her eyes wide. As far as I know, none of the kids ever did anything that might hurt her. In most cases, if she asked us to do something, she never had to ask twice. We had such respect and admiration for her. We knew what she went through with Eric to keep the family together. How could we do something to disappoint her? I felt that way, and I believe all of us felt that way.

We'd run into kids from Panama in New York. I saw a lot of them turn to dope. I remember one guy whom I'll call Lorenzo. I was friendly with him in Gamboa. He came from a good family, went to school and had been a good kid. In New York, he used to come over to our house a lot. He was my brother's age, and the three of us would sit and play cards. Then all of a sudden, he began to change. He started looking as if he were in a daze. He suddenly looked older. ''What's the matter with you?'' I asked one day. He said he was getting high every now and then. After a while, he just stopped coming around the house. Dickie and a friend went looking for him. They found him one day in a stupor on the street. He said he was hooked on drugs and didn't want their help. I don't think they ever saw him again.

Our family was close, and everyone seemed to be looking out for the others. My uncle Clyde Scott, my mother's brother, was a major influence on me. He was about 28 and had recently come out of the Air Force. Like Mr. French, he was a stern man, but a guy you respected. No messing around with him. I don't think we had been in New York a week when he took Dickie and me for a walk through the streets and laid down the do's and don'ts. I remember he told us:

"There's nothing out there in the streets.

"You came here to make something of yourselves.

"You didn't come here to disgrace the family.

"You didn't come here to get into things that you don't need to get into.

"Don't eat from someone you don't know—you have no idea what's in the food.

"If there's something you want, go to somebody in the family."

I remember we crossed a bridge about a mile from our apartment and we walked around Yankee Stadium. Uncle Clyde hadn't finished instructing us yet:

"You've always been selective in your friends; continue to be that way.

"We carry ourselves properly, and we do what we know is right.

"Know what you can do. Don't try to follow other people or try to outclass anyone.

"Know within yourself what you're capable of doing and try to do it.

"Don't let anything like women or drink stand in your way."

Now, that was laying the law down.

Although our father gave us little, the kids in our family were fortunate that we did have strong and good male influences that we respected, particularly Mr. French and Uncle Clyde. In later years, I would have several more.

When I started playing pro baseball, Clyde used to preach, "All these guys that you see in the major leagues, they're not out there because they didn't work at it. Work is the only way you can hope to get there."

My brother and I got jobs. He was employed in Macy's department store as a clerk in the paint section in the basement. I found a job in a grocery store as a stock boy. After I got paid the first time, I went alone to the Apollo Theater, a legendary place for music. It's on 125th Street in Harlem. I wanted to see James Brown. I had the money in the top pocket of my jacket, and three guys came up the street toward me and one bumped into me. "Oh, excuse me," he said. Well, I walked up to the ticket window and went for my money—it was gone. Those guys had pickpocketed me. It was one of my initiations into New York City.

That first summer, I went to the beach at Coney Island and the movie theaters. That's always been my big thing. I love the movies. I enjoyed detective movies best, and Charlie Chan was my favorite.

Another step toward the Americanization of the Carews was taken by Mrs. Allen. She thought we should discontinue calling our mother "Olga." "Here," she said, "you call your mother 'Mom.' "

Mrs. Allen also was instrumental in choosing the high school that I would attend. She gave me a choice of three and explained the virtues of each. Being the scholar that I was, I chose the school closest to my home, George Washington.

Mrs. Allen tried in another way to prepare me for school in New York. In Panama, I had gone to schools in which Spanish was the primary language. Most people spoke English as well, but the English spoken by the people I grew up with was heavily accented because of the strong West Indian influence there. It was broken English, and with a lilt.

Mrs. Allen wanted me to learn to speak English well. She said we wouldn't get anywhere in America by speaking Spanish. So no Spanish was spoken around her house. And even when her nieces and nephews were around and started speaking Spanish, she'd tell them to stop.

Change is hard. I guess there's nothing harder. I felt comfortable with the way I spoke, and it was hard to correct it. But I tried. I became conscious of what I said and how I said it. When I caught myself saying something wrong, I'd stop and say it slowly. Like the word, "ask." I used to mix up the last two letters and say "aks." A lot of foreign-born people and blacks who aren't careful with the language say "aks." Sometimes, even today, when I come to it, I have to slow down to say it right. And I had the darnedest time with the "th" 's because we'd never say "this" or "that." It would be "dis" and "dat." "H" 's were also a problem. I couldn't come right out and say, "He has to go." I'd drop at least one of the "h" 's, and it would come out "He 'as to go." "Thick" would come out "tick." Instead of "building" I'd come out with "billin'," and I'd say "human beans" when I was talking about human beings. My sentence structure wasn't much better.

There was one teacher at George Washington named Mrs. Donohue, an elderly lady, who took an interest in kids from the Latin countries. We'd stay a half hour or forty-five minutes after school with her working on English. I started picking it up. I couldn't understand how so many other kids were content with speaking broken English. They knew the difference. They just didn't want to work on it.

Some people may not realize how difficult it is to begin *thinking* in a second language. I had trouble trying to analyze in English and not in Spanish what I had read in class.

At first I found myself not participating much in school. As time went on, I got into it.

The New York public schools generally place an immigrant student back a grade. They say the teaching is different in the foreign country. I wonder if Henry Kissinger, who entered George Washington when he came from Germany in the 1930s, had the same problem. Well, I was supposed to be in the twelfth grade, my senior year. But I was put into the eleventh grade. I was unhappy about it, but had no choice. It didn't bother my mother, though. All she wanted was for me to get a high school diploma. That was very important, especially to someone like her who had never gone past the seventh grade. She wanted me to go on to college, too.

I missed Panama a lot during my first year in New York. I'd walk around the streets and wish I were back home in familiar territory. The whole transition was tough—everything from the language to the overcrowding to the rats. The first time I saw a rat was in that bathroom we shared in the first apartment we lived in. I had seen something rustling around in a large paper bag. I looked in and saw this animal. I went upstairs and told my brother, "I think there's a puppy downstairs in a bag." He came down with me. He looked and then fell apart laughing. "That's no dog—that's a rat, man," he said. Shortly after, we moved into a nicer apartment and my encounters with rats were reduced to a minimum.

I've always had the capacity to sink into my own private world when I need to. I can compare it to baseball. When I'm at the plate, it's me, the ball and the pitcher. Everything else is blocked out. No matter what else is going on in my life, I can usually eliminate those thoughts when I'm concentrating at bat. A catcher for the White Sox named Jim Essian once said about me that he has never seen anyone so *quiet* at the plate. Like I'm tunneled in. Well, that's the way I was at times in New York. I enjoyed staying around the house. I used to go into my room and put on the stereo. I'd put on mostly Latin and calypso music, the music I had listened to back home, and I'd blast it away. I'd put my books down and just lie around and listen. Or I'd study with the music on.

My life was school, work, home. When the bell rang at three, I'd go home; then I'd go to work, finish at nine and return home. I never wanted to run around. I was shy and never pushed myself on anyone to make friends. There were times when I wanted to get involved—even with girls. But I couldn't walk up and start talking. And so I never dated.

In New York I played basketball in a playground near my house, and in summer I swam at Coney Island. But for two years I did not play baseball. I didn't try out for the school team because I was too involved in keeping my studies up. In summer, I didn't know where to go to play with anyone. I didn't know anyone who played baseball. And there was no room to play baseball in the neighborhood where I lived.

Yet I still had a burning desire to be a professional baseball player. And perhaps that was another reason why the streets held no temptation for me, and why I didn't experiment with liquor or drugs. I knew what I wanted.

Although we lived near Yankee Stadium and the Polo Grounds, I went to only one baseball game in my first two summers in New York. I watched games on television and that satisfied me. Also, I didn't have much chance to go to games. I couldn't go on weekday afternoons because of school, I couldn't go on weekends because I worked and I didn't go at night because my mother didn't want us walking the streets alone after dark. But one Sunday afternoon my brother and I saw the San Francisco Giants play. I'd heard about the Polo Grounds primarily because of Willie Mays and the New York Giants. Now the Mets played in the Polo Grounds, and Mays was with San Francisco. On the day I went, I think everybody was there to see Willie play. I remember I sat out in the bleachers to watch the guys come out. The locker room was situated under the bleachers. I just wanted to get a glimpse of the players, and Willie. Many of the kids were yelling for autographs. I wasn't. I wasn't into that. I just wanted to see if Mays actually looked the way he did on the baseball cards, with the big smile. When he came out, everyone was shouting, "Say hey!" That's what they called him, "The Say Hey Kid." Everybody used to walk around the streets yelling, "Say hey!" But when he came out, he wasn't smiling. And he wasn't signing autographs. Maybe he was in a bad mood, but then I decided that he was just all business now, and let it go at that.

# Chapter III

DURING MY last year at George Washington High School I came to know a fellow named Ozzie Alvarez. We took the bus to school together and we were also in some classes together. I told him that I had played baseball in Panama. He belonged to a team in a park league known as the New York Cavaliers; it was a city sandlot team in the Bronx Federation League. In the spring of 1964, Ozzie and another friend, George Mercado, invited me to work out with the team. Of course, I had my baseball glove from Panama. I had kept it oiled and saddle-soaped because I knew I'd be playing baseball again one day. The Cavaliers worked out in Crotona Park, in the Bronx. I know the coach, Sid Pack, was surprised that I could hit the ball so far for being so skinny—I weighed only 150 pounds, and I was just about six feet tall. I went out for shortstop. He told me to try second base because he didn't think my arm was strong enough for shortstop.

I made the team and became the regular second baseman. We played teams all over the city. Sometimes the park commission scheduled games in a field across from Yankee Stadium known as Babe Ruth Field or Macombs Dam Park. You'd be out there in the infield and suddenly a cheer would go up across the street, and someone who had a transistor radio would holler, "Mantle just parked one," or "Roger just unloaded."

Competition in the league was good. Kenny Singleton, now an outfielder for Baltimore, played in the league at the same time I did. Many teams had men, and I was still only 17. But I held my own. Singleton says he remembers that I was on base all the time, always stealing.

There was a kid on my team named Steve Katz. His father, Monroe, was a bird dog for the Minnesota Twins. A bird dog is a guy who checks out prospects, usually as a hobby or for a few dollars, and makes recommendations to a scout. The scout is either part time or full time and paid by the parent club. Steve told his father about me, and Monroe watched me play. He then told Herb Stein, the New York–area scout for the Twins. Herb is a guy who had hopes of a major-league playing career, but he broke his ankle and then spent three and a half years overseas during World War II, and that was the end of his dream. The next-best thing for him was trying to discover someone else who could make the big leagues. His regular job is as a detective for the New York City Transit Police. He introduced himself to me after a game I played. He had been in the stands watching. Stein told me that I had a pair of wrists that exploded with the pitch. He said he liked the way I could hit an inside pitch to left field, unusual for a left-handed batter.

One time he told me I was the most nonchalant player on a ground ball he'd ever seen. I'd pick the ball up and get comfortable before I threw it. I felt I had enough time to make the play, and I usually did. But it made other people nervous. Later, Stein told me he'd be in the stands and saying to himself, Get rid of the damned ball, Carew!

Stein began following me all over the Bronx. If we played on a Saturday one place, he'd be there. If we played on a Sunday some place else, there was Herb Stein. He'd buy me lunch and talk about my playing pro ball. I liked him, and we developed a friendship.

This business of a scout's following me was fantastic. Ozzie Alvarez and I would be on the phone a lot talking about what was going on. I had always been rather secretive and, well, I just didn't want anyone knowing about it yet. Not even my mother. So I would whisper on the phone to Ozzie. The whole conversation was baseball. But because of my whispering, she grew suspicious. She was still worried about me in New York. Every day at 3:30 she'd call from work to make sure I was home and not in the streets. Or if she couldn't get me, she'd call at supper time, just before she came home from work. She was gone from 7 in the morning until 7 at night. When she was home and answered the phone, it was always that one voice, Ozzie's. One day she said to me, "That boy calls every night. Be careful." He kept calling, and I kept whispering, and she kept worrying. So one day she answers the phone and again it's Ozzie. Mom says to him, "Don't you call back here anymore." And she hangs up. I finally had to explain the whole thing to her. Of course, she knew I was playing baseball now. I no longer had to work on weekends, because my brother knew how much baseball meant to me and he had said, "Go ahead, Rod. I'm working. I can give you an allowance."

I must have been hitting .500 in the Bronx League, and this was rugged competition. Now a scout from the Tigers showed up and began following me around. Then all of a sudden I had about six or seven different clubs interested in me. The Braves, the White Sox, the Red Sox, the Pirates. They all had scouts out to the games. I wanted to sign a contract at the first chance I had, but I talked with Uncle Clyde and Sid Pack, my coach, and I decided I'd better figure this thing out. I determined that I did not want to go with an established topflight club, because it might take me a long time to move up the ranks in the minor leagues. I thought an expansion club might be best. Even though the Minnesota Twins had been the Washington Senators and were not an expansion club, I still felt they were a young team and the turnover of personnel would be greater there than with the big contenders.

And I liked Herb Stein. Stein brought in the Twins' farm-system director, Hal Keller, to see me play one day. The Twins didn't want me to know this, because they didn't want me to do anything out of my usual routine, but just before a doubleheader at Crotona Park Sid Pack leaked the information to me.

"Rod," he said, "there is a guy from Minnesota here to see you. He'll be in the stands."

Then I got nervous. Oh, Jeez, here's my chance. This guy's a big shot. I've got to go out and try to have a good day. If I don't do well today, I might blow it. I felt that this guy was probably there to decide on signing me. I knew I might get an opportunity to sign with somebody else, but I didn't want to get involved with going to tryout camps. I had heard that players were like a herd of cattle at those camps. Some guys I knew had gone and they didn't even get looked at.

Well, I kept searching the stands to pick this guy out. There must have been, oh, 200 spectators. I tried to figure out what he might look like, but I couldn't.

The first time up, I doubled. I stood on second base and I was *still* looking for him. I really don't know what I was looking *for*. I said to myself, Where is he? Where is he? Next time up, I doubled again, 2-for-2. I said, Well, if nothing else, I've had a good start. Third time up, bam, a triple against the outfield fence. Drove in a couple of runs. I hit

another double the next time up. I also fielded well at second base, and we won. I had gone 4-for-4. I was feeling
great. At least I had one good game. We were on the bench
drinking soda pop and waiting to start the second game
when Sid said, "Rod, I'm going to put you in center field."

"Center field!" I said. "I've never played center field. I
don't know anything about the outfield." I didn't know
what Sid was trying to do to me.

"The man wants to see what you look like in the outfield.
Wants to see what your reactions are out there," said Sid.

So now I was standing out in center field and trying to
think about the way guys played it. I tried to line myself up
in the middle. I called over to the guy in right field, "What
do I do?" He said, "Don't move." After you're used to
playing the infield, everything from the outfield looks about
twenty miles away. I was in a lost land. The first ball hit in
the game is hit to—where else?—left center field. I didn't
want to call for it. But it was high, and I had a lot of time to
get close to it. I'm thinking, All I've got to do is drop a fly
ball. But I caught it. Then a guy hit a ball into right center
field. It hit off the fence, and I automatically picked the ball
up and wheeled and threw to third base. My instincts just
took over. I didn't even think about where to throw. But I
held the batter to a double. I really wasn't sure whether I
had done right or wrong. Should I have thrown to second,
since the runner was just coming into that base? And my
throw hadn't been particularly strong.

First time up, I made an out. Then I came up with the
bases loaded and hit a grand-slam homer. It was unbelievable. I couldn't do anything wrong at the plate. I think I
wound up 4-for-5 for that game, and I had 3 or 4 stolen
bases. So I had 8 hits in 9 times at bat for the day.

Hal Keller saw me after the game. He was a huge man,
weighed close to 300 pounds. He once was a catcher with
Washington, and he's the brother of Charlie "King Kong"
Keller, the old Yankee outfielder. Hal Keller's voice came
from deep down in his chest. "Very impressed with you,

young man," he said. He said I had shown him some base-ball sense in the way I had reacted to that ball I threw to third base. The Twins were coming into Yankee Stadium in a couple of weeks, he said, and asked if I would work out with them before a game.

All the guys heard about it. Everyone was excited. You're going to work out with the Twins at Yankee Stadium?

On that day, Herb Stein picked me up at home and drove me to the ball park. He told me to just relax. I brought my glove and cleats and baseball cap; I wasn't sure if they'd give me a cap. The clubhouse man gave me the first locker by the door and handed me a Twins traveling uniform. I dressed and walked down the long runway leading from the locker room to the dugout, and then when I stepped from the dugout onto the field, I heard some kids yelling, "Oliva, Oliva!" I looked around and they were yelling at *me*. I thought, They think I'm the star! Then I turned around and said, "I'm not Tony Oliva." One of them said, "Hey, he's not Oliva. What's he doing in Oliva's uniform?" As it turned out, the clubhouse man had given me one of Tony's uniforms, with his number 6 on the back.

I didn't know what I should do or where I should go. I stood on the dugout steps and watched the guys play catch. I had read so much about the Killebrews and Allisons and Batteys and Olivas and Versalleses.

It was around 6 o'clock. Dusk. The lights weren't turned on yet. I looked around. The park seemed immense. The grass was beautifully cut. Since it was early, few people were in the stands, and so it seemed there were miles of empty seats. I felt about two inches high.

Oliva, who is Cuban, came over and introduced himself in English. I told him I spoke Spanish. Then he said in Spanish, "Just go and hit and run and take ground balls. Don't be afraid." He jogged to the outfield, and I noticed his funny knock-kneed way of running.

Zoilo Versalles called me to play catch with him. He

asked what position I played. Second base, I said. He said, "Good, because you no can play shortstop." I didn't know what to say. Then he added, "I be here a long time, kid. So forget about shortstop."

Earl Battey walked by and said, "Hey, how's it goin', skinny kid?" Even *that* was nice. A lot better than being ignored.

Someone called me to get into the batting cage. I stepped in and just started whacking the ball. I hit a couple right out of the park. Over the 407-foot mark in right center. I was nervous, but still hitting the ball solidly. I was just about to take another swing when one of the guys yelled, "Five swings, kid—you don't cheat around here." I didn't know how they ran it. I didn't know how many swings you were supposed to take. I jumped out of there in a flash.

In the second round of five, I kept blasting the ball all over the place. Now guys are coming over and kidding me: "Hey, did you see this skinny kid hit the ball? Check that guy's arms." Don Mincher and Rich Rollins felt my muscles. I wasn't sure how to respond. I didn't say a word. I don't think I even smiled.

The first two pitches of the third round I hit into the outfield stands. Suddenly someone is hollering, "Get that kid out of there! The Yankees might see him!" It's Sam Mele, the manager. "Let him go field ground balls." I was pulled out of the cage and sent to second base.

In the clubhouse after the workout, some of the other players introduced themselves. One was Harmon Killebrew. I had expected him to be a much taller guy. Everyone had read about "the Killer," and you'd figure he was a monster. He turned out to be a gentle guy. He was about five-ten and stocky. He wasn't wearing a shirt, and I noticed that his body had no flab—all solid muscle.

The team trainer, Doc Lentz, came by. In years to come, we'd develop a warm friendship. He said now, "I heard you did real good out there, kid. Sam Mele really likes you." He told me to fold the uniform when I was finished and give it to him—"and keep the cap." He said the Twins would be in touch with me. He gave me a ball autographed by the team and a ticket to the game. I remember that Jim Roland pitched that night—pitched a good game, too; but I left before it was over. I was anxious to tell my mother. When I told her what had happened, she didn't believe me. "C'mon, Cline, a *tryout* at Yankee Stadium?" I got mad at her—I could get mad fast—and said, "You'll see." And I went into my room.

At the Cavaliers game the next week, Herb Stein was there again. He said the reports had been good. The Twins hadn't made an offer, though. A few other teams had mentioned bonuses of $1,000 or $2,000 if I'd sign with them when I graduated from high school. They wanted me, but for as little as possible. The most persistent team, other than the Twins, was the Red Sox.

On the night that my high school class graduated, June 24, 1964, Herb Stein went with me. He seemed jumpy. He told me later he was looking around to see if other scouts were there.

When the ceremonies were over, Herb suggested we go to dinner. So my mother, Uncle Clyde, my sister Deanna and I got into Herb's car and went to the Stella d'Oro Restaurant on 238th Street. A nice Italian restaurant. The nicest restaurant I had ever eaten in. Monroe Katz met us there.

"Go on and eat," Herb said to us. "It's on the Twins." Now, we couldn't sign anything until midnight of the day my class graduated. So Herb's stalling around, hemming and hawing, and talking about what the deal will be. He offered a $5,000 bonus, with $7,500 additional when I made the Twins, and a $400-a-month salary as soon as I reported to the Rookie League team in Cocoa, Florida.

I looked at my mother and Uncle Clyde. This was big money to us. But Clyde had said we should be cautious.

"I'm not sure," I said. I wanted to sign immediately, but I also knew Herb was anxious to have me; otherwise why would he be here?

Now it's past midnight, and we're still talking. We're the only people left in the restaurant. The manager wanted to close the place. All his waiters were standing around. Herb said to the manager, "Please, my friend, I'm a major-league scout and I'm trying to sign a player," and the guy said okay.

Stein said, "Look, Rod, I'll call a scout for you. Or you can call him yourself. See what his offer is."

He gave me the number of a Red Sox scout. I called and spoke to him and told him the Twins' offer. He said he'd have to get back to me. Well, I wasn't about to wait another day.

"Okay, Mr. Stein," I said. "Give me your pen."

As it turned out, Herb had had me call the one scout he knew didn't carry a club checkbook. In later years Herb also told me that there was no way he was going to let me out of that restaurant without my signing the contract. First, he said, he believed in me. Second, and maybe more important, he had just spent sixty bucks of Calvin Griffith's money on the meal, and he was afraid to let me get away after *that*—knowing how closely the Twins' owner watches his wallet.

A few days later, Herb took me to get my airplane ticket for Florida. I'd be leaving before the week was out.


ABOUT A year before I signed, my mom began getting letters from my father. He wanted to come and live with us.

Mom asked the kids how we felt about it. "Well, it's up to you," I said. "If you want him to, there's nothing I can do." But I wasn't looking forward to it, I can tell you that. Our life was as peaceful as we had ever known it. None of the tension, none of the cussing, none of the beatings. I thought my mother was happy too.

I guess Mom still loved him. He was also going to bring Deanna and Dorine. They had been living with him. One thing about him, he was always pretty good to the girls. He got them presents at Christmas and for their birthdays, and didn't mistreat them physically the way he did Dickie and me. He promised Mom he would act differently toward her and the boys. Mom agreed to take him in.

We went to meet them at the airport. I had no feelings whatsoever about him. I shook hands with him. We were cordial enough, but not warm.

At first he was all right around the house. He was just feeling his way. My godmother helped get him a job as a painter with a construction company. But then after a few weeks he started up his bad act all over again. He was cussing around the house and verbally abusing us. Then he began wandering off into the streets, just as he had done back home. He wouldn't come home until late, if he came back at all, and there was the smell of liquor about him. It killed me to see what it did to my mother.

Now, he wasn't about to take a belt to Dickie or me anymore, since we had gotten pretty big. Eric's about six-three, but Dickie is six-five, and I had grown to six feet tall. One day he was mouthing off and I said to him, "I don't have to accept anything or take anything from you anymore. You are now in *our* home. If you don't like it, then you can leave. We did without you for over a year, and we can continue doing without you. We came here to make something of ourselves, and you're not going to spoil it."

I felt good to be able to stand up to him. This was quite a change in my life. I wasn't in prison anymore. I could speak freely, and I had rights. I'd finally come of age and could handle myself and didn't have to worry about getting whipped.

Now he was really in a rage. I told him I wasn't going to take any more of his guff, and if he wanted to do something about it . . .

He turned and came at me with clenched fists. My

brother stepped in the way. I held my ground. I knew I could handle myself with him now because I had that thing inside of me—a desire to really take him on—to whip him. We got close to blows one or two other times.

I'd get so mad. Why do I have to hear this? Why do I have to live with this? Why does this thing have to be a constant in our lives? He hadn't changed at all. He was still the same person.

I started shying away from him. I never said anything to him. Not a word. He would make comments sometimes, as if he wanted to start a regular conversation, but I wouldn't answer. I would have left the house, but I wanted to finish school. I didn't want to be out on my own yet.

All this time I was observing the relationship between my parents. I was realizing that Eric never took my mom to a movie, or anywhere else. She loved going to movies. She'd go by herself, or we'd go together, she and Dickie and the girls and I. I wasn't about to tell her how to run her life at this point, but I sure didn't understand why she kept him around. She was working. Dickie was working. The girls were working. I would be working full time soon. We had managed without him. When we went to dinner with Herb Stein, I did not ask my father along. I didn't want any part of him.

And now that I was about to leave home for the Rookie League, it was a welcome experience: for the second time in about two years I was getting away from my father, getting relief from him.

And after the Rookie League, I would go right into the Marine Corps for six months' active duty to fulfill my obligation. Even though I wasn't a citizen of the United States at the time, I was a permanent resident. I would spend another five and a half years going to reserve meetings. I signed up for the reserve program rather than take the chance of being drafted for two years.

I had no communication with Eric at all after I left home.

He'd try to find out how I was doing when I started moving up the ladder in baseball. He'd question others in the family about me. After I made the Twins, I decided to live the year around in Minneapolis. I never wanted to go back home and to my father again. I was finally on my own.

# Chapter IV

THE CLUBHOUSE in Cocoa, Florida, was small and crowded with players. Lockers were bunched together. Equipment was stacked all over. There was barely room to move. On the first day of practice for the Cocoa Rookie League, there must have been 80 guys knocking one another over trying on their new uniforms. The rookie teams of the Twins, Tigers, Astros and Mets were together. We had come from all parts of the country—star high school and college players. And one sandlot player from the Bronx Federation League. There was a mass of arms and legs. Guys were pulling on and tugging off pants and shirts. They were very picky. Most didn't want baggy uniforms. I didn't care. Just give me a uniform. My team was called the Melbourne Twins, though we never did play in Melbourne, Florida. We stayed in Cocoa.

I shouldn't have been in such a hurry to get my uniform,

because it wasn't very long before I was embarrassing myself.

It turned out that I had two left feet at second base. I couldn't catch anything in the field. I could hit—right from the start I was ripping the ball, and guys were amazed, coaches and players—but fielding here was something else. It really baffled me. I had played Little League, and I was one of the best fielders. In New York, I was adequate, and Hal Keller told me I had good instincts.

Some players had developed a polish in college that I didn't possess. I also had a fear of the ball. A lot of guys won't admit it, but I think all of us are afraid. If you've ever played any kind of baseball, you know you're afraid of a bad hop hitting you in the face. It's natural. You flinch. That's the biggest fear, I believe, of a lot of infielders, especially when they're young. You're supposed to bend at the knees and get low for the ground ball. I had a habit of either turning my head or looking up just enough that I'd miss catching the ball.

Ellis Clary and Freddie Waters, coaches there, took turns fungoing ground balls to me every day. "Keep your eye on the ball! Don't turn your head!" They tried to get me to relax my hands. To *flow* with the ground ball instead of battling it. Some days I'd be so exhausted from practice that I couldn't eat dinner. I'd flop into bed and conk out.

When the games against other rookie teams began, I wasn't a starter for the Twins' team. Some days I wouldn't even get into the game. It was frustrating. I wanted to play, but I was making such slow progress in the field. Not only wasn't I fielding ground balls well, I was having trouble with the double play. When executed well, the double play is a thing of beauty. And it all revolves around the pivot man, who in most cases is covering second base. With a runner on first and no more than one out, a ground ball is hit, say, to shortstop. He flips the ball to the second baseman, as the runner tries to throw him off by sliding into him. The second baseman tries to 1) get out of his way by coming across the base as he is 2) taking the throw and 3) throwing the ball to first to complete the double play—three things in nearly one motion. Some guys do it so gracefully that it's thrilling. For example, I love to watch Bobby Randall, the second baseman for the Twins now, do it. I never saw Bill Mazeroski turn the double play, but I've heard people say he was so quick with the release to first that he was like a phantom. The ball was there and the next instant it was gone. But for me at Cocoa, Florida, in June of 1964, when I was 18 years old and in my first couple of weeks of pro ball, trying to make the double play was like trying unsuccessfully to pat my head and rub my stomach at the same time. The harder I tried, the more frustrated I got.

What relaxed me was my hitting. I always thought I could learn to field. People learn to field, but very few people could learn to hit as naturally as I did. I kept that in the back of my mind.

In practice, I would hit line drive after line drive to left field. I wasn't a pull hitter. I could hit the ball all over, but I hit mainly to left. When I began to play in competition there, guys would shift toward left, but I could always hit the ball with a spin, a downward spin, and the ball fell just beyond them for a hit. It was a natural thing, that spin. Maybe it had something to do with my wrist action. I don't know. I just went up there and swung the bat because that's what I thought hitting was all about. At that level, you don't worry about looking for a curve ball or looking for pitches on the corner of the plate. Not with these kid pitchers I was playing against. Most of them just threw hard. They'd throw and you'd swing. That's what baseball was all about for me then. In a few years I'd learn that I knew as little about hitting as I did about fielding. As I moved up, the pitching got better and I had to adjust or fall by the wayside.

I remember on the very first day in Cocoa, Freddie Waters gathered us around in a circle on the field. He said that baseball ought to be fun, but that it was also work. And that the few of us who would make it to the major leagues would make it there on a combination of ability and sweat. I took that seriously. Waters said that our legs were very important and that was why he wanted us to do sprints. I don't remember how many sprints we were supposed to do a day, but some guys used to goof off. A guy might run one sprint. When the coach asked how many he'd done, he'd answer, "This is my fourth, Coach." But there were other guys, I remember, who were slow, but tried their best to improve their speed. Even though I was fast, maybe the fastest runner in the camp, I felt I couldn't let down if I was going to get anywhere. Every day I tried to run ten sprints more than required.

In some ways, I was afraid of the future. Ellis Clary said to a group of the infielders one day, "All you can do is work and practice, and who knows . . . you might make it quick or you might spend several years in the minors." He said he had seen some guys, some good ballplayers, spend six or seven years in the minors before getting to the big leagues. Some never made it up at all. I didn't like the sound of that.

I really didn't have much of a life outside of baseball. There were two reasons for that. One was my deep desire to improve as a baseball player. Also, I was never one to follow the crowd. Some of the guys would go out drinking. I didn't drink much. Never really liked it. I might try a beer, take a few sips and I'm ready to say good night. Now, we had a midnight curfew. You were supposed to come through the main entrance of the apartment complex we lived in by midnight. Some guys would have dates, maybe two in a night, and they'd come back late. They'd try to take the screen off their window and have someone throw them a rope so they could climb in.

I never stayed out past curfew. Even if I had wanted to, it was not advisable for a black kid to be running around during the night in the South in those years. Except for that, I didn't give much thought to the racial situation in the South. I know I should have, but I didn't. And I had never in my life experienced any problems with race. In Panama, I accepted the separation of races as the way of the world. And I was happy there. In New York, I stayed in my neighborhood and never had a problem of any sort. Even though I was the only black on the Cavaliers in the Bronx, I was treated as an equal. Even more than equal, since I was a standout player. And at camp so far in Cocoa, the guys were terrific. Another fellow and I were the only blacks in camp, but there was no atmosphere of racial discrimination. The guys played ball together, played Ping-Pong in the recreation room together, ate together, joked together. In fact, I was even beginning to come out of my aloofness. The only awkward moment at the complex occurred the evening I arrived, and it had nothing to do with race. I was told I'd have a roommate, which was fine with me. No one was in the room when I walked in, but I knew something was fishy; even someone as unworldly as I was could tell that. There was incense burning, and the room was lit with a purplish light. On the walls and on the dresser were photographs of men in various poses. I went downstairs and asked the man in charge to come up and take a look at the room.

He opened the door and started to laugh. "Aw, you got the fag," he said. "He's the cook."

Cook or no cook, I didn't know what to expect. I knew I needed my rest, and I wasn't about to sleep with one eye open.

"I'd appreciate it if you'd move me," I said.

"Sorry, kid," the guy said, "but we're all filled up. Two to a room. It's just a matter of luck who you get as a roomie. But something else should open up soon."

"Look, can't you put three in a room for a short while?" I asked. "Who knows what might happen? I'm here just to play baseball."

I finally persuaded him to move me out that night.

During the first few weeks the atmosphere had been terrific. The guys would always invite me out—me and the one other black player on our team—and we'd drive to the beach or take in a movie or shop in downtown Cocoa. One of the white guys I went with was Jim Blackledge. His nickname was Blackie. I remember I picked something up in a store one time and said, "How do you like this, Blackie?" And he said, "Who are you calling Blackie, Blackie?" We cracked up. Things were going fine.

But one day I went along with two white teammates to a barbershop in Cocoa. I sat down to wait for them. The barber came over and said, "Sorry, boy, we don't allow no niggers in here." He wanted me to sit outside while my friends got their hair cut. I was stunned, as if a ton of bricks had fallen on my head. But if someone didn't want me, then I didn't want to be around. I was no militant. I didn't even know what a militant was. The only race problems I had seen were on television, when police would sic dogs on blacks in Mississippi. And I never wanted to be the center of a fuss. I was embarrassed. My teammates said they were leaving, that they weren't going to get their hair cut unless I sat inside. I said I'd wait outside, that there was no sense in creating problems. Other blacks might stand and argue. That wasn't my nature. I'm changing now. But then, well, this was my big chance to play pro ball, and that was my whole purpose in life. Nothing else mattered nearly as much. So I backed off at the barbershop.

It was no secret how whites in town felt about blacks. You could *see* it. It seemed as if every time we walked past a white person he or she would turn and look. And would kind of squirm away from you. It was like "What are *you* doing here?" Maybe it was because I stayed on the sidewalk when whites passed. I used to see black kids step off the curb when a white person went by. I never did that, but these kids were from town and I imagine they knew that they had to stay in their place.

After a while I asked myself, Why are we so different? Aren't we all God's people? If a black wants an education, why shouldn't he be able to get a decent education? Why shouldn't a guy be able to eat in the same restaurant with others? What's food? You eat food, it goes in and fills you and then it comes out as waste. I used to wonder if we had some kind of disease that they didn't want to catch. What's wrong with me? Do I have something on my skin?

I remember seeing the movie of Jackie Robinson's life, and the incident in which some fans threw a black cat onto the field. A similar incident happened to me. It was in 1965, and I was playing for Orlando in the Florida State League. We had a night game at Leesburg. I was sitting at the edge of the dugout and heard two guys in the stands making smirky remarks. Then I noticed a little black dog on the field right near me, and these two guys were calling it, "Here, Nigger, here, Nigger." I made believe I was ignoring the whole thing. But I was burning up. Well, I went to play there two more times, and these same two guys would be there. If I didn't get a hit I'd hear them say, "They made an easy out of you, coon." Everything was "coon" this and "coon" that. Whenever I went to the plate, I'd hear "Get that coon out." Every time I got up to bat I wanted more than anything to get a hit. I did well there, too. I'd double, and I'd stand on second base and feel as happy as hell. But I didn't show a thing. After my last game, I walk out of the clubhouse and these guys are waiting for me. I thought I was in for it. "Hey, Carew." They came over. They said they had given me a bad time and I had never once said a word to them and they wanted to shake my hand. I said, "No problem." And shook hands. Maybe that's the way you do it—convert them one at a time. Or two at a time. Some I guess you just can't convert at all. The next year I played in Wilson, North Carolina, and one of the white players invited me over to his house one night for dinner. The next day he found a note in his mailbox with three K's on it. I found the same thing in a letter to me; it said, Stay out of white peoples' homes.

While playing for the Wilson, North Carolina, team, I saw my first BLACK ONLY and WHITE ONLY signs. They were above washrooms at a truck stop in Lynchburg. This was better than some stops, though, where we weren't even allowed *into* the restaurant, to eat *or* use the washroom.


I HIT .325 in the Rookie League. I finished a close second for the batting championship to a guy named Larry Seneta. He was in the Tigers' organization. Larry was a husky guy and a good hitter. We became friends. I always thought he had a shot at making it with the Tigers, but it never materialized for him. He went higher but didn't hit and then got hurt and got out of the game. Looking back, I find it a strange thing that on the way up you just can't tell who's going to get to the majors. There were guys I played with at Orlando and Wilson, in Class A ball, who did make it. Guys like George Mitterwald and Ted Uhlaender. But when people ask me, What does it take to make it? I'm not really sure what to answer. I know it takes talent to make the majors. I know it takes work. I know it takes desire. And I know it takes a lot of luck. You can't get injured too seriously. You can't get down on yourself too badly. You have to have the right people helping you, taking an interest in you. Now, what proportion of which is crucial? I don't know and don't pretend to. I was the only player on my Rookie League team to make the big leagues. I would never have predicted that. Some guys really busted themselves to improve. Some wanted it just as much as I did.

After the Rookie League, I had impressed the Twins enough that they invited me to Minnesota to spend the last ten days of their season working out with the team. Jerry Kindall was the second baseman then, and he showed me some moves around second base. My locker was next to

Tony Oliva's, and we became friendly. Even though he was the batting champion, he took me under his wing. He drove me around and showed me the area. After workouts at Metropolitan Stadium I went into the stands to watch the game. This was my first taste of Minnesota fall weather, and I wasn't prepared. I had only a light jacket. It got cold, and I'd return to the motel, which was just a few blocks away, and watch the game on television. Or just listen to the radio. The Yankees were staying at that hotel. I saw Mantle and Ford, and I remember running into Hector Lopez, an outfielder–third baseman who had a solid ten-year career in the majors. He was then the only player from Panama in the major leagues. He was the hottest thing in Panama, as you might guess. I introduced myself, and he said, "Yeah, I've heard of you. You're the kid from Panama the Twins are talking about." Imagine that! I drifted off on a cloud.

The next season I packed my bags and quit baseball. Several times. But never for more than a few minutes. I had been moved up one notch from the Rookie League to Orlando, which is A classification. As the season went along, I grew very unhappy. I developed an attitude. It began, I guess, when I thought that some of my teammates on the Orlando team were jealous that I was doing well. I would hear sly remarks. These guys knew about my having been up to Minnesota. They began calling me "Calvin's bobo." Or "Mr. Griffith's boy." If I'd get a hit that wasn't a line drive, they'd snicker, "Blooper ball." I was hitting well over .300, best on the team.

One day I didn't feel well and didn't play. One of the guys made a side-of-the-mouth remark like "Now here's a Jake," or something like that. "Jake" is the name for a guy who fakes an injury so that he doesn't have to play hard, or play at all. Now, there *were* times when I felt I was hurt and didn't want to play. I've never felt that you should do or die. Why play injured? If you can't perform, sit out and give yourself a chance to heal. I had also come to learn that, in baseball, blacks have a reputation for claiming injury. That's the old racial slur about lazy niggers. It's just worded differently. I think it may go back to the inability of some whites to identify or empathize with blacks. Blacks aren't really human beings to them. If a white guy is hurting, they can understand that—but they can't with a black. Whites are also less patient with blacks, and management is quicker to give up on a black than on a white player. I've seen white guys get a little headache and the coach will say, "Yeah, take the day off." This is true, in my opinion, all the way up the ladder. From Orlando to Minnesota. When I was a rookie playing for the Twins, Mudcat Grant, who was a veteran pitcher then, said to me one day, "Rod, I'm going to tell you something. For a black guy to survive in the major leagues, he has to go out there and play if his leg is broken, if he's dying." He added, "Look around: you don't see many black guys sitting on the bench up here. You go out there and play until they drag you off the field."

One day in Orlando a couple of guys were talking on the bench. This was before the game, and I was scratched from the lineup—sore leg or something. I overheard, "Aw, he's just protecting his average. Jake's at it again."

I stood up and said, "Stick it up your ass." And walked into the clubhouse. I had had it. I began packing my bags.

The way I heard it later, the batboy, who was the son of the general manager, Bob Willis, went rushing out to his father on the field and said, "Dad, Dad, Rod Carew's packed his bags and says he's going home." So Willis comes bursting through the door while I'm cleaning out my locker. Willis is a powerfully built guy with a puffy face like an ex–street fighter. But he had a nice way about him. "Rod, where you goin'?"

"I'm quitting baseball. I'm going home."

He said, "Look, if you walk out, they're gonna throw me

out. The owner's gonna shoot me. Calvin has singled you out as his next superstar."

He asked me to sit down and talk. I told him what was going on in my mind. He thought I had a point, but he felt I was being oversensitive, that the remarks made to me weren't racial slurs or jealous statements, but attempts to prod me to do even better.

Whether that was true or not—and I wasn't convinced— it gave me time to cool down and to consider my actions.

Willis said, "Rod, you have a great future; you have a chance to play in the big leagues. Why spoil it?"

"I'm tired of these guys picking on me," I said. But I was cooling down, and Willis' words sank in. I was doing fine on the field. I was hitting, my fielding had improved, I was stealing bases. I was in the papers every day. I'd get a couple of hits or I'd steal a base to win a game. I was on my way to fulfilling a dream. Bob Willis was right: why destroy my chance? I put my uniform back on.

I was never one of the boys to begin with. I had always been a loner, and I remained that way. I stayed in my room a great deal and enjoyed sitting alone listening to music— jazz rock, mostly, Wes Montgomery or Nancy Wilson. Or I'd read sports magazines. I would go to the movies alone. I know I gave some people the impression that I was standoffish, but I just didn't enjoy some of the locker-room pranks—I didn't like guys smacking me on the back or a guy giving someone a hotfoot.

I was also a kid. I was immature. I was getting a lot at a young age, and I couldn't cope with some of the things. I was homesick and called my mother frequently. I had been a mama's boy. When I had problems with my father, I knew I could always go to her. When I was sick, which was often, she was there to comfort me. Sometimes now I'd tell her I wanted to come home—even with Eric there. She'd tell me to do whatever would make me happy, but to think it through first. She'd add, "Everything will be all right." That old phrase. It sounded good in my ears.

This is the team I played on in the Elga Little League in Panama when I was 12 years old, in 1957. The photo is from the file of my uncle Joseph French, who was my earliest baseball mentor and coach of this team. Mr. French wrote the names of the players on the picture. José Stennet is the brother of Pittsburgh Pirate infielder Rennie Stennet. Below is my uncle with his wife, Edith. (COURTESY JOSEPH FRENCH)

I'm on the left, with my aunt Doris Broomes and my brother, Eric, Jr., at Panama City airport just before my brother and I departed for our new home in New York City. It was June 30, 1962. I was 16 and was wearing my first suit and dress hat. (COURTESY OLGA CAREW)

My mother, Olga, in our Upper Manhattan apartment shortly after our arrival in the United States. My mother was by far the single most important person in my life. (COURTESY OLGA CAREW)

Harmon Killebrew, right, watching a game from the dugout with manager Sam Mele. Mele was my first big-league manager; Killebrew, of course, was our leading slugger in my early years with the Twins. (COURTESY MINNESOTA TWINS)

Dave Boswell, onetime Twins pitcher, warms up in Metropolitan Stadium. Boswell's carrying a pistol touched off a furor on our team bus in 1967. (COURTESY MINNESOTA TWINS)

With Tony Oliva before a game. Oliva was my on-the-road roommate for much of his major-league career, and my best friend on the Twins. This photo was taken in 1977, when Tony had become a Twins coach. (COURTESY MINNESOTA TWINS)

Manager Gene Mauch with a fungo bat. Mauch's nickname for me is ''Pro,'' and I have the highest respect for him as well. (COURTESY MINNESOTA TWINS)

George "Doc" Lentz, Twins trainer, works with me to strengthen my knee, injured in a collision at second base. This is in August, 1970, two months after the play. Below, a month later, I'm taking batting practice. I was wearing sneakers to relieve pressure on my knee. (COURTESY MINNESOTA TWINS)

Although Billy Martin is a controversial figure, I have a tremendous respect for him. Martin was both a manager and coach for the Twins in my early years, and an important and beneficial influence. (COURTESY MINNESOTA TWINS)

Marilynn and I in our courting days, 1969.

Stealing home against the Yankees in 1971. Yank catcher Jake Gibbs (41) tries to tag me as Jim Holt tries to back away from the play. I tied the major-league record for most stolen home bases in a season, 7, in 1969. (ASSOCIATED PRESS)

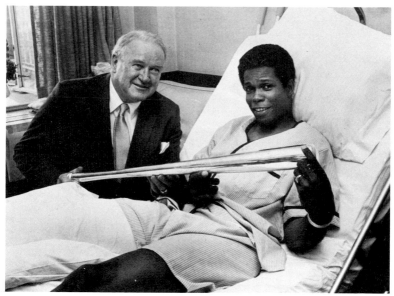

Joe Cronin, then president of the American League, visited me in June, 1970, in the hospital, where I was recovering from my knee injury. Cronin presented me with the silver bat emblematic of winning the 1969 American League batting title. (COURTESY MINNESOTA TWINS)

Making a public appearance before a grade-school class in a Twin Cities school. (COURTESY MINNESOTA TWINS)

Here I'm making the double play at second base as Graig Nettles of the Yankees slides. (ASSOCIATED PRESS)

In Venezuela in 1972, I took time out from my job as player-manager of a Winter League team there to instruct a group of boys in hitting fundamentals. (COURTESY MINNESOTA TWINS)

I think back to those days, and to how emotional I was. I can't imagine ever being that young.

I LOST the batting title of the Florida State League on the last day of the 1965 season. A guy in the Cincinnati chain named Harvey Yancey beat me out by two points, .305 to .303. I stole 52 bases and was second in the league in that department as well. Unfortunately, I tied for the league lead in another department—most errors by a second baseman: 28.

Overall, though, it had been a terrific year in my baseball career. So I was knocked for a loop the next spring when I learned that I would be sent to Wilson of the Carolina League. Wilson was A ball. I was sure I'd be promoted to Double-A or Triple-A ball. There were guys on the Orlando team who batted 60, 70 points below me who were promoted over me.

I began the season in a state of confusion. Besides my displeasure at remaining on that level of ball, I had also missed the first part of the season because I had to complete thirty days of active military duty.

At the Wilson airport, a driver picked me up to take me to the park. He told me that everyone was really excited that I was there and that he'd heard so much about me and knew I could help the Wilson club.

I had my problems at Wilson too.

It began with my fielding. Old Lead Hands was at it again. Vern Morgan was the manager. He and I grew very close. In fact, I became in some ways like a stepson to Vern and his wife, Ann. Vern was to become a Twins' coach when I was in the major leagues. He was a career baseball man who had played in the big leagues—third base with the Cubs—only long enough for a cup of coffee, as the saying goes. Maybe it was because of Vern's ability as an infield teacher that the Twins wanted me in Wilson. Vern spent many, many hours hitting ground balls to me, talking to me about my fielding. He told me that I was nearly a major-league hitter, but that I wouldn't make the big leagues unless my fielding improved. He kept reminding me that if I didn't play in the big leagues, I'd have wasted my talent.

Then the "jaking" thing popped up again.

I had jammed my foot, and it was swollen. I couldn't get my shoe on. I went to a doctor and he thought I might have torn tendons. The foot was inflamed. But the club wanted me to make the road trip to Rocky Mount. I said I wasn't going and said why. And I didn't go. Well, I guess I was getting temperamental. Maybe I should have gone with the club, even though I wasn't going to play. But I felt it was better to rest my foot. It was my career I had to worry about. The other guys couldn't have cared less about it. I was alone in the world, I felt. I had to look after myself and do what I felt was best for me. Why should I risk permanent injury and jeopardize my career? Was I supposed to prove to these guys that I was a man? I thought I was man enough *not* to have to prove it. I had a lot at stake. I had a chance to make something of myself and do something for my family. That was my first consideration. The team came second. Besides, I was hitting something like .320, and I thought I was doing my part. Then I heard guys calling me "Jake." Boom, I went off.

I went to Morgan and said I was going home. All my other thoughts went out the window—about my career and family. I just flew off the handle.

"Rod," Vern said, in the tone of a Dutch uncle, "to hell with those guys. Don't listen."

The next day the guy who was going to pitch for us came in and said, "Rod, I need the win tonight, and I need you in the lineup to get it." He had a roll of bandages in his hand. "Let me tape up your foot for you." I realized he wasn't kidding. I couldn't believe it, but I was moved by it. I played, I was hurt, but I played. I got a couple of hits and then in the ninth inning, with the score tied 2–2, I won the game with another hit.

For the rest of the year, I got along just great with everybody. I ended up hitting .292, and *not* leading or tying for the league lead in errors.

That winter I was invited by the Twins to the Florida Instructional League. I was told the Twins wanted me to get as much playing time as possible. It seemed as if everything I did there was right. One day Calvin Griffith was in the stands. I got a couple of hits, fielded balls cleanly at my position and stole some bases. Afterward we met and he said, "You're a good-looking player. You have a chance to make our team in the future."

That didn't thrill me as much as one might think. I remembered what Clary, the coach in the Rookie League, had said about its taking some guys six or seven years to make it through the minor leagues to the majors. Mr. Griffith didn't say he thought I had a chance of making it "next year." Or "the year after next." He said "the future." What did that mean?

For good or bad, there was a new dimension to Rod Carew, literally. It was in my cheek. I had become a chewer of tobacco. You could spot me on the field by the lump on the side of my face.

I had never chewed before in my life. I hardly knew what tobacco was. The first time I tried it was in the Cocoa Rookie League. Some of the guys gave it to me as a gag to see what would happen. What happened was that I got nauseated. At first it tasted like hay, and then I swallowed some juice and, oh, it had the most bitter taste, Burned my throat, I got sick to my stomach. But I didn't throw up—I got drowsy. I was on the bench and I fell asleep. Fred Waters, the manager, woke me up. He said, "If you can't handle the things men can handle, don't play with it." He was a chewer too, and this remark was meant to be funny. In my state, though, I didn't laugh very hard.

Two years later I tried chewing again. Wilson is in tobacco country, and chew was readily available. During the
summer months in North Carolina, the weather was so hot
and sticky you'd find yourself drinking water or Coke every
minute you could. I might drink twenty-five cans of Coke a
day. I'd run up to the clubhouse for a Coke between every
inning. So my stomach got heavy and bloated, and when I
bent for a ground ball it felt as if I had a medicine ball inside
my shirt. I felt lousy.

I learned that tobacco kept your mouth moist and you
didn't need so much liquid. I began messing around with
chew—or chaw, or snuff, as some guys call it—and I became a pro at it. Now I enjoy having a wad in my mouth
most of the time. I wrap gum around the wad to keep it
together. I chew four or five packs a game.

It could be considered a dirty habit because of all the
spitting that's required. You chomp down a few times and
then you let fire with a stream of juice. Sometimes you walk
along the dugout and you can step into a puddle made from
a guy's having sat there and chewed for twenty minutes.
(Tobacco-juice pranks are common among chewers. For
example, a guy with a new pair of cleats will walk onto the
field and he'll have them baptized immediately by the chewers.)

Some stomachs might be too queasy for chewing tobacco—might be too queasy even for the *subject*—but it's
really been a positive thing in my life for several reasons.
One, as I mentioned, was that it keeps my mouth moist.
Another is that it helps keep my weight down during the off
season. Since I'm chewing, I'm not hitting the refrigerator
all the time and noshing. If I feel hungry, I put a chew in
my mouth, and spit into a paper cup.

I'm convinced that chewing makes me a better hitter,
too. I get a steadier view of the pitcher when I've got a
hunk of tobacco in my right cheek. It makes my skin tight.
When your skin is tight like that, you can't squint, which

means your eye is watching the ball more clearly and steadily.

IN TWO and a half years, I had played in three pro leagues and was a top batter in each. In a fourth, the Instructional League, I had impressed the boss, Mr. Griffith, at first hand. Every coach I had said I had the tools to be a big-leaguer. In the spring of 1967, I was invited to training camp with the Twins. About 50 guys are asked to come, and 25 guys are eventually kept. The others are sent back to the minors for more seasoning. I had been invited to the Twins' camp twice before, and twice had been sent down. Even though I knew it was rare to jump from Class A to the majors, I was confident I could do it. There may have been a little arrogance showing, in fact. One day Bob Allison said that he had heard I could really go. Allison, the six-foot-four, 225-pound left fielder, had been a star fullback at Kansas State in 1953 and 1954. He said he'd like to race me. I told him, "Bob, forget it. I could beat you backwards." That may have scared him off, because we never raced.

Meanwhile, unknown to me, a uniform was hanging in a locker in Denver that bore the name CAREW on the back. The Denver Bears were the Twins' Triple-A farm club. A number of the bigwigs in the Twins' organization expected me to be in Denver for the upcoming season.

In training camp now, I discovered that I had a few problems: namely, fielding, running and hitting. That was all.

Ground balls still plagued me. The Twins' infield coach, Billy Martin, had me throwing balls off a cement wall to try to relax my hands and arms. Throw and catch, throw and catch—so I wouldn't have time to think and get stiff waiting for the ball.

Then I found I didn't know how to run the bases. I was running with my head down and running through signs.

That is, a coach would be signaling me to stop at second. But I wouldn't see him, and I'd run to third, where I'd be thrown out. I had to learn to run with my head up. Once, I almost passed one of my teammates on the bases. Another thing I found was that in big-league competition, pitchers have pick-off motions that are so fine that you'd better know what you're doing when you get on base. I didn't. In the first few spring-training games against major-league teams, I was picked off almost every time I got on base. Some of it was my carelessness, but some of it was experimentation. I had to learn how long a lead I could take in order to steal a base. I learned I couldn't get very far off at all.

So besides my spotty fielding, my missing signs on the bases and my getting picked off, all that was left of my game was hitting. And for the first time in my life, I was in hot water there, too.

In the minors, pitchers just reared back and threw their hummer. In the majors, they're technicians. They're working on you. High inside curve ball first, then a low outside fastball. A change-up. A sinker. Low, high. Outside, inside. In the minors, when the pitcher began to lose control he'd have to slow his pitch a little, and the batter dug in, licking his chops. In the majors, pitchers have sharper control, so they don't have to let up like that.

Mostly, though, I was handcuffed by the breaking ball. I was overstriding, and I'd swing off balance. If I didn't strike out, I'd tap the ball weakly. I was looking bad! In games, other teams began to get the message. I remember Hank Bauer, the Baltimore manager, telling his pitchers, "Throw the kid breaking balls." When they'd try to sneak a fastball by me, I'd get a base hit. You could almost see the steam coming out of Bauer's ears when that happened. In the minors, I rarely struck out. But now, in two early practice games I struck out four times—all on *called* strikes. In the 23 preseason games, I struck out 22 times,

14 with my bat on my shoulder. I was being fooled so badly by breaking balls that I couldn't get the bat around.

In the field, I was very quiet. Yet I knew they wanted a holler guy. When you're chattering it seems as if you're hustling. The Twins' manager, Sam Mele, said to me one day, "Kid, talk up—otherwise you're going to get lost."

And Martin called me aside. "Rod, if you don't open up a little you're not going to have any chance of making the club," he said. I started chattering a little bit, just to let them know I was around. But it really wasn't my nature to do it.

They may have thought I was being moody. I know my reputation preceded me. I can tell you one thing: I can't say that Mele ever said anything that wasn't kind or helpful to me. I remember one practice game in which I made a particularly dumb play at second base. Sam told me in a nice way what I should have done. Sure enough, about a week later it happened again and I did it right.

What to do about the curve ball? I knew that some guys never learn to hit it, and that makes the difference between the big-league hitter and the plumber. I tried several ways to work it out. I waited as long as I could on the pitch and then snapped my wrists. I tried not pulling the curve, but going up the middle or to left field—the opposite field for a left-handed batter. I took extra batting practice and called for curve balls. Most guys don't really care to hit breaking balls in batting practice. Guys just want to get fastballs and pound them out of the park. But I thought I ought to work on my weakness. Since hitting had never been a problem with me, I thought I could eventually work this thing out.

At this time the Twins had two veteran second basemen, Frank Quilici and Cesar Tovar. During the 1966 season, Tovar and Bernie Allen, who had been traded over the winter, had split most of the second-base play for the Twins. Quilici, who had been called up from the minors to help the Twins win the pennant in 1965, had been returned to the minors in 1966, but was up now for another try. Frank was not the most talented player, but he was gritty and smart and hustled. Mele liked him. Tovar was a guy who could do a lot of things well and play a lot of positions. They were tough competition for me.

Dismal as some of spring training might have seemed at times, I had bright moments. In my first start at second base, for example, against the Phillies at Clearwater, I made a leaping stab of a line drive, started two double plays and stroked a few hits.

And Calvin kept his confidence in me. In mid-March, although I was batting only about .240, he said, "Carew could be the American League All-Star second baseman if he wants to be." Wants to be! I wanted nothing more. Well, I wanted one thing more—to make the club. You can hardly be the American League All-Star second baseman if you're playing in the International League.

Guys started to get cut from the squad. The clubhouse man has a list of guys they're going to cut. After a workout, he'd walk over to a guy's locker and say, "The manager wants to see you." Like the Grim Reaper. I sat by my locker. I watched the clubhouse man out of the corner of my eye. A whole row of guys watched out of the corner of their eyes. When one guy got the news, the other guys would look to see who would be next. Some guys walked into the training room, or the john, thinking if the clubhouse man didn't see them he'd forget about them, which was never the case.

I survived the first cut. When I got back to my hotel, I had a team brochure with me. I put a check beside the names of the guys sure of making the club, and put an "X" by the guys who had a slight chance or no chance to make the club.

At the second cut, five or six more guys went. I returned to my room and crossed off their names. It was a little sad to see these guys leave, but my feeling was, better them than me. But you felt the gloom, and saw tears in the eyes of those leaving. The young guys who had made it so far said to those cut, Well, I'll be over there in Wilson, or Denver, in about a week or so to join you.

Just before camp was about to break up, at the beginning of April, Billy came over to my locker and sat down. "Rod," he said, "they're going to make the big cut today." I waited for him to continue. "Your name is on the list to go north with us."

Before I could get too excited, Billy added, "But you have to realize that we're going to have to cut three more guys after a thirty-day stay with the club. We can carry twenty-eight guys until the end of May. Go out there and work hard."

I wasn't aware of the behind-the-scenes drama that was going on. Sam in fact had planned to send me to the minors. But Griffith went to Mele and insisted that I go north with the club. This is unusual for Griffith, or any other owner, generally. The field manager is left to make decisions of this nature, and if the owner doesn't like the manager's decisions, then he can drop the axe. But Mele knew his job was in jeopardy—he had won a pennant in 1965, but the team had dropped to second in 1966, and Calvin was supposedly unhappy. If all went well with the team, the Twins were going to be in the pennant race again. And Sam wanted an experienced man at second, not a rookie.

But the day before the season opener, Sam called me aside and said, "Rod, you might be the starting second baseman in the first series." This was against the Baltimore Orioles, *World Champions*. The previous October on television I had watched the Orioles demolish the Dodgers in four straight games.

Well, that night I couldn't fall asleep. I kept the television on until something like 2 or 3 in the morning. Mudcat Grant was my roommate, and he had gone out like a light. I kept the sound of the television low and it didn't bother him. It didn't bother me either, because I hardly knew it was on. I thought about the next day, about the possibility of facing Dave McNally, who would pitch for the Orioles. I still wasn't sure of starting. It was still up in the air whether Quilici, Tovar or I would be at second. But I thought about facing McNally, who had been a top 20-game winner. He was supposed to have a blazing fastball. And then I thought about the rest of the Orioles, Brooks Robinson and Frank Robinson and Boog Powell . . .

Before we took the field for batting practice, Sam called a meeting of the club. He wanted to go over signs. From his hip pocket he pulled out the lineup card. "Zoilo's leading off and playing short," he said. "Carew's batting second and at second base . . ." Bam! Right off. My stomach flopped upside down.

The starting players were introduced on the public-address system, and we lined up at the foul line. In some ways I felt like an outsider. When the announcer said, "Zoilo Versalles," there was a big hand—he had been the Most Valuable Player in the league two seasons back. When I was announced, I trotted out to the politest little applause you've ever heard. Well, the fans weren't about to waste their heavy artillery on an unknown rookie. When Tony Oliva and Harmon Killebrew and Bob Allison were called, the fans let loose.

Zoilo went up and out. Now I'm standing at home plate. I was fidgety in the box, trying to settle myself down a bit. I knocked the dirt out of my cleats. I took a deep breath to relax. Then I looked at the third-base coach, Billy, to see if he wanted me to take a pitch or swing.

The sign was to swing if the pitch was good. The pitch was good, but I didn't swing. I wanted to see McNally's velocity. He threw me a good steamy fastball. McNally was a lefty, and that should have been of special concern for me. But in those days the lefty-righty aspects of pitching and hitting never crossed my mind. My whole outlook on hitting was watching the ball and swinging. Whether it came from a lefty or a righty never troubled me. As I got older, I began to give it more thought because people talked about it. I wish I had never considered it. Sometimes thinking at the plate can be hazardous to your performance.

A breaking pitch came in next, and I swung and bounced out to second base. In the bottom of the first, I'm standing at second base and I can't shake my nervousness. There's a runner on first, and Frank Robinson is up. *Frank Robinson.* He looked so big up there. He's a tall, strong guy, and he's whipping the bat around, and his stockings—he's got that thing where the stirrup socks are high and he's got a lot of white showing. He looks menacing. Then he takes that big hitched swing and he bounces a ball up the middle. It was the kind of ball I should have backhanded easily. But I couldn't get started after the ball because my legs were shaking. I'm like in mud. When my legs finally do get going, I get just close enough so that the ball bounces off my glove and goes out into center field. I guess it should have been called an error—an error on my legs. But it was scored a hit. Strangest thing, after that I had no trouble in the field that season. I think I fielded my first 105 chances in the major leagues without an error.

I got my first major-league hit the next time up. McNally threw me a soft slider and I hit it right past him into center field. They stopped the game. The umpire called for the ball and handed it to me. A souvenir. My first hit in the big time. Then I tossed the ball to Doc Lentz, who kept it for me. The guys on the bench congratulated me. I got another hit and finished the day 2-for-5.

After my first game in the big leagues I'm hitting .400. That night I thought, Well, even if I never get another hit up here in my life, at least I'll be able to say that at one time in my major-league career I was a .400 hitter. Me and Ted Williams.

I got a hit my first time up in the Twins' home opener

against Detroit. Big, enthusiastic crowd. The applause for the hit sounded sweet in my ears. Jim Lemon was the first-base coach. "Way to go, Rodney," he said. Then he told me the usual: take a little lead; watch the line drives; don't get doubled off; check the outfielders to see where everybody's playing. The pitcher was Earl Wilson, a right-hander. A pretty wily guy, been in the majors six, seven years. I thought I'd take a nice-sized lead and steal a base. Make a big first impression for the local fans.

I took two steps and was about to take a third when Wilson suddenly wheels and fires to first. I was dead. The ball was there before I knew it. I couldn't even slide back. Norm Cash was the first baseman. He put the tag on me. "That's a way to go, Rook," he said, laughing.

Opening-day hometown crowd. First inning. I felt like crawling under the base. I was so embarrassed I didn't even want to go back to the dugout. But I came back to the bench and waited to catch hell. Sam didn't say a word. In days to come, Billy would discuss with me how to read pitchers. How to watch their motion. How not to be fooled by them. But in the next couple of weeks, I got picked off about seven times. Bam. Bam. Bam. It was horrible. Yet I was starting to learn. Right-handers were tougher than lefties. I had to watch their shoulders. When they opened it up—when you could see their chest—they were going to throw to first and not throw a pitch. Some guys hold the ball a long time in the stretch position and wait for you to get fidgety and off balance; then they nab you. Luis Tiant and Jack Sanford were really tough for me.

I knew I had to listen if I was going to learn. My next major lesson dealt with Stu Miller, at the end of April. Miller was going on 40 years old and had been pitching in the big leagues for sixteen years. As a relief pitcher with the Orioles, he was rough. He threw all this soft stuff, and he threw with a herky-jerky motion. I had heard so much about him. He had three speeds. Slow, slower and slower still. He relied on guys' being so anxious to hit his balloon that they'd twist themselves into knots. Even the way Miller *looked* made you anxious to hit. Very slight build. He was the guy who was once blown off the mound by a big wind at Candlestick Park.

I wasn't in the lineup this game. It's now the bottom of the ninth and the score is tied 2–2. We load the bases with one out. The Orioles bring in Miller. Mele looks down the bench and points his finger at me and says, "Grab a bat. You're hitting."

Before I get up the dugout steps, Sam stops me. "Wait on him, Rod. Don't be too anxious."

The ball Miller threw reminded me of a milk train. It kept making stops all along the way. As Sam suggested, I waited and waited and waited. When the ball finally reached the plate, I swung and got good wood. It bounced right past Miller, over second base and into center field for a single to win the game.

Miller had seemed to be throwing from center field. But other pitchers in the league, like a Sam McDowell, seemed right on top of you. McDowell was a tall, lanky lefty— about six-five, 190. By the time I faced him, he was already the American League leader in strikeouts, as well as walks. A lot of guys bailed out on him, as they would on Nolan Ryan and Bob Veale. Batters didn't enjoy facing fastball pitchers like those guys. They threw it 100 miles an hour. Veale was like McDowell, tall. And by the time he came down from his windup, you were thinking, Jesus Christ, what's he doing so close?

But as hard as some of these guys throw, I've never been afraid to walk up there and face them. I don't care how close he comes to me with a pitch. If I were frightened, I wouldn't be able to go up there and hit. I don't think you can be intimidated and be a good hitter. The word on Henry Aaron, for example, used to be, Don't knock him down, because then he gets mad and concentrates on the pitch even more.

Pitchers excuse their knockdown pitches by saying,

"Well, you can't hit while on your back." And there are guys who you see are scared at the plate. Sometimes for good reason. Some of them have been hurt. Look at Tony Conigliaro. He was a young guy and got smashed in the face with a pitch. A few seasons later he was out of the game. Another guy it affected, I think, is Paul Blair, of the Yankees. He was hit in the head with a pitch and was out for a while, and when he came back he was a different guy at the plate. He's still good, but he isn't the terrific threat he once was. He went from American League All-Star center fielder to hitting below .200 in the space of two years (he's improved since then, I'm glad to say).

I've been fortunate that I haven't had a serious batting injury. I find the fastball pitchers a great challenge. I've had luck with most of them. Guys like Denny McLain and McDowell never gave me the trouble that good breaking-ball pitchers did.

Pitchers try to make you flinch, and if you don't, then it begins to erode their confidence—"Gee, maybe this guy is better than I thought. . . ."

Some guys, though, simply have your number. Of course, some hitters hit pitchers as if they owned them, too. There was a second-string infielder with the Phillies named Tom Hutton who was about a .200 hitter but got a hit off Tom Seaver almost every time he looked at him. I'm that way with Catfish Hunter. Catfish will tell you that. He has said I have no real weakness as a hitter. He says I swing with the pitch—that's why I have no holes.

Well, Rudy May might say the opposite. I had no confidence hitting against Rudy May. Telling you bluntly, I had no confidence at all when I faced him. I would walk up there and I would say to myself, I'm just going to make a right turn and go back to the dugout. When Gene Mauch took over the Twins in 1976, he asked me if there were any pitchers I had particular problems with. I said one. Rudy May. And when May pitches I'll usually take the day off.

What does May have? He's a six-foot-two left-hander with a good fastball and good breaking stuff. He's an excellent pitcher, but other guys hit him. And I hit pitchers who are as good as or better than Rudy. Like Catfish in his best years. Both of those pitchers move the ball around on me—inside, outside, low, high, fastball, breaking ball. But Rudy could throw the ball underhanded and probably get me out. One reason, I think, is that he hides the ball so well. It seems that I can't pick up his pitch until the ball is nearly on top of me. I tried everything against him—choking up on the bat, moving around in the box: nothing worked. When he was traded in 1977 from the Orioles to Montreal in the National League, my reaction was, Great, put him over on another island.

After the first month of my rookie season, a lot of guys were looking like Rudy May to me. Even though I had that big hit off Miller, and those opening-day singles in Baltimore and at Met Stadium, I was hitting only about .220, and I knew the final cut was coming up. I started putting pressure on myself. I knew I had to do better. Billy had told me that the Twins felt if I could hit .250 and play a decent second base I'd be kept. Then I got a few hits and I'm up to .240. There are three days left before the cut. And I'm playing every day. They're giving me the chance to make it or cut my own throat. Now Washington comes to town for two games. Suddenly everything that's thrown up I bang back for a hit. I go 5-for-5 the first game. Next day I single the first time up. Then I make an out. Then I come back with three straight hits. I ended up with a 9-for-10 series against the Senators. It's early in the season and you don't have that many times at bat, so the points on the batting average can pile up: I went from .240 to .340. When I look back on it, I wonder if I just loosened up. Before, I may have been trying too hard and taking too many pitches. Being too picky. I had gotten into the habit of taking the first strike, too. Now I went up swinging. That's the opposite of Ted Williams' theory. He has this thing about the strike zone, and that you should be very, very selective about what pitch you hit. That was certainly a proper theory for him. For me, I swing at anything that looks good. Of course, Ted was strictly a pull hitter; I spray the ball. So a pitch on the outside corner and low, a pitch he'd let go by, I might slap down the third-base line for a double.

I thought my chances were good now for making the club. But when the final day came down, I still wasn't sure. The club had been carrying 28 guys. Three had to go. On the day of the final cut, May 11, I'm sitting at my locker dressing for batting practice. The clubhouse man, Ray Crump, comes out of Sam's office and I see he walks over to John Sevcik, the catcher, and taps him on the shoulder. This is it. One down. Two to go. Sevcik comes out of Sam's office and his head is hanging down. Now Crump walks over to Ron Keller, a pitcher, and taps him on the shoulder. Then he goes to a third guy—I don't even remember his name—and taps him. Suddenly I felt light as a feather. Nobody ever said, You made it, Rod. But nobody ever said I hadn't, either.

Everything fell into place after that. I was no longer nervous. I felt I was a big-league ballplayer now. I'm hitting. I'm stealing a few bases. I'm playing well in the field.

I'm also learning the tricks of the trade. Fields are doctored, I discover. The White Sox have sinker-ball pitchers like Gary Peters and Joel Horlen and Tommy John, so the groundskeepers are instructed to soak the front of the batter's box; when the ball is hit, down it goes plunk and practically stops dead. Boston was a power team and didn't run much, so the Fenway Park baselines were made soft to handicap teams that did run; the turf had been loosened up so much you'd think you were running in sand.

A first baseman will sometimes talk to a runner to distract him, to enhance a pickoff attempt or to slow him up when the ball is hit.

And a first baseman like John Mayberry, then of Kansas City, would tag you a little harder than normal when there was a routine pickoff throw. He'd whack you in the shins. He thought it might slow you up just a bit. We had a guy on the Twins, Jimmy Holt, who had bad feet. The whole league knew it. If you dropped a piece of cotton next to Jimmy's feet, he'd hit the ceiling. So all the first basemen would give Jimmy an extra-hard tap on the toes. Anything to make a guy feel uncomfortable. I'd say just about everyone in the league is looking for that little edge. They say it's a game of inches. So if a guy can be slowed up one inch because you stepped on his toe, well, that's the way they play the game.

Catchers have a lot of tricks. To try to throw off your rhythm, some catchers tip your bat when you're getting loose just before the pitcher winds up. Another guy might pull on your socks. Other guys will throw dirt on the batter's shoes. Thurman Munson does that to me a lot. He also talks to me all the time, especially when the pitcher is delivering. "Rod," he'll say, "what am I doing wrong at bat? Am I lunging at the ball? Am I too slow? Am I not attacking the ball?" And zip, the ball is coming in. Carlton Fisk chatters when you step into the box. "How many hits you gonna get today, Rod? Where do you want the pitch?" It can throw you off. You've got to block out the noise. That's the kind of stuff I had to learn to handle in my first few months in the league.

Once I made the team, and was able to breathe a little easier, I looked around and noticed that other guys were having their own problems. Sam Mele more than most. Experts, or so-called experts, were predicting that the Twins should be one of the strongest clubs in the league. Besides our power hitters, we also had picked up Dean Chance, a good right-handed pitcher, in an off-season trade, and we had several fine young pitchers in Dave Boswell, Jim Merritt and Jim Roland, along with proved veterans Jim Kaat, Jim Perry and Jim Grant. On paper, we were great. But on the field, we were struggling to play .500 ball. By the end of May, Detroit and Chicago are in and out of first place and we're 6½ games back and guys are grousing. A bunch of guys are mad at Sam for every conceivable reason. You name it, they're mad at him for it. As I said, I liked Sam. He was a soft-spoken guy who was always decent to me. Now it's in the papers that Sam has lost control of the team. I guess they meant that guys weren't putting all out for him. All I know is, I was. We lose a close one to Cleveland on June 8, and on June 9 Baltimore kicks our fannies 11–2. And Sam is fired. Cal Ermer, the manager at Denver, is in.

Our problems aren't solved. We still can't get a winning streak going. And guys are still unhappy.

In Detroit, we're on the team bus going from the airport to the hotel. Dave Boswell always used to carry a little bag with a couple of guns in it. They were handguns. Dave had some pretty weird habits. So now Boswell pulls one of these things out and starts pulling the trigger. It isn't loaded, but Tony Oliva jumps up and is really upset. "Don't be playing with that thing on this bus," Tony said. Dave yelled out, "Well, you guys can play with guns in Cuba; why can't we play with guns here?"

All of a sudden, things just broke loose. Jim Grant said, "This is no place to be playing with guns." Ted Uhlaender, who is Boswell's buddy and is sitting beside him, pipes up, "If all you black guys want to stick together, all us white guys are going to stick together." Then Sandy Valdespino backs up Tony and Grant. Uhlaender jumps up and he's about to go at Sandy. Other guys jump in and hold them apart.

I sat and watched this whole thing with amazement. Ermer had to make a stand, and he fined Oliva, Boswell and Uhlaender $250 apiece. In those days, that was a pretty good chunk. I don't know what those guys were making, but it wasn't anything like the big money we make now. And they had families to support. I know I was earning only $7,000 a year then—the minimum salary for a major-leaguer. I was living in a hotel room and trying to send money home every week and barely making ends meet. So $250 hurt. And I think it might have shaken us up. Sometimes an incident like that can have a positive effect. Maybe we started taking things more seriously. Whatever, we won 12 of our next 15 games.

We were seeing teams for the second time around, and I thought they might have been getting my number. It was a battle, an uphill battle for me, made especially tough for me because I was attending Marine reserve meetings one weekend a month. So when I'd get back to the team, my timing would be just a little off. And then you go up against a Sudden Sam McDowell, who is throwing aspirin tablets anyway—every pitch is doing something different. The ball is going to be running away from you, or running into you. You're in trouble.

I wasn't confiding any of my anxieties to anyone, except in a few instances to Oliva. Tony O. was really the only guy I communicated with. He was like a big brother to me. He would try to prepare me by telling me what different pitchers threw and what their balls did.

From the first time I met Tony, he was always Oliva the person and never Oliva the American League batting champion. In 1965 when I went to the Twins' spring training camp for the first time, Tony and I became buddies. He had just won the league batting title as a rookie, and I was only pinch-running and working out. But we'd go out and eat and sit in a room and talk and play cards with Earl Battey and Sandy Valdespino and some others. It never crossed Tony's mind one bit to act the part of a hotshot player. He was always the same. Laughing, free-spirited, generous, understanding.

Tony was a guy who came from a poor little farm in

Cuba. He was signed by the Senators and brought to the States. He couldn't speak a word of English. When he began playing for Wyethville in the Appalachian League, his manager wrote two messages on a piece of paper for him so that he could order in a restaurant. One message read, "ham and eggs." The other message read, "fried chicken." That was all he ate for three months, until he learned a few other words. Then he got cocky and one evening in a drugstore he saw a nice chocolate candy bar and pointed to it. He took it up to his room, unwrapped it and bit into it. He almost gagged. It was chewing tobacco.

We roomed together for eight years. He has been my closest friend on the team. But when I was in one of my moods, I might not even talk to him for a couple of days. It seemed like water off a duck's back for him. It never turned him against me. If I were in his shoes, I probably would have demanded a new roomie.

And what a beautiful hitter to watch. Unbelievable. He could hit anyone, right-handers or left-handers, consistently. And he almost always hit the ball hard. He could hit to all fields, and with power. I've seen him hit pitches that amazed me at times. I saw him hit pitches that were so low they were like lying on a tee, and he'd put them 450 feet into the stands. He stood up there in his knock-kneed manner and just ripped. He hit with his weight on his front foot, which is unorthodox. He's a pretty big guy, about six-two, 195, and has a strong torso and big arms. He won three batting titles—the first two in his first two years in the majors—and probably would have won more if it hadn't been for his knee injury.

It's a funny thing, but I saw him dive for a ball in right field only twice. The first time, he dislocated his shoulder, in 1968. The next time, in June of 1971, he damaged the cartilage in his right knee. The second time, he shouldn't have been diving at all. I didn't think he had any chance for the pop fly, but he tried. He landed on his knee. That's when the pain started. From then on, every time he swung he was in pain. He took as many as ten shots before a game during the season to relieve the pain so he could play. Before each game he took two or three painkilling pills. Yet he led the league in hitting that year. And all this time people were saying, Tony is not really hurt that much; after all, look how he's hitting. It was the old story that a black guy can't really get hurt. The knee was operated on once. He said he felt fine afterward. But the next spring the knee got worse. The knee swelled repeatedly. It had accumulated fluid. Tony was in terrible pain. He played only 10 games that season and underwent another operation in July. Two bone spurs and over a hundred little bone chips were removed. He kept them in a bottle to prove to people that he really did have an injury. He compared those little bone chips in the knee to someone running around with pebbles in his shoe. The pain can get excruciating. Tony was worried sick that his career was over, at age 31. He played a few more years, until 1975, but was primarily a designated hitter. He had to change his swing because of the weak knee; he was never again the same hitter.

People used to talk about Mickey Mantle and his physical problems, his bad knees. I couldn't understand because I'd never seen it and never experienced it. But then I roomed with a guy with bad knees for years and used to listen to him cry like a baby at night. I'd be asleep and sometimes I'd hear Tony moaning and groaning. Or he'd get up and be in agony from the pain in his leg. I'd see him get up during the night and go down to get ice, wandering all over the hotel trying to find ice to put on his knee. I'd look at his leg and I'd see the scars and the way it was all wracked up and I'd wonder how he could continue on.

If you see Oliva's knee, you won't believe it. It's just a mass of flesh. After several operations, there was no bone left in the knee. So many times I watched him run down to first base and I could see how much he was hurting. But he would not give up.

With every step he took I felt the hurt. I'd see him in the winter and I remember him telling me, "When the weather comes good all over, my knee won't be stiff no more. Then I start to hit out the bullets."

And he'd tell me, "I have the confidence still at bat. One thing I always know: if one time I miss, the next time I go smoking for sure."

As time went on, the knee got worse. He'd be at the park at 3 o'clock when he wouldn't have to be there until 5. He'd work out every day lifting weights for the leg, getting into the whirlpool, having the trainer massage the leg. In the last three years, during the off season, he worked out from 10 to 4 every day except Sundays. The boredom—forget about the pain—must have been monumental. Every day, every day, he'd be at it, hoping to get back into the outfield. The doctors kept telling him, "No, there is no chance." He was now strictly a designated hitter, but he couldn't accept that. He didn't want to be half a ballplayer, he said.

Tony bought every kind of massaging machine on the market. On the road, he carried a suitcase with different machines in it to work on his knee. He'd be lying in bed watching TV and massaging. He'd get up early in the morning and all you'd hear was "Hmmmmmm," a real loud vibrating sound. He'd just sit there and rub his knee.

Every time you'd go past his locker, you'd see Tony putting something on his knee. People from Latin America sent him old home remedies. I remember one ointment made from snake skin. If another player came around and said anything to him about it, he'd get upset. "Go, guys," he'd say, "get away from my locker. What are you looking at?" But I could get away with kidding him because we were such good friends.

One day I saw a can of STP he had and was rubbing the

contents on his knee. I couldn't believe it. "Tony," I said, "what are you trying to do, get fifty miles per hour out of those things?" He laughed and kept on rubbing.

BY JUNE of my rookie year, I was leading all other American League second basemen in hitting, and people were talking about my making the All-Star team. Before the season, Reggie Smith was the guy everybody was picking for Rookie of the Year. In preseason articles about the major-league rookie crop of 1967, I was never mentioned. Now Reggie was having a slow start and I was getting noticed.

When we played in New York, my parents came to the game. I think it was the first organized game either ever saw me play in. Photographers took a picture of us standing by the dugout. My mother and father were looking over my shoulder, and then my mother began to cry. I knew it was from happiness. I just looked at her and I said, "I told you I'd be a ballplayer and make you cry one day."

I didn't even want Eric there, but they were living together and so I got them both tickets. When I first saw them behind the dugout I said, "Hi, how are you guys doing?" But I didn't talk to him at all. I can't remember if he said anything to me or not. I'm sure if he did I wouldn't have been listening. But he was beaming, and he was laughing.

Later in the season I invited them to Minneapolis for a week. They had a good time. I know Eric enjoyed being Rod Carew's father there. He received a lot of attention. People were telling him how well I was doing and how bright my future was. He was also amazed that I had set him up in a nice hotel, and that all he had to do for anything was sign his name. If he's going to be my mother's husband, I decided, I can be civil to him—especially since I was no longer living with the man. But there was no smoothing over all those years of unhappiness with him. And though it may not be fair, the only thing I really remember about his visit is that afterward he never bothered to thank me for it.

At the All-Star break in mid-July, we had climbed to second place, and I made the All-Star team. Not only did I make it, but I was the starting second baseman. The only rookie to start, and I think I was the only rookie on the American League team. When I got the telegram from the league office, the first thing I did was go to Calvin Griffith's office to thank him for the confidence he had shown in me.

My batting average now was .315, fourth best in the league behind Frank Robinson, Al Kaline and Carl Yastrzemski. Even though I was up there with them, the thought of playing on the same team with guys of that caliber made me nervous again. Robinson had impressed me with his unselfishness as a hitter. He used to try to move the runners into scoring position even if he had to take an out to do it. Whenever a runner was on second base with nobody out, Frank tried on the first or second swing to move the runner to third, to get him into better scoring position. And only after he got two strikes would he go back to his normal way of hitting. And Kaline—I loved the way he played right field. The way he got to the ball, like a cat; and his throws—the consistency—they were always on the money. But the most incredible guy of all that season was Yaz. He won the triple crown, leading the league in batting average, homers and runs-batted-in. He never got cheated all year. That is, he never got fooled by a pitch. You never saw him take a half swing, a mediocre swing. He was ripping at everything. Every ball he hit, he hit like a rocket. And he played left field as I've never seen anybody play left field. Making catches and throws and charging the ball. You didn't run on Yaz. You didn't try to take the extra base on him.

The All-Star game was in Anaheim, California. In the clubhouse, I didn't say a word. Few people spoke to me. I was just happy to be there. Tony, Harmon and Dean

Chance had made the team too, and they were all starting. So I didn't feel completely left out. When we went onto the field to warm up, I looked across at the National League side and saw all those great players—Ernie Banks and Willie Mays and Bob Gibson and Henry Aaron and Roberto Clemente and Don Drysdale. We took the field first. I could feel my heart pumping. Big, brand-new stadium. There is a capacity crowd of 46,000. The largest crowd I've ever played in front of. There are supposed to be 55 million people watching this game on national television. My friends and family back home are seeing this. So I'm standing at second base and my knees are knocking together. I wonder if anyone can see my legs knocking—or hear them. Talk about nervous. I thought I had gotten over my nervousness. Not at all. I think that that game was the most exciting thing to happen to me in my entire career. But for all my awe, I still had the confidence now that I could play on the same field with these guys. I respected their longevity, and their achievements, but I felt I belonged.

I fielded a few chances flawlessly. I was 0-for-2 when I came up my last time. I pulled one off Ferguson Jenkins. If it doesn't go foul, I've got a home run. I was standing at the plate watching and shouting at the ball, "Stay in there." It hooked and went foul. On the next pitch, I backed Lou Brock against the left-field fence for a long out. I didn't get a hit, but I had played well in my first All-Star game. After I was taken out, I sat on the bench and watched the whole game. Everyone who came out of the game sat around to watch. No one disappeared into the clubhouse. It was a thriller, going 15 innings, and we finally lost on Tony Perez' homer.

When I returned to Minnesota, Calvin called me into his office and presented me with a $3,000 bonus, which I was grateful for. But at times I wondered in the next few months if he had second thoughts about it. My average began to drop, and I committed some blunders on the bases. One

time, I tried to steal third with a 3-0 count on Harmon
Killebrew, our top power hitter, and was caught to end the
inning. Well, there was nothing dumber than that. Harmon
would have had the hit sign, and the pitcher had to come in
for a strike or walk him. Ermer gave me hell for it, and I
deserved it.

Harmon never said a word to me about it. He is a quiet
man, and a true gentleman. He commands respect. He always went out and did his job and never complained
(though I understand he stood up to management in contract negotiations). Harmon never argued with an umpire.
It just wasn't his nature.

Harmon had to be one of the strongest men in baseball.
He hit some of the longest home runs in history. Once he
hit a ball that seemed to be rising as it cracked into the seats
in the left-field upper deck in Metropolitan Stadium. Unob-
structed, that ball might have carried 600 feet for all I know.
When Harmon retired in 1975, he finished with a major-
league career total of 573 home runs—fifth behind Henry
Aaron, Babe Ruth, Willie Mays and Frank Robinson. Harmon's grandfather was supposed to have been a legendary
Union Army strong man during the Civil War. I'd have to
believe it, knowing his grandson.

The Cinderella story came true for Harmon. He was discovered in 1954 while playing high school baseball in remote Payette, Idaho. A U.S. Senator from Idaho, Herman
Welker, told his friend Clark Griffith, owner of the Washington Senators, about this great young player in his consti-
tuency.

Griffith, more out of friendship than from genuine interest, had Ossie Bluege check the kid out. Bluege was head
of the club's farm system. Harmon was a high school senior. In the game Bluege saw, Harmon hit two tremendous
homers and boomed a triple. Bluege signed him as fast as
he could. It was a $35,000 contract, huge for those days. It
made national headlines. That money included Harmon's

salary for his first two baseball seasons. It also meant he would have to spend two years with the Senators and could not be sent to the minors. If you signed for $4,000 or more in those days, they had to keep you on the parent club's roster. So Harmon played in his first major-league game when he was 17, but mostly warmed the bench for two seasons. Eventually, he did play a few seasons in the minor leagues. But in 1959, his first year as a regular big-league third baseman, he hit 42 homers, to lead the league. He would lead the league in homers five more times, and lead in RBI's three times.

Harmon, though, also struck out a lot, as many sluggers do. When the Senators moved to Minnesota in 1961, Harmon found that people booed him. I guess fans expected him to hit a home run every time at bat. When I came up to the Twins, I found it amazing that the fans would boo such a great player. There was one guy who sat in the grandstand just below the press box every Sunday. He had a pair of leather lungs and you could hear him bellow all through the park. Whenever Harmon came to bat, this guy would holler, "Here comes Harmless Harmon!"

When this happened, or when others booed him, I'd often look at Harmon to see if he would blow up. He never lost his temper. But I thought, God, if he's one of the best home-run hitters in our time, and they do that to him . . . Then I thought, But he can *accept* it, too. In later years when I was booed for my fielding at home, I remembered how Harmon had taken the abuse gracefully; he was an inspiration to me.

NINETEEN SIXTY-SEVEN was the year known as "The Great Race." Five teams were in it up until the last week, and four teams had a chance to win the pennant on the last weekend of the season. Chicago led for most of June and July. We led for most of August and the first part of September. The Tigers took over first place in mid-September. Boston was never more than a game or two off the pace. California never fell totally out of the picture either, and if they had put together a big winning streak in August or September they might have taken the whole thing. It was neck-and-neck. You'd be checking the scoreboard from the dugout to see how the other teams were doing. I'd go home and catch the late scores from California on the television news. I'd be anxious before games now, and think about coming up in clutch situations and not letting the team down. Whether it was the heat of the pennant race or not, I developed a bad case of hemorrhoids and lost 10 pounds during that summer. I had an upset stomach all season. I've heard about other guys getting nervous and developing physical complaints. Joe DiMaggio says he got ulcers because of the pressure he felt as a player. Roger Maris' hair fell out the year he broke Babe Ruth's home-run record. I know Bill Russell and Gale Sayers used to vomit before big games.

As the race came down the stretch, I was made to feel important. On the weekends that I went to reserve meetings, Calvin had a small jet waiting at the airport for me after the game so that I could make the meeting on time.

In mid-August, I missed two weeks because of Marine summer camp. Almost as soon as I left, we went on a winning streak and climbed into first place. I realized that no one is indispensable, particularly a rookie. Harmon was headed for a 44-homer season; Tony would be among the league's top ten hitters; Allison was slugging; Chance was on his way to 20 wins and Kaat to 16. Tovar played anywhere we needed him and performed solidly. He took over at second when I was gone. When I came back from the reserves, I felt rusty. I was called "The Invisible Carew" because of my absences. Even if I hadn't been a rookie, being away like that makes you feel like an outsider when you return.

The season was coming down to the wire. On September 7, *four* teams were tied for first. And the second-division teams were knocking off the first-division teams. None of the contenders could put any kind of winning streak together. During the final week, two straight wins by any of the top four could have pretty much clinched at least a tie for the pennant. So, Boston lost two straight to Cleveland; Detroit was losing to Washington, New York and California; the White Sox lost five straight to Kansas City and the Senators, and we lost two out of three to California.

Still, we were in first place, one game in front. We would end the season over the weekend with a two-game series at Boston.

On the eve of the series, we had a minor team riot. We got together in the clubhouse to vote on World Series shares. A bunch of guys didn't want to vote Sam Mele anything, not even a quarter share. Uhlaender, Boswell and Jim Merritt were leaders of that group. The pro-Mele guys countered that if Sam wasn't entitled to anything, neither was Ermer. It was upsetting for me. Sam had been with the club for half the year. I thought he should get a full share, and I said so. I couldn't believe that some guys who had played for him for years were voting him out completely. The result was that Mele got nothing. Ermer was voted a full share, which I think he deserved. I was concerned that this infighting might beat us before Boston had the chance. My God, we're going into the biggest series of the season. The pennant's riding on it—and we're squabbling.

We had to win just one game to ensure a tie for the title. Before the first game, Ermer told us, "Forget tomorrow. Win today. We've got to give everything now."

Fenway Park is a little old bandbox of a park. It's got humpbacked bleachers, and the stands are so close the fans seem to be right on top of you. And there's that big, inviting left-field wall only 315 feet down the line; they call it "the Green Monster." It's a terror for pitchers. Saturday came up sunny and beautiful, and the park was really jumping. The fans were cheering so loudly I thought my ears would burst.

You have to remember, the Red Sox had finished seventh the season before, and they had been a 100–1 shot to win the pennant this year. They hadn't been in a World Series since 1946. They often came close, but then faltered on the last days of the season. Now their fans were saying this was "the impossible dream."

Jim Kaat, who was called "Kitty," as you might imagine, was the starting pitcher for the first game. He's a big, red-haired left-hander from Zeeland, Michigan, a small Dutch community. His dad was a shopkeeper who was called "Honest John." When Kaat graduated from high school, he was only five-eleven, about 170 pounds. Within about two years he had grown to six-five, 235. This season, 1967, was his ninth in the big leagues, and he had developed into one of the best pitchers in baseball. In 1966, his good fastball helped him lead the league in wins with 25. But in the course of that season he also caught a one-hop bouncer right in the mouth. It knocked out his upper front teeth. When I first saw him in the spring-training clubhouse in 1967, I remember him taking his new dental plate out of his mouth and walking around and smiling like a madman with that huge gap. It was very funny, and I thought, These guys are just kids after all.

There was another unusual thing about Kaat. Although he was an excellent fielder—he is amazingly quick off the mound for a man his size—he had trouble throwing accurately to the bases. He had great control when pitching, but when, say, he tried to nab a runner at second on an attempted sacrifice bunt, the ball would likely end up in the hands of the center fielder.

Kitty was 16-and-12 going into the opener of the Boston series, and he was pitching well. However, in the third inning, with a 1–0 lead, he threw a fastball and then let out a howl. He had popped a ligament in his pitching arm.

He had to leave the game. The Red Sox then took it to some of our relief pitchers, and we fell behind. I came up with the bases loaded at one point and had a chance to send us ahead by a few runs; I lined a fastball down the third-base line, and smack into Jerry Adair's glove. It killed the rally. Yaz had a big homer that game, and that made the difference in the final score, 6–4. So now Boston is tied with us for first place. One game is left to play. Meanwhile, Detroit is splitting a doubleheader with California. Detroit still has a chance to tie for the pennant if they can win a doubleheader Sunday.

Chance was our pitcher in the final. Jim Lonborg, a strong right-hander with 21 wins, went for Boston. The pressure was so heavy that the fans this afternoon were quiet. It was strange—there was a capacity crowd of over 35,000, but sometimes the only sound you heard was the chatter of the infielders.

We did everything wrong. Zoilo threw to a wrong base and let a run score. We left a base open with no one covering it. There were wild pitches. We left guys on base. An important ground ball hit a stone and bounced over my head for a hit. And Lonborg was pitching great. And even though we had scoring opportunities until the end, we just couldn't get it done. Right from the start, I thought Dean Chance had a bad case of nerves. He wasn't the same Dean Chance who had won 20 games this season. I went out to the mound to talk to him once during the game. His face looked drawn. He was sweating more than he normally did, and you could see a glassy look in his eye. Usually, he'd have all the confidence in the world. Dean was a hell of a nice guy. You read a lot about Dean, and it's true that he knew a lot of people in Hollywood, but he never drank, never smoked, and Dean never did anything to hurt anyone and never talked behind anyone's back. He'd normally joke when he was out on the mound. He'd say to me, "Don't worry, Supe, I've got him." He called me Superman. I never knew why. When I went out to talk to him now, he just nodded his head. Didn't say anything. They rapped him hard, and when he was knocked out, he walked straight into the clubhouse, showered, changed his clothes and left the park before the game was over. I think he felt he had let us down, that he didn't win the big game for us. We lost 5–3. After the game, some guys were saying, "Well, he didn't have the guts to stay around." I felt otherwise. I felt that Dean knew he didn't have it today and felt just awful facing us.

I could certainly sympathize. In my last 12 at-bats, I had gone hitless. This covered the last three games of the season, the biggest games of the year. My consolation was that I had hit several hard shots, but they had been right at somebody; so I wasn't about to get down on myself. I mean, we lost the pennant by one game, and each of us could have found something to blame himself for—that maybe somewhere during the course of the season he might have cost the team a game. And on the plane coming home, everybody was down in the dumps. No one cared that the Tigers had lost their last game of the season to give the Red Sox the championship outright.

I finished the year with a .292 batting average, sixth in the league. Several weeks later, in the voting for Rookie of the Year, I received 19 of the 20 votes. Reggie Smith got the other. But I really didn't have much time to gloat. I had an appointment at the Mayo Clinic in Rochester—and if there is one thing that can humble you, it's lying on the operating table for a case of hemorrhoids. Overall, though, it had been some season. Even though we hadn't won the pennant, I had a lot to be thankful for. Especially for a guy who hadn't even been expected to make the team that year—and who had had a uniform waiting for him in the Denver clubhouse.

Danny Thompson, making the double play, was the Twins shortstop in 1974. Thompson and I were the double-play combination known to teammates as "Salt and Pepper." Danny died tragically of cancer in 1976. (COURTESY MINNESOTA TWINS)

Late in 1975 I was moved to first base. It was an attempt by management to help lengthen my career, since playing first base is in many ways less demanding than second base. (COURTESY MINNESOTA TWINS)

Umpire Al Clark tries to break up a fight between me and Detroit pitcher
Dave Roberts on April 30, 1977. I thought Roberts had intentionally hit
me with a pitch, so I retaliated. (MINNESOTA TRIBUNE)

Leading off first base, I'm studying the pitcher's motion in order to get
the best jump for a possible steal of second base. (COURTESY MINNESOTA
TWINS)

Hal McRae, above, and George Brett. I was involved with these two Kansas City batting stars in
what was probably one of the most exciting races
for a batting title in recent years. It was 1976; going
into the final weekend of the season, each of us had
a chance to win the title, and we played against
each other in those last three games. Brett won the
title. (COURTESY KANSAS CITY ROYALS)

June 26, 1977. The Twins scoreboard
has just flashed the news that I have
gone over the .400 mark in my batting
average, and I wanted to acknowledge
a standing ovation from the capacity
crowd. (COURTESY MINNESOTA TWINS)

Unlike most batters, I have numerous
stances. Where I stand in the batter's
box and the position in which I hold the
bat vary with the pitcher and the circumstances of the game. (COURTESY
MINNESOTA TWINS)

One of my greatest pleasures in life is
making solid contact. (COURTESY MIN-
NESOTA TWINS)

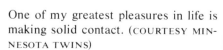

The follow-through is complete, as it always should be. My head is down and I've attempted to follow the flight of the pitch as I swung. (COURTESY MINNESOTA TWINS)

I have an unorthodox way of bunting, in that my hands are together when I make contact. But the style has proved effective for me, and bunting has become one of the most important weapons in my hitting arsenal. (COURTESY MINNESOTA TWINS)

Al Kaline, in his prime as the Detroit Tigers' star hitter. Kaline's ''whippy'' bat so impressed me that I adopted the bat model as my own. (COURTESY DETROIT TIGERS)

Carl Yastrzemski. His timing, reflexes and patience result in his never being cheated at the plate. That is, he invariably takes a good cut at the pitch, and is rarely fooled. (COURTESY BOSTON RED SOX)

This gives some idea of what it's like to face Nolan Ryan, who throws the ball harder than anyone else I've ever faced. (COURTESY CALIFORNIA ANGELS)

Steve Mingori is an off-speed pitcher, as opposed to an overpowering pitcher like Nolan Ryan. (COURTESY KANSAS CITY ROYALS)

Mark Fidrych, the Tigers' irrepressible "Bird." Besides his unique mound habits—such as crawling around to smooth the dirt—he has a very effective fastball and excellent control. (COURTESY DETROIT TIGERS)

Luis Tiant unwinds. I've had success against him because I just follow the "chute" from which the ball comes, and I don't watch all the hand and arm gyrations that he uses. (COURTESY BOSTON RED SOX)

Sparky Lyle, relief specialist and winner of the 1977 Cy Young Award, has one of the most exceptional sliders in the game. (COURTESY NEW YORK YANKEES)

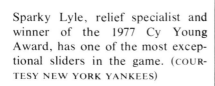

The Carew family shopping in downtown Minneapolis. I'm carrying my daughter Charryse in my right arm and Stephanie in the left. This was in the summer of 1977. In November, Marilynn would give birth to our third daughter. (TIME-LIFE)

# Chapter V

IN DOWNTOWN Minneapolis there is a lively little nightclub named King Solomon's Mines. It's a racially mixed place with a good band and a nice crowd. I enjoyed going there. I no longer felt reluctant to enter such a place, as I had in Cocoa, Florida, or Wilson, North Carolina. Race problems exist in Minneapolis, but compared with many other cities in the States it is racially relaxed.

One night shortly after the 1968 season began, I went to the "Mines" with a friend named Xavier Caldwell, who was called "Tiny," probably because he's six feet four. We stood at the bar. It wasn't long before we noticed two good-looking white girls sitting nearby. Tiny decided to introduce himself. One of the girls caught my eye. Her hair was long and black and shiny. She looked like a Spanish princess.

Tiny's opening line was "How would you girls like to

meet Rod Carew?'' He didn't say, ''Can I buy you a drink?'' or ''Let's dance.'' I guess he thought they'd rush into our arms at the magic word. Whatever, it didn't quite work.

''Who's Rod Carew?'' the dark-haired girl asked.

''Who's Rod Carew!'' said Tiny. ''He plays for the Minnesota Twins!''

''Big deal,'' she said. ''If Tony Curtis walks in, bring him over instead.''

Now, I didn't hear any of this. But Tiny came back and said, ''Rod, the girls really want to meet you.''

We went over. While Tiny was trying to hustle the one named Judy Lawrence, I talked with the other, Marilynn Levy, the one with the long hair and the sassy attitude. That is, I tried to talk to her. But she gave me a hard time, wasn't friendly at all, very sarcastic. ''You're a baseball player? I never heard of you. Who did you say you play for?'' And when I told her, she said, ''So what?'' I was intrigued. I liked the idea that she didn't care whether I was some kind of big deal or not. She knew nothing of baseball and had never heard of Rod Carew. She looked me over and decided that I was cocky. She thought I strutted like a peacock. Why not? I was establishing myself as a major-league baseball player. My name was all over town. I had a fine bachelor apartment now—I had made my home year round in Minneapolis—and attractive women were calling me. Life was great. I was on top of the world.

''You know what I think of you?'' Marilynn said after a while. ''I think you're a funny duck.''

I didn't know what a funny duck was. Never heard that expression before. I thought, I don't need this. There are a lot more women where this one came from. So I thought I'd just toss her back in. But before going, I told her she was a flake, a common baseball expression for ''oddball.'' The night wore on, and I kept looking over at her. As she

was leaving, she walked up to me and said, "Hey, what did
you mean by 'flake'?"

I said, "What did you mean by 'funny duck'?"

I'm not sure we've ever figured them out.

I asked if I could walk her outside. We stood by her car
and talked. She told me she worked as a dental assistant
and that she rarely went to nightclubs, but that this was her
birthday, May 30, and Judy had suggested she take Marilynn for a celebration drink.

When I asked for her phone number, Marilynn said, "I
don't give out my number to people I don't know. I mean,
what if you're a guy just out of jail, or you robbed a gas
station this afternoon? I don't know anything about you."

"I'm clean," I said. "No prior record."

Now, when I first joined the Twins, some of the older
black players told me you've got to watch your p's and q's.
And if you want to stay in the big leagues, you can't be
seen dating white girls. But I felt now that I had earned my
so-called freedom to associate with people of my choice. If
the Twins don't want me on those terms, I felt somebody
else would.

Marilynn and I began dating after that meeting, and I
never had any problems at all with the Twins' organization
about it. The obstacles we met came in other sizes and
shapes.

Marilynn wasn't the first white girl I had dated, but I was
the first black man she had ever gone out with. Her last
name, Levy, meant nothing to me. It was a Jewish name,
but I never thought of anyone as Jewish or Polish—or black
or white, for that matter—unless it was forced upon me.
And Marilynn? Well, she was pretty sheltered. She was 23
years old and had never gone out with anyone her family
didn't know. In fact, she went steady with one boy from
the time she was 14 until she was 20. She was raised in the
Jewish area of North Minneapolis and was programmed,
she says, to marry a Jewish boy—preferably a doctor, of

course—raise children, clean house and take care of her husband. As I understood later, her going out with me was considered a fling for her.

She was open about the fact that dating a black man was a problem. Not for her, she said, but for her parents. She didn't want her parents held up to ridicule or embarrassment by their friends and relatives. So we dated in secret throughout much of 1968. It was all right with me. I mean, I didn't care if her parents knew or didn't know. I wasn't serious about her.

So we never really dated in the conventional sense. We met places. We'd go to Solomon's Mines, or we'd meet at a theater. Or she'd cook dinner for us at my place. Then I'd take her to her car and she'd go home.

When we took a drive together, Marilynn might see a car that looked familiar and she'd duck behind the dashboard. One time we were in King Solomon's Mines and Marilynn thought she spotted a guy she knew from her neighborhood. She left me in a flash and stood at the other end of the bar so that this guy wouldn't see us together.

One time, for some reason, she didn't have her car and so I drove her home. We're in her driveway talking when a car pulls up behind us. It's her parents and her sister. Marilynn says, "Oh, God" and drops to the floorboards. It happened that her sister, Louise, was driving. Louise had met me; knew my car, a Thunderbird, and was thinking fast, because suddenly the car pulls back out and disappears. Then I pull right out, and we drive down the block.

"Look, Rod, I know this is humiliating for you, and I'm getting heart failure," said Marilynn. "This has to stop. It's been nice, but we're going to have to call it a day."

I didn't feel as though I were being humiliated. I thought it was Marilynn's problem. And strange as it may seem, we never talked about race. It didn't come up. I felt she had to work it out herself. But if she felt that way, well, it was goodbye and chalk another one up. Back to my little black book. That's just the way I felt about it.

MEANWHILE, MY baseball career was on the rise, generally, but then something would happen to throw it all out of kilter. In 1968, my second year with the Twins, I was again chosen to start at second base for the American League All-Star team. Yet a few weeks before the game, I was about to jump the club.

This is what happened: At the end of June, 1968, I returned from two weeks of reserve camp. I took about a week's worth of batting practice, and now I felt I was in shape to play again. I had been hitting .356 when I left. Quilici had been at second base while I was gone, and he hadn't been hitting very much. The team wasn't going particularly well. We were in Cleveland and had a night game. I told Ermer, the manager, that I was ready to play. He said, "I'm going to give you more time to get yourself in shape." I got upset. And true to the form of some of my childish ways in those days, I decided to jump the club. That afternoon I paid my incidentals at the hotel. A player normally pays his incidentals when the team is leaving town. Then I went back to my room. A reporter saw me leaving the cashier's window and called the room. Oliva, my roommate, was lying in bed and answered the phone. The reporter wanted to know what I was doing. Tony held the receiver. "Tell him I'm on my way to the airport," I said.

I wasn't leaving, though I had thought about it. And my telling Tony to say this was a kind of joke, but not a very good one. It wasn't professional, and I wasn't respecting the professionalism of reporters. Well, this reporter called one of the coaches. And two coaches went out to the airport to intercept me. Meanwhile, I never left the room.

When I got to the park that night, the players were joking

about "the invisible Carew," and they put up signs: HAS ANYBODY SEEN ROD CAREW? And WHERE'S CAREW?

I went to Ermer. "Cal," I said, "I think we'd better have a meeting so I can apologize to the players." I did, and I felt it closed the incident.

But I still wasn't in the lineup. I sat on the bench and didn't say anything. Luis Tiant was pitching a masterly game against us. The score was 1–1 in the top of the tenth, and Tiant had struck out 19. Then we got a runner on third with none out. A right-handed hitter was up. Tiant's a right-handed pitcher. I had hit Tiant in the course of the season as if I owned him. And now I was the only pinch hitter left on the bench. And since I bat left-handed, I thought this was a perfect time to send me in—but Ermer didn't. We wound up losing 2–1 in the bottom of the tenth. After the game, a reporter asked Ermer why he hadn't had me pinch-hit. He said because he was punishing me. I thought the job was to win the game, not to punish me—and besides that, I had apologized to the entire team before the game. So what was he trying to prove? Apparently I wasn't the only one who questioned Ermer, because he was fired after the season. (Martin replaced him.) We had finished 24 games behind the Tigers, who won the pennant. I had no more problems the rest of the season, and although my average dropped to .273 from .292 my rookie year, I still was among the top batters in the league. (That was the so-called Year of the Pitcher, in which Yastrzemski was the only player in the American League to hit above .300— finishing fast for .301.)

MARILYNN AND I had broken up sometime around the end of the 1968 season. But shortly before I was to go to spring training for the 1969 season, I walked into a night spot called The Filling Station. Marilynn was there with some friends. She looked sensational. She was dressed in a black pantsuit with a white blouse. She really looked good. I thought, Well, why not? I'll send over a bottle of champagne.

Not long afterward, she came over and thanked me. This is a Friday night. I told her I'd be leaving on Monday for spring training. I said, "I'd like to see you before I go. Just for a talk. I think I understand now how you feel about your family." It's true. I had been talking to some friends about Jewish people and their concepts of marriage and kids and not marrying out of the faith.

"I'll leave it up to you, Marilynn," I said.

She said, "I'll let you know."

That Sunday afternoon she came to my apartment. After a while I said, "I'd still like to date you."

"Well, it's still got to be under those same terms, Rod. I just can't put my parents through any more changes," she said. Her parents were having marital problems at this time.

"If that's the way you have to do it, okay," I said. "I can handle it."

"You're going to spring training and you'll be gone for six—seven weeks. We'll see what happens when you get back."

I called her several times from spring training, and when I returned to Minneapolis we started dating again.

I was still seeing other girls, but Marilynn had my heart. And I think I had hers. I told her once, "Marilynn, you're the only woman I would allow to fold my wash." She took my wash that she had just folded and threw it at me.

"What? You let *other* girls fold your wash!"

And there was no explaining the phone calls I'd get when she was there and I'd whisper to the caller.

It got pretty stormy. We broke up a hundred times. I was stubborn and she was obstinate. The immovable force against the irresistible object.

One time, we had an argument over something or other and the next day my doorbell rang and Marilynn was there with a grocery cart filled with all of the gifts I had given her. Whenever I'd make a road trip, I'd return with something for her—jewelry from Greenwich Village, a stuffed dog from Disneyland, a sweater from Chicago. She put all this stuff in the cart with the keys to my apartment, which I had given her, and said, "Take it. I don't want it."

That blew over too.

One afternoon in the spring of 1969, we went to Loring Park near downtown Minneapolis. It's across from the Guthrie Theater and the Walker Art Center—a beautiful park with a duck pond and lamps along the sidewalks. The sky was blue, no clouds. The sun was warm. We fed bread to the squirrels, and we sat on a blanket and talked and we were oblivious to the whole world. At this moment, I was no baseball player. I was no black man. I was just a guy who was in love with a beautiful woman in a beautiful setting on a gorgeous day. We had a picnic of fried chicken and Coke. I think that was the moment when both of us knew we had something really special. But we didn't even hold hands—we were too greasy from the chicken.

Then Yolanda came into our life. She had been my girlfriend, or what passed for my girlfriend, in Panama. I'd take her to a movie Dutch treat and then sit a few rows behind her so that none of my friends could suspect us of necking. Some kids used to crawl around the seats trying to catch couples kissing. Well, Yolanda happened to be in Minneapolis, and my mother had given her my number. She was nothing more to me than an old friend. I told Marilynn about Yolanda and suggested the three of us go out to dinner.

Marilynn said, "Broads. Every time I turn around, there's broads. If they're not calling, they're writing letters."

Well, I convinced her that Yolanda was harmless. We went out, the three of us, and Marilynn was very cordial. I thought we had a nice time. But as soon as I dropped Yolanda off, Marilynn said, "I would like to choke you." One night, Marilynn and I were having a wonderful dinner at my apartment, but the phone rang every fifteen minutes. I didn't answer it. I didn't know who was calling. It could have been Calvin Griffith. Finally I decided to take the phone off the hook.

Marilynn got up and said, "I'm leaving."

"But I've taken the phone off the hook!"

"Look, Rod, I'm a one-man woman. I want that man to be mine and I will do the same. I don't want to share a man with the rest of the world out there. And at this stage of your life I can't see you settling for one girl, and I can't blame you. Why are you bothering with me? Go about your business and be happy. Let me alone. Your career is just blossoming. There are girls dying to go out with you, and we're sneaking around corners."

"Maybe that's what it's about," I said with a laugh. "Going around corners, the mystery, the adventurous Marilynn Levy. . . ."

I liked having one woman, one main woman, the woman you could talk to, confide in, feel that she is central to your life. As much as I liked one woman, I also enjoyed the company of other women. It was the age-old dilemma. And up to this time, I had taken nothing seriously with women. But the longer Marilynn and I dated the more serious we became.

I RECEIVED one very disturbing phone call a few months into the 1969 season. It was from my sister Dorine. She said Eric was acting up again with Mom and Mom was really miserable. It bothered me very much. I remember going into Detroit a couple of days later and the thing with Eric kept building up in my mind. I was miserable during batting practice that evening. Guys would say something and I'd snap back. They'd say, "Oh, he's got the red ass today.'' I sat on the bench before the game and thought about the situation at home.

The game started. I made an out. But my mind was not on the game at all. I was thinking, I've got a problem and what am I going to do about it? I certainly couldn't solve it there by going out and playing. Guys on the bench were talking, yelling and screaming and I was sitting there saying to myself, That son-of-a-bitch. Oh, that son-of-a-bitch. I was on the on-deck circle and I was shaking my head: What should I do? What can I do? I swung at the first pitch and grounded out. When I hit first base, something snapped inside me. "I'm going. I've gotta go."

From the time I hit the dugout I was unbuckling my pants. I went right down the stairs and right up into the clubhouse, and by the time I hit the clubhouse door, my shirt was coming off, my hat was off. By the time I got to my locker my shoes were off. I just kicked them off. My socks were coming down. Everything came off practically in one swoop and I jumped into the shower.

One of the guys was getting coffee and looked at me and I barely noticed him. He must have gone down to the dugout immediately, because Billy Martin, who was the Twins' manager then, came charging in and screamed at me, "What's the matter with you? What the hell's going on?"

"I gotta go. I've got a problem, a personal problem, and I've gotta go."

He started yelling and swearing at me. He shouted at the other player, "Lock the clubhouse door and don't let him out."

I said, "I don't care what you say, I'm going."

Then he saw I was shaking. He wanted to know the problem. I wouldn't tell him. I felt it was my problem and I should try to solve it any way I could.

Billy and I argued and argued. Finally, he said, "Okay, go ahead."

I returned to the Sheraton-Cadillac and called my mom. I told her what I had done. I sat on the bed and told her I was coming home. "No," she said, "stay and play the game."

"I've already left the game," I said.

She insisted that she could handle the situation herself.

I lay in bed all night thinking about it. The next morning I called my mom again. She said everything was all right and that I shouldn't worry. "Keep your mind on the game," she said.

"All right, but if anything happens, I want to know," I said.

At the park that afternoon Doc Lentz said to me, "Rod, go in and talk to the manager. Tell him what the problem is. You don't want to just run away from things like that. Try and sit down and talk with someone."

I told Billy I was sorry if I had acted like a brat. I told him the problem had to do with my parents. He was understanding, and there was no hassle with him after that.

Billy also told me something Marilynn had been telling me: "Open up a little bit so people can get to know you, Rod. If you don't, you're just going to go through your career and life without people respecting you or wanting anything to do with you. If you would open up some, people would have a better understanding of Rod Carew."

I was calling my mother every day after that. I learned that Eric had taken off. He'd gotten his own apartment. Sometime after, Mom told me that he was on the phone crying and wanting to come back. I said, "If you let him back in the house, I'm not going to be your son. I'm tired of seeing you go through life being miserable and putting up with this kind of stuff from him." He never came back into the house again.

In that 1969 season I was having my best year as a professional baseball player. I led the league in hitting from early in the season.

I had changed my style of hitting from the previous season, my second season in the big leagues. I had batted .273, the lowest average I've ever had. I was trying to hit the fences, and I wasn't capable of doing it very often, to say the least. Although once in Kansas City I hit a 500-foot homer off Catfish Hunter. I thought that was tremendous. Harmon came up next and hit one about 50 feet farther. He made mine look cheap.

When Billy Martin became the manager of the Twins in 1969, he told me, "Rod, that long ball is not you."

If I could score 85 to 100 runs a season, he said, it would mean more to the club than if I hit 10 home runs. Now, home-run hitters were supposed to be the guys who drove Cadillacs. Singles hitters drove Fords. So you saw little guys going for home runs, squeezing the bat down at the handle. But line-drive hitters were then beginning to make their value felt. A guy like Pete Rose was starting to get a lot of publicity. People would come out to the park to see Rose. Rose wound up driving not a Cadillac, but a Rolls-Royce.

I also added a new wrinkle to my baseball repertoire at Orlando in the spring of 1969: stealing home. Billy and I talked about my being more aggressive on the bases. Although I stole a lot of bases in the minors, I had stolen only 5 and 12 in my first two seasons with the Twins. He thought the team should put more pressure on opponents than we had. He said I could use my speed to advantage in a game situation in which we needed a run and the guys weren't hitting. I had stolen home once before in the minors—I had decided on the spur of the moment, and I could have gotten killed if the batter had swung. All I knew about stealing home was that Jackie Robinson had done it so spectacularly. I remember seeing newspaper photos of him, with a big hook slide and a lot of dust around home plate and the catcher lunging at him. That spring, Billy worked with me for hours on stealing home. He suggested I take a slow, walking lead, instead of the lead in which you come to a stop. How far I should lead depended on how far the third baseman was playing off the bag, and whether the pitcher took a stretch or a windup. That walking lead was essential: you'd have momentum already started toward home.

We had it timed to the split second. If a pitcher wound up—instead of pitching from a stretch—and took six beats from the time he began his windup to his release, we determined that I ought to make it home safely. We also had the batters practice getting in the catcher's way, without being called for interference.

I also concentrated on staying low when running. I think you can propel yourself better that way, and get a fuller use of your arms and legs, than when you're running straight up. I learned that by running track in high school.

You know, few guys ever steal home. Some of the best base stealers don't. Maury Wills never stole home in his entire career. I don't think Lou Brock ever did either. It takes a different kind of timing than when you're going, say, from first to second. I guess it also takes a certain amount of nerve; Billy told me I could not have any fear within myself of getting hurt. And I didn't, because I felt in control. "As long as you give the hitter the sign and he flashes it back to you," Billy said, "then he should know that on the next pitch you're coming and he shouldn't swing." Ideally, the batter is right-handed, and he ought to be trying to protect the plate and obscure the catcher's vision a little bit. Billy said, "And you can't be afraid of being thrown out, because that's going to happen occasionally. You have to do it recklessly."

Roger Nelson was a lanky right-hander nicknamed "Spider" because of his long dangly arms. He was pitching for Kansas City in the second game of the 1969 season. I arrived at third in the fifth inning. We were losing 3–2, two outs, and Graig Nettles batting. I took a modest lead, watching the third baseman and watching the pitcher. Spider Nelson went into a bi-i-i-g windup. All arms and legs. I counted. Nettles took a pitch. I signaled that I wanted to go. Martin and Nettles got the message. When Spider went into his windmill act again, I took off. When Nelson saw what was happening and finally untangled himself, he threw high, and I slid home safely. It was my first steal of home in the major leagues. I couldn't wait to try it again.

Ten days later, we're playing California. I was on third in the seventh inning. The score was tied, and Hoyt Wilhelm, the old knuckleballer, was pitching. His knuckler takes all day to arrive at the plate. It looked appetizing. I flashed a sign to Billy that I thought I could go. He flashed back an okay.

Harmon was at the plate. I flashed him the sign. It's a tap on my belt buckle with my right hand. It appeared he answered by tapping his belt buckle with his right hand. Wilhelm started into the windup. I went. I was coming down the line, and I was amazed to see that Harmon was preparing to hit the pitch: if he swung, I'd end up a double down the left-field line. Suddenly out of the corner of his eye he saw me, and he held back in the nick of time. I came sliding in and beat the knuckleball home. It proved to be the winning run of the game.

Before the next game, I made sure I sat down with the hitters and got the signals straight once and for all.

Eleven days later, I stole home for the third time in April. Two weeks later I stole home again.

It was really getting exciting now. Whenever I got on third, the fans were yelling, "Go, go!" The other team's dugout was yelling, "Watch him!" "Hold him on!" Everybody was anticipating something.

In June I stole home two more times. I now had six steals of home this season. That tied the American League record held by Ty Cobb for steals of home in a season. Pete Reiser of the Dodgers set the major-league record in 1946 with seven.

In the second inning against Chicago, on July 16, I was on third when Jerry Nyman went into a windup. He just forgot I was in the game. His teammates were hollering, "Hold him on, hold him on!" Too late. I slid home with number seven.

But generally it was getting harder and harder to go now. Everyone was watching me when I got to third. Pitchers were taking a stretch now instead of winding up.

But about a month later against Seattle I had the opportunity to go for number eight, the record. Skip Lockwood, a right-hander, was pitching. I got a great jump on him, and I slid by the plate as the ball popped into the catcher's mitt. But the umpire called me out. I couldn't believe it. J. C. Martin was catching, and he couldn't believe the call either (he didn't tell me that until the next day). I think the umpire's vision was blocked, so he automatically gave me the thumb.

That was my last good chance to steal home in 1969.

I stole home nine more times in the following eight years. One was against Cleveland and Ed Farmer, and it won the game in the bottom of the tenth inning. Five, or exactly one-third, of my steals of home, were in the first inning. It seems that pitchers don't expect you to take a risk so early in the game and perhaps kill off a potential rally. One-third of the games in which I stole home were one-run games, and we won four of them. I never stole home with two strikes or three balls on the batter. I never tried it when there were no outs.

I didn't really begin to steal many bases at all until my third season in Minnesota. We had had the big hitters—Oliva, Harmon, Rich Rollins, Allison and Zoilo—and there was little sense when I was on first in taking a chance of being thrown out, thereby taking the bat out of their hands. In later years I began to steal second and third with increasing frequency.

I had terrible growing pains that year, 1969. The thing

with my family in New York was a constant thorn. And then I placed pressure on myself to play better and better. I was very sensitive and wouldn't take slights easily. Ron Perranoski and I almost got into it.

Perranoski and I never saw eye to eye while he was a relief pitcher with the Twins. I don't remember what the incident was, but guys held us back one time from going at each other. One time, when I was in a slump, we were in Kansas City and I was so discouraged that I told a reporter, "I'm quitting." When Perranoski heard it, he said to a reporter, "What's Carew going to do, become a brain surgeon?" I had to laugh at that one myself.

Another relief pitcher who rubbed me the wrong way was Dave LaRoche. He was always complaining. I thought it was unnecessary and told him so. He got huffy and so I suggested we get this settled. We went into a little broom closet and began whaling away at each other, until guys came in and broke it up.

Then in late summer of 1969, I had an incident with Dave Boswell. I had been leery of Dave since the time in my rookie year that he was fiddling with guns on the team bus. Then one time Emmett Ashford, the black umpire, called some close pitches balls when Dave was on the mound. Runs scored. Boswell got yanked. As he's walking back to the bench, he says, "That goddamn nigger." Some of the black players jumped up. Jim Grant was off the bench, and so was Earl Battey. I was still a rookie then, so I was doing a lot of watching and listening and let the older guys go at it.

Dave was a good guy, but he was also mouthy. Basically he tried to get along with everybody. But everyone agrees he's a little flaky. For example, he used to sleep in bed wearing a motorcycle helmet and a leather jacket and dark glasses. When he went to play winter ball in South America, he took several canteens of water in his suitcase because he was told to be careful of the local water.

One time I had come from two weeks of reserve meetings, and as soon as I returned to the lineup I pulled a muscle. I hadn't been ready to play. I was hurting and having trouble running. Some guys started saying, "Jake" and all that stuff. Now we're in a ball game in Kansas City and Dave's pitching. I was hurting, so I wasn't in the lineup. Kansas City got out in front. Then I pinch-hit and singled to tie the game. Now I go in to play second. Bob Oliver hit a fly to center and it dropped in front of Tovar. Boswell was ranting and raving on the mound because he thought Cesar should have had the ball. Next pitch, Oliver took off to steal second. I went to cover the bag, even though I couldn't move too well. The throw from the catcher was to the third-base side, and as I caught it and came back to make the tag, I was pulling my left leg out of the way so that I wouldn't get spiked. Oliver was safe. Boswell was mad. He said I wasn't aggressive on the play, that I had let Oliver slide in easy. The next guy got a base hit, and they won the game. Boswell was fit to be tied. In the clubhouse he was saying something about that chicken-shit son-of-a-bitch cost me my ball game.

Everybody thought he was going to try to punch me. Allison told me, "Rod, I want you to get dressed. Get dressed with everybody so we can all leave together. Don't hang around here with Boswell, because he's in a mood to pick a fight with you."

I entered the team bus with most of the other players. Boswell stayed in the clubhouse drinking beers. I went out and had dinner with Tony, and then we went back to the Muehlenbach Hotel where the team was staying. Tony went next door to Tovar's room to talk. I was tired and was just getting into bed when suddenly *bang!* My door comes falling down and here's Boswell. He'd kicked my door down. I jumped up, and he said, "Come on out here, you son-of-a-bitch." He smelled of beer. Tony and Tovar had heard the door coming down, and they came running. Allison and Killebrew hurried down the hall. They were all trying to settle Boswell down.

Nothing else was said about it, and the press never found out. Dave and I stayed far away from each other until one day a couple of weeks before the season ended. We go into Seattle and he's pitching. He's getting his brains beat out. But he's hanging in there. I think I went 4-for-5 that day and drove in a couple of runs, including the winning run. And Boswell wins his 20th game. In the clubhouse afterward, he comes over and hugs me and says, "Thank you, man, that's great. I hope you've forgotten what happened in Kansas City."

"Boz," I said, "I'm not perfect. I make mistakes. But I didn't appreciate what you did."

He said, "Well, I'm sorry." And then he kissed me on the side of my face.

For the rest of the time he was with us—three or four years—Dave and I got to be pretty decent friends.

One guy I felt I really did let down one time was Killebrew. It was in the final weeks of the 1969 season. Harmon was going for the RBI championship. On this day, the field was muddy, and there was a play in which I had a mental lapse. I slowed up on a hit by Tony and was thrown out. Harmon was at the plate, and he lost a chance to drive in a run. Billy Martin was furious at me. He said, "You should go over there and apologize to Killebrew."

I thought I should too. I told Harmon that I was sorry, that I had made a mistake. "Aw, Junior, don't worry about it," he said. "You're going to get me a lot more RBI's before it's over."

The season ended with Harmon winning the RBI title, which I was thankful for. I took the batting title with a .332 average, 23 points ahead of Reggie Smith, who came in second. But in the play-offs (the league had now split into two divisions) I went 1-for-14 and struck out four times. Maybe I was trying too hard. But nobody else hit against Baltimore either. We lost in three straight games.

That winter I was disappointed to learn that Billy Martin had been fired. He came head to head with Calvin Griffith and neither would budge. One had to go, and it wasn't going to be the owner of the club.

The first time I met Billy Martin, in the Twins' executive office, he did not appear the rough-and-tumble guy I had heard about. He seemed rather slight. But he was a battler. He'd do anything to win. I remember seeing World Series films of him sliding hard into Roy Campanella. As a manager, he backed up his players and always beefed with umpires if he felt he should.

You had the feeling that he wouldn't back down from a fight. Once, Boswell was causing some trouble in Lindell's A.C., a night spot a lot of ballplayers frequent in Detroit. Allison pulled Davey outside to cool him down. And Boswell threw punches at Allison. Martin came out. Now, Boswell is six-three, 190; Martin is five-ten, 160. But they tell me Billy knocked Boswell out on his feet.

Later, when Billy was managing the Yankees, he had some angry differences with Reggie Jackson, as everybody knows. Reggie is a giant compared with Billy, but if they had ever come to blows, Reggie would have had to kill Billy to keep him down. The harder you hit Billy the more he'll keep coming back at you.

For all this, Billy is a gentleman, and a really fine manager. He's smart, knows how to handle players and is aggressive. He has a theory that aggressive, running teams force opponents to make mistakes. He must know what he's doing. He's managed first-place teams in Minnesota, Detroit and New York. Billy and I also became good friends. He helped me tremendously on the field and off, giving me meaningful fatherly advice when I really needed it.

In August of 1969, my mother and my sister Dorine came to Minneapolis for a visit. I couldn't pick them up at the airport because I had to be at the ball park. I asked Marilynn to get them. She said, "How am I going to know which one is your mother?" I said, "Ask every black lady who comes off the plane. One of them should be my mother." She looked at me as if I were nuts. I laughed and said, "You'll know her because she looks just like me." And it's true, I think. Marilynn drove my mother and sister back to my apartment, and they had a chance to talk.

The next day the four of us went shopping, and my mother and I were carrying packages and walking behind the two girls. Out of the clear blue sky my mother says, "That's the girl you're going to marry, Cline."

My mom liked her; so did Dorine. They talked easily with her, saw that she was level-headed, that she was good around the house, cooked well and cared for me and did not, like some other women, date me to share the spotlight. *Spotlight!* Marilynn didn't want to be *seen* with me in public. Mom seemed to think that her little boy would be in good hands with this girl. Not only that, but years before, in Panama City, my mother had her hand read by a streetside palm reader. The woman said, "Your son is going to meet a girl that you know nothing about. There will be no regrets."

My mom had no qualms about my dating a white woman, or one who was Jewish. She has always said she wants just two things in regard to me, that I be happy and that I show her respect. Her philosophy about kids is, Parents raise their children, give them what they have to give them, tell them the right things; and, when they get to the age when they can choose, then you've got to let them build their own lives, don't meddle.

Neither Marilynn nor I had discussed marriage. I sometimes thought I wanted to be a playboy. But for all those thoughts, I'd come back from road trips and I'd feel lonely. Guys were anxious to get off the airplane and be met by their families. I remember how much Tony Oliva looked forward to seeing his wife, Gordette, and their kids. I'd straggle along because I thought, I'm going back to an empty apartment. I could easily call a girl to come over, but it wasn't the same as having someone waiting at home.

So sitting there, talking with my mother, I said, "I think I will marry Marilynn." She said, "Well, I hope you don't keep her hanging." I asked what she meant. "I hope you don't just run around with her and keep her on a string and then run off, because it was told to me that you're going to marry this girl and everything's going to be all right."

Around this time Marilynn decided that she ought to be frank with her parents about me. "I'm tired of sneaking around," she told me. "My parents will just have to accept what I want to do in life."

Her mother did know that Marilynn and I were friends. I let Marilynn drive a car that had been lent me by a Ford dealer—he gave one to each of the Twins. Marilynn's mother questioned her about me, and she said, "He's a friend." I wasn't new in this regard. In the high school Marilynn had attended, there was a large minority of blacks and a few were friends of hers. But they weren't best friends, and none were boys. Mrs. Levy was not happy with Marilynn's newfound friendship. She smelled something and warned Marilynn to be careful.

Now Marilynn decided to confront her mother at work, so that that discussion could be brief. Her mother was a saleswoman at a department store in downtown Minneapolis. As I understand the story, Marilynn met her during a break and they sat on stools at the lunch counter.

"Mom," Marilynn said, "you know my friend that I mentioned, Rod Carew?"

She said, "Yes, the *shvartzer*." (That's Yiddish for black.)

"I'm going to date him," Marilynn said.

Mrs. Levy looked at her and then began to cry.

"Mom, it's only dating."

"But from a date comes serious, too." Mrs. Levy was born in Romania and came to America as a young girl, but her English can sometimes sound like my mother's.

For weeks afterward, whenever my name was mentioned, Mrs. Levy broke into sobs. Marilynn said, "I'm a big girl. I don't care what you say or what your friends say; if you want to sit here and cry, go ahead."

As time passed, Mrs. Levy realized Marilynn was dead serious. One day she said, "Marilynn, your friend, Rod Carew, is he nice?" She was softening.

From the start, Morrie Levy, Marilynn's father, a small real estate broker, took the whole thing better. "If you know what you're doing, fine," he said. "I just don't want you to get hurt."

Her two brothers urged her to stop dating me, that it could only cause unnecessary problems. Her close friends said the same thing. None of them, though, shut her off. Behind her back some of her acquaintances called her a tramp. They considered any white girl who dates a black man a tramp.

We weren't going to let any of that affect us, though I wonder if subconsciously it created tensions that led to some of our arguments.

At any rate, I started visiting Marilynn's house. Her mother was at first kind of distant, but she saw, as she told Marilynn, that I was well spoken and "cleaned and pressed."

One day in the car I said to Marilynn, "Let's get married." She laughed and said, "Rod, you don't just go 'Let's get married.' " Well, we discussed it. Race didn't even come up. Womanizing did. Marilynn thought it best that we go slow. But as weeks went by, more and more I'd say, "Should we get married?"

"I don't think so," she said. "I don't think we're ready." She meant, I don't think *you're* ready. But the more we talked about it, the more attractive the idea became for us.

Finally, I said, "Marilynn, go pick out a ring. Get an engagement ring and I'll pay for it."

She said, "That's all I'm going to do—go to a jeweler's and buy a ring and then I'm going to get stuck with the bill, right? Oh, no, if you want to get engaged, *you* pick me out a ring."

Shortly afterward, on the afternoon of April 14, 1970, I picked up Marilynn at her office and took her to lunch. We went to the A & W Root Beer drive-in on Highway 100. We parked, we ordered and then I pulled out a diamond engagement ring I had bought.

I leaned over to kiss her. She said, "Wait a minute." She scratched the ring on the window glass to see if it was real. This was her idea of a joke.

Marilynn went back to work and was showing the girls the ring when one of them said, "Oh, it's on the wrong hand." Marilynn said, "Does that mean I'm not engaged?"

She called and told me what had happened. I said, "Well, how was I supposed to know which hand? I've never done it before."

That night was the first night of Passover, the Jewish holiday that celebrates the Jews' liberation from slavery under the Pharaohs. I was invited to the family Seder, or ceremonial dinner for Passover. It was the first family affair of theirs I had been invited to. I was to pick up Mrs. Levy at work, then meet Marilynn at her home, where she would tell her mother about the engagement.

We didn't know what her reaction would be. Mrs. Levy and I had a pleasant conversation in the car. We arrived home and Mrs. Levy went upstairs to her room. Marilynn came in a few minutes later. She looked around as if she were a burglar. "Where is she?" Marilynn asked.

"Upstairs," I said.

"Did you say anything?"

"No."

"Rod, if she says anything wrong—I'll never forgive her."

Just then Mrs. Levy came out of her room. Marilynn went up the stairs. When she got near the top, she just stuck out her hand. Mrs. Levy understood. She kissed Marilynn; then she came down and hugged me and said, "Take care of my baby." She was crying, but I think now they were happy tears. I know she felt I was good to her daughter. She knew that I had thought of Marilynn when I was on the road, and brought home little gifts and treated her with respect. She thought that we were genuinely in love. She accepted me. I didn't know how the rest of the family would take all this. The Seder was at Don and Arlene's home. Don is Marilynn's older brother; Arlene is his wife. They lived in a split-level house with large windows. When I pulled up, all I could see was nieces and nephews looking out the windows.

There must have been 50 people there. Everyone seemed excited and happy for the holiday. As we came in, the kids held up a sign they had made. It read, GUESS WHO'S COMING TO DINNER? I'm sure I was blushing, though of course no one could see it.

When Marilynn's mom took my hand to introduce me to people, she whispered, "Rod, you're *shvitzing.*" I didn't realize how clammy my hands were.

I could smell the chicken cooking in the kitchen. It reminded me of a holiday at my grandmother's home in Gamboa.

For the Seder, several long tables had been put together in an L shape from the dining room to the living room to accommodate all the people.

The men had taken off their suit jackets and loosened their ties. I was still too stiff to do that. Prayer books were passed out, and I participated—when I could. They asked me to read one small section. In English, of course. The Hebrew was left to the others. Marilynn would explain quietly what was going on during the reading.

My biggest problem was the yarmulke, or skullcap. My hair was kind of puffed out, and the cap kept falling off. I tried sitting at an angle so that it would stay on. Then my neck became cramped. I straightened up and the yarmulke fell off. I tried a different angle. It fell off again. Marilynn noticed, and solved the problem by fastening it with a bobby pin.

When the service was over, I said I had an announcement to make. Everyone grew quiet. "This afternoon," I said, "Marilynn and I became engaged." It was the shortest and longest speech I've ever made. It was only a sentence, but I felt it took about five years to say it. The family seemed happy about it and we were congratulated. However, someone later asked Marilynn, "Are you doing this because he's a baseball player?" She said, "You know me all my life, right? What do I know from baseball?"

And there was one aunt who called Marilynn aside and said, "Don't ever bring him to *my* house." In later years that aunt and I became friends, and I've spent many enjoyable hours at her home.

Mr. Levy was not at the Seder because he and Marilynn's mother had been divorced. Marilynn was anxious to call and tell him about the engagement. We went into the bedroom, and as Marilynn spoke to him she became so choked up she began to cry. I got on the phone and Mr. Levy said, "You know you'll have problems, Rod. But I hope you two know what you're doing. Be good to my girl. And keep your name clean and pay your bills. One other thing, Rod—*mazel tov*." Good luck.

I thanked him for his blessings. That meant a great deal to us, to have the support of Marilynn's mother and father.

We returned to start dinner. The first dish served was gefilte fish. I had never had it before. Marilynn told me to add a little horseradish. Only a little, because it was spicy. I wasn't a big fish man to begin with. In fact, I was mostly steak and potatoes. I took a bite of the fish, and Marilynn said, "Well?" I whispered, "I'm not crazy about it." I realized there were a number of eyes at the table moving from that piece of fish to me. I took another bite.

The chopped liver showed up next. I never conceived of eating liver chopped up. I thought you ate it in one big slab. The matzo balls, the texture of the matzo balls, was odd, but they went down all right. When we finally got to the chicken, I knew I was home free. And by then, I had also had a few glasses of sweet wine, which helped.

Sitting there, I realized that I knew very little about Jews, about how they are as family and what their traditions mean to them. All that I had known about Jews before Marilynn was in relation to the Nazi concentration camps in World War II, and that Jews were business people. In New York, all the stores would be closed on Jewish holidays.

I had never seen such hugging and kissing in a family, such a feeling of closeness, as I did here. I noticed how they openly said to one another, "I love you." I liked it. My family never expressed themselves in that manner. Marilynn has said that if she didn't tell her father every day that she loved him, he'd be crushed.

After dinner, the children came up and sat on my lap and asked what they should call me. I said I didn't know, since I wasn't married to their aunt yet. They wanted to call me "Uncle Rod." I said that would be great.

I have had good times with the kids over the years. We've gone on picnics and I've taken them for ice cream. I've picked them up from the dentist's office.

I remember that some of the kids wanted to do my fan mail. Much of the fan mail is requests for autographed pictures. So the kids wanted to sort out those requests from other letters.

When the engagement news hit the papers, we received some nice letters. Then one of my nieces picked up a nasty letter which began, "Dear Nigger." It referred to the "white slut" and all that garbage. I started getting several of those a week. None of them would be signed with correct names. They'd be "KKK" or "I Hate Niggers," on plain stationery or with hotel letterheads. Letters like those arrived all season long. I got to the point where I didn't want to look at my mail any longer. Then one letter arrived which caused concern. It said, "I'll see you at the ball park tomorrow, Nigger, and while you're out at second base, I'm going to shoot you."

The following day turned out to be a day off. I figured, A harmless nut. But I kept thinking and wondering just how harmless the guy was. I decided to do something. I showed the letter to Don Knutson, one of my best friends. He ran the apartment complex I lived in, which was owned by his father. Don said, "I have a friend who has contacts in the FBI. We'll talk to them." Two FBI guys came over. They said they would try to trace the writer, and that they'd keep in touch.

I took Marilynn out dancing that night. Afterward, just before I dropped her off, I said, "I forgot to tell you something." And I told her about the letter. She panicked. "Why didn't you tell me? We didn't have to go out tonight."

I said, "I'm not going to let anyone feel that they're getting the better of me. They can't force me to stay home by threatening me."

"Promise you'll call me when you get home, Rod," she said.

"You kidding me? It's one in the morning. I'm going to call and wake up the house?"

"Well, I'll call you."

When I got in the door, the phone rang. It was Marilynn. "Yes, I'm home all right," I said.

I watched a little television and went to bed. It's about 2 A.M. and I'm starting to fall asleep and all of a sudden—bang! I jumped out of bed and dived to the floor. Somebody must be here! I went down into a crawl the way they teach you in the service, and I started sliding around in my apartment. I crawled to the door. I could see it was still double-bolted. I checked the windows. The windows were closed. I lived on the fifteenth floor. No way to climb in there. I went into the bathroom and there I saw the problem. The toilet seat had fallen down. I breathed easier. But I still didn't fall right off to sleep, I'll tell you that.

We had a night game the next night. I found myself moving around a lot at second base. I wouldn't stay in one place very long. It was the first time in my life I had ever been threatened. I hadn't told anyone with the club. So I'm moving back and forth and trying not to make it look too obvious that I don't want to be a sitting duck.

The game ends and I'm grateful. Nothing happened. Not even a paper bag popped.

My life was threatened one other time. It was in 1975. We were in Boston, and I was hitting well against the Red Sox. I answered the phone in my hotel room and the caller said, "Is this Rod Carew?" I said, "Who's calling?" He said, "Is this Rod Carew?" I said it was. "Well, nigger, I want to tell you something. I don't want you to go out there and get any base hits or anything, because if you do, you're either going to have your legs broken or you're going to get shot." He hung up. I got to the ball park and I told our manager, Frank Quilici, about it. Frank called the park security officer and he said he would alert his men.

I'm feeling a little shaky when I get up to the plate the first time. I ground out. I'm 0-for-3 when I come up to the plate in the eighth inning. It's a tight game, and I'm saying to myself, Should I try for a base hit or should I look for a walk? I figured this guy must mean business if he takes the time to call me at the hotel. So, the first pitch is a ball. I take a strike. The count goes to 3 and 1. Should I look for ball 4? I said, To heck with it. Roger Moret was pitching, and he threw me a fastball down the middle. I lined it through the box for a hit. I run to first—running fast. Now I'm standing on first base and there's not very much space to hop around. So I figure, If it's going to happen, there's little I can do about it now.

The next morning the phone rings and wakes me up in the hotel room. "Nigger, you didn't take our advice, did you?" And he hung up. I knew I couldn't worry about it anymore. I went right back to sleep. Never heard from him again.

A black man in a synagogue is not an everyday occurrence, and Marilynn and I have had some unusual moments in temples. I remember the first time. I went to someone's bar mitzvah and I was the only black person there. I sat in one of the front rows, and I could just feel the eyes of people behind me burning in the back of my neck. I said to Marilynn, "I feel people staring." She said, "Honey, it's only because you're so good-looking." I said, "True enough, but next time let's get a seat in the back anyway."

We went to one synagogue and a rabbi from out of town was delivering a sermon. Now, he knew about Marilynn and me. Yet he spoke about how interracial marriages should be condemned. I was embarrassed. Marilynn's family was outraged. After it was over, they gave the rabbi hell.

It's hard to know what it's like to be the odd person in a crowd unless you've experienced it. I once took Marilynn to an all-black club. She was the only white person there. At one point, she turned and said, "I never realized how it was. It's like I have a light bulb under my chin."

Marilynn now lived with just her mother and sister. Then the strangest thing happened: I moved in with the three women.

This is how that came about. On June 22, 1970, we were playing Milwaukee at County Stadium. My batting average was something like .376. I walked up to the plate and the Milwaukee catcher, Phil Roof, said, "Rod, if you don't get hurt, you're going to have a hell of a career."

The very next inning, on what seemed a routine double-play ball, Mike Hegan came barreling toward me to break up the play. I threw to first and thought I was well out of his way. But he seemed to veer far out of the baseline and smashed into me. We went tumbling. My leg snapped back and it went *crack!* It felt as if it had been broken in half. The pain was excruciating. I rolled over in the dirt. The umpire at second base, Jake O'Donnell, had heard the crack and vomited. Bill Rigney, now the Twins' manager, rushed out and said to me, "C'mon, you gotta get up. You'll be all right." And I'm dying. I hobbled off the field. In the clubhouse my knee was swollen so badly they had to cut my pants down the side to get them off. I was flown to Minneapolis and that night underwent an operation to remove some cartilage and to repair torn ligaments. I was running a fever. And what pain! I was crying. I was hallucinating. After the operation, a cast was placed on my leg. But for several days I felt nothing in the leg. I looked down and was really scared that they had amputated. The Twins' doctor, Harvey O'Phelan, said, "Rod, your leg looks pretty bad. There is an outside chance you may never play again. Some athletes have not come back from an injury of this magnitude." That hit me like a bomb. Things had been going so well. I was only 25. Now I had to wonder what else I might do with my life. I imagined going to college and studying engineering. I had always liked drawing, and I was fascinated by the locks and bridges of the Canal back home. In military service I was a combat engineer and helped build bridges. But I really couldn't picture my baseball career at an end—not yet. A weird scene occurred in the hospital one day when Joe Cronin, American League president, presented me with a silver bat, emblematic of my having led the league in hitting. Usually, these ceremonies are held at home plate. But I couldn't even get out of bed!

In a hospital, each day has forty-eight hours. You do a lot of thinking, a lot of sleeping and a lot of looking at four white walls. The hospital wouldn't release me even when I was feeling better because there was no one to care for me at home. One day Marilynn said, "Mom and Louise said it would be fine if you'd want to come live with us until you get better."

I wondered what effect the opinion of neighbors and relatives might have on Mrs. Levy. Marilynn assured me it was all right.

So I moved in with the Levys, cast, crutches and Afro.

The Levys lived in a town house, with a mezuzah on the door, religious artifacts in the house and paintings of rabbis on the wall. Yet I felt right at home. They placed a bed in the living room, and all three of them catered to me. Marilynn accused me of acting like the star of "The King and His Maidens." I loved it.

Soon I could hobble outside on my cast and play catch with the kids in the street. A Little League field was near the apartment complex, and one evening I saw a game. It sickened me. The parents were screaming at the kids instead of encouraging them. I couldn't believe they would put such pressure on young kids. I saw one boy strike out, and his mother hollered until he cried. I never went back.

I think sports can really be worthwhile for kids, but only if it's fun for them. Participation in sports can help kids communicate with others their age. At its best, it encourages friendships. Sports may also give a kid a good sense of himself, as it did for me. But kids should not be pushed into sports if they aren't inclined that way. I thought it was the worst thing in the world for parents of some of the Little Leaguers I saw to be screaming at their kid that if he doesn't get a hit he'll get no allowance, or no dessert. I can't see at all what one thing has to do with the other.

A few weeks after my injury, I received a letter from Mike Hegan. He wrote, "I'm sorry you got hurt, but if I had to do it all over again, I would, because I thought I was doing my job in trying to break up a double play."

I've never held a grudge against Mike. We simply had a

difference of opinion on how he should do his job. The first time I saw him on the field I said, "You may have been trying to do your job, but I don't think you took me out cleanly." I had an occasion once when he was coming into second base on another double play when I could have hit him square in the face with a throw, and didn't. I had a clear shot, because he didn't slide right away. I went for the double play instead.

Life with the Levys continued virtually without a hitch. And Mrs. Levy treated me like a son. Marilynn and I had some of our smoothest and most tranquil moments—until I took her to a ball game at Metropolitan Stadium. My first game since the injury. I couldn't wait to get to the park. But I guess I didn't realize just how frustrated I was over not playing. It was murder to sit in the stands. People came by and asked me questions. And then Marilynn—who had now been to a number of games and was catching on—kept asking what was going to happen. Was that a bunt sign? A steal sign? It was like the third degree. I said, "Try to figure it out for yourself. It's no fun if I tell you everything." I was impatient with her. I wanted to be *out* there. After three innings I couldn't take it anymore. I left and watched the rest of the game on television in the clubhouse.

We were leading our West division by a wide margin, eventually coming in nine games ahead of second-place Oakland. It would be our second straight division title. Now, in 1970, we had what appeared to be another terrific chance to make the World Series, and I feared I might be a spectator.

But my leg began to respond to the extensive physical therapy. There was an outside chance that I could make it back for the very end of the season. Although my right leg was still very stiff, I was activated in September. I pinch-hit at Kansas City, and grounded out to the first baseman. I tried to run, but every step was painful. I ran three-quarters of the way down, and then stopped. I heard some boos.

I got another chance to pinch-hit, in the play-offs, and struck out. Baltimore knocked us off in three straight again, by scores of 10–6, 11–3 and 6–1. No contest. It was sad—the team was down, and there was nothing I could do about that; besides, I had no idea what the future held for me. At least in baseball.

But about three weeks after the 1970 play-offs, the flake and the funny duck were married. The date was October 24, nearly two and a half years after we first met.

It was a civil ceremony in the Levys' town house. Just the immediate family was there—with the exception of Don Knutson, my best man, and two of Marilynn's best friends. We kept it a small wedding ceremony primarily because it allowed Marilynn's dad to be there. He did not get along at all with his former in-laws, who weren't invited to the ceremony but would be coming to the reception. He did not attend the reception. Judge Eugene Menenko presided at the wedding. Marilynn had on a beautiful wedding dress, and I wore a black tux. She looked gorgeous, and it never showed that she was a nervous wreck and that I had to hold her up during the whole ceremony. I wasn't a total pillar of strength myself, since I had my bad leg. During the ceremony, "Take My Hand," "Sunrise, Sunset" and "The Impossible Dream" were played on the stereo.

A reception was held afterward at the Normandy Hotel. Tony Oliva and Charlie Manuel, an outfielder with the Twins, were the only ballplayers to attend. The rest of the players lived out of town. A number of people from the Twins' office came.

In preparing for the reception, I had spoken to the baker of the hotel about a cake. He said, "For you, Rod, I'll make something special. Leave the cake to me." The cake turned out to be enormous and had a fountain in the middle. Speaking of liquid, the bar was *flowing*. The band stayed later than it was supposed to. The big part of the evening for me was to dance to "The Anniversary Song."

The one unfortunate aspect was that Marilynn's father was not there. And when her brother Donny cut in on me to dance to ''The Anniversary Song,'' he said to Marilynn, ''This is for Dad—Dad told me to dance this one with you.'' Marilynn broke up.

My mother, my sisters and some nieces and nephews had come in for the wedding. Marilynn persuaded me to invite my father. She said, ''Well, no matter what, Rod, he is still your father.'' So I sent Eric an airplane ticket. By now, my parents had separated. My brother, Dickie, delivered the plane ticket to him. As I should have expected, Eric did not come. We never even heard from him.

Seeing Tony and his wife, Gordette, at our reception raised some thoughts in me about the similarity in our situations. He's a ballplayer and black, and Gordette is white (though not Jewish). Funny, but I had never discussed with Tony what it was like to be in a mixed marriage. And we were such good friends, and roommates on the road. I did know that he had also received hate letters concerning him and Gordette. But when I decided to marry Marilynn I know nothing anyone had to say about marriage mattered that much to me. I mean, I was sure that you just had to learn on the job.

# Chapter VI

AFTER THE 1970 season, I went first to the Florida Instructional League and then to Venezuela to play in the Winter League to try to strengthen the muscles in my knee which had atrophied during my recuperation from the injury.

On my first day in St. Petersburg, Florida, Del Wilbur, the coach, began hitting me ground balls. I knew then I was in trouble. The leg felt stiff. On double-play balls in games against some of the St. Louis Cardinal kids, I was looking out of the corner of my eye at the runner and almost forgetting to catch the ball or tag the base. If the play was close, I'd go for the force-out and forget the double play. I'd just bail out of there fast.

To compound matters, I had a disturbing racial situation in Florida. Marilynn was with me now. We went to a restaurant one night in St. Pete. As we're walking out, some older man says to his wife, "What's that white girl doing with the nigger?'' I stopped. I said to him, ''Mister, this lady is my wife. She's not *that* white girl.'' He jumped up and raised a big stink, as if I were picking on him. He called the manager. Just then a white busboy pulled on my sleeve and said, ''I heard him say that.'' When the manager arrived he recognized me, and all of a sudden everything got smoothed over. The man didn't apologize to us, but the manager did.

That whole thing shook us up. We were leaving Florida soon for Venezuela, anyway, and under the circumstances the timing was just right.

If anything, things got worse in Venezuela. The man who hired me to play for his team in Caracas reneged on financial arrangements. He wasn't paying me as much as he had promised. The playing conditions were horrible. The field was lumpy, and the park lights were so weak the players should have worn miners' hats.

I developed fluid on my knee. What was I going to do now? I told the owner of the team that my leg was bothering me and I thought I had to go home. He said, ''Oh, we have doctors.'' I thought, Nobody's going to mess with my leg here.

Also, Marilynn was getting leery of being down there. When she went out, guys followed her through the streets. One afternoon, my team had a game out of town. I stayed behind. Marilynn and I were in the apartment when we realized somebody was trying to jimmy the door. They probably thought I wasn't home. I opened the door and the guy took off. I chased him, but I couldn't run well. Marilynn was scared. We had to come up with something that would get us out of town, a plausible excuse.

I told the owner that Marilynn was sick and had to return to Minneapolis. I said I had to go with her. He said, ''No, no, we want you to play. We'll have somebody fly with her back to Minneapolis.'' I said, ''No, no, no, that's my wife. I've got a responsibility.'' We came home and I didn't go back.

I worked out over the winter. I went down to the hospital and used the pool. I swam a lot and took therapy and fooled around with weights.

In spring training, 1971, everybody was wondering if my leg was all right. I was one of those people wondering. As the season began, the double play was the big stumbling block. I had this terrible fear of getting hit again, that somebody's going to slam into me and it's going to end my career.

You had tough guys like Frank Robinson and Walt Williams and Carlos May and Rick Reichardt coming down the baseline at you. They'd come in hard and come in rolling to knock you over.

That was the way they felt they should break up a double play. Boog Powell came down one time, and Boog is six-four and weighs 240. I saw Boog—*felt* Boog—coming down, and I said, "Oh, no," and I backed off second base on a double play and threw the ball away, for an error. It should have been an easy double play, and I would have had a lot of time to get out of the way.

Despite the fans' screaming, I could hear these guys coming down the base path like a herd of elephants. I don't care how big the guy was or how small, I could hear. I could hear a guy's breathing when he was coming down there. And I was having nightmares and dreams that if I got hit again it was all over for me. One time I sat straight up in bed. I had replayed that thing with Hegan in my dream.

I was doing poorly at the plate as well. At the start of the 1971 season I went 0-for-17 before I got my first hit. I had told the guys that when I got my first hit I'd kiss the base. I doubled and I got to second base and did what I promised. They were all laughing in the dugout.

It's May and I'm hitting around .200 and my concentration is all messed up. Then all hell breaks loose. There was one double play that I blew that was really easy. I came into the dugout after the inning, and as soon as I hit the dugout steps, Bill Rigney, the manager, jumped all over me. He started hollering, "For crying out loud, if you don't want to play, don't play." I said, "I'm going to tell you something. If you don't want me to play, take my name out of the lineup and I won't go out on the field." In years past, I probably would have just walked out and left, because he was embarrassing me in front of my teammates—right in front of everybody on the bench. Now I stood my ground. I told him point-blank: "If you don't like it, tell me to take my uniform off. You're the manager. I'm the one risking permanent injury, not you. It's my career in jeopardy, not yours."

All the guys are sitting on the bench, and their eyes are going back and forth between me and Rigney as if they were watching a tennis match. I wasn't going to let him put me down in front of the other players. I stayed in the game. Afterward, I stormed into his room and told him, "Don't ever try to embarrass me in front of my teammates. Respect me as a man the way I would respect you as a man. If you have anything to say to me, call me into your office and chew me out and I'll accept it—but never do it in front of my teammates."

I looked at him and I said, "I'm going to tell you something. I'm hitting .227 right now, but at the end of the season, Bill, I want you to check the stats and I'm going to be in the top ten in batting."

Well, he didn't say anything when I said those things to him. I just walked out of the office. I didn't say too much to him the rest of the season.

The papers were full of how poorly I was doing and that I was gun-shy. It got so bad I didn't even want to open a newspaper. You know, with newspaper guys it's too often the case that they see no middle ground. They don't see ballplayers as fallible human beings who are trying and sometimes succeeding and sometimes not. You're either a hero or a bum to them. If a guy is going poorly they ought to find out why, try to look deeper inside him. Let the people know that a guy might be going bad because he is playing under some kind of strain.

It's the same thing with your manager. Rigney never sat down with me and said, "Okay, let's talk about this fear. Let's try to see what the root of the problem is and try to solve it." As much as we're grown men and professional athletes, we need that. We are human beings. Just as we need understanding when we're going bad, we need a pat on the rear end when we're going good. We want to be appreciated for what we do well. We're no different in this regard from anyone else.

Rigney had been sniping at me all along for my play at second. God knows he had reason to be critical. But he never went out to second with me and said, "Let's go over some of these things." And he had once been a second baseman with the Giants.

In fact, I had been doing something wrong on my throwing release. I reared back and threw to first from behind my ear. I recalled something Billy Martin had told me in 1969 when he was the Twins' manager. He said I should throw from where I catch the ball, using a lot of wrist. I eventually started doing that.

Before that, though, Rigney decided he would try me at third base or left field. That was foreign territory for me. I wanted to stay at second and work out my problem. I beefed. The papers called me a crybaby.

But I went to third for a game. I felt so strange there. I remember a pop-up that I started on one way, then the wind took it another way, and I finally chased it to the mound and caught it falling to my knees. The guys on the Indians' bench were doubled over with laughter. I would have been too. The next day, Rigney returned me to second.

Some days, I'd come home from the park and wouldn't say a word to Marilynn. I was going badly, and I felt like going off alone into a cave. She didn't understand my silence. She took it personally. We fought. Some days I didn't come home until late. I'd drive around, or sit in a movie theater by myself. Marilynn was beside herself with worry and rage at me. I just couldn't open up to her or anyone else and tell all the things that were eating me up. I had always been a loner and always kept things to myself.

Besides Rigney's upsetting treatment of me, I also didn't think he got the best out of other players. I know he never got the best out of me. Of the major-league managers I've had, Mele, Martin, Quilici and Mauch could get a hell of a lot out of a player. They gave you the impression—they gave *me* the impression—that they cared about you. They gave you a push. But Rigney was concerned only with himself. When we needed a pinch hitter, he'd walk up and down the bench with his hands in his back pockets. All of a sudden he'd turn to a guy and say, "Go win it for me." He never said, "Go win it for us." It was always, Win it for me. And he could tell people nice things about you one minute and the next minute he'd be on the air telling the world what kind of lousy ballplayer you were. You were never sure where you stood with him.

I remember an incident in Detroit. Leo Cardenas was playing shortstop for us. Cardenas missed an easy double-play ball, and when Leo hit the front step of the dugout Rigney was screaming at him. In front of everybody.

Rigney belittled Tovar. Cesar is the type of guy that never gets mad at anybody, goes out there and plays his heart out. I think Tovar was just beautiful. Well, Rigney used to put Tovar down all the time. Rigney just liked to needle. Some players did like Rigney, though. Danny Thompson, the shortstop, was one. Rigney gave Danny a chance to play. But if you were in Rigney's doghouse, you were in for a lot of trouble.

I'm sure that my anger toward Rigney had some good effects in the field. I forced myself to get tougher at second base. I started blocking out some of the fears in my mind. I tried to work harder than ever.

Guys had started taking advantage of me. They weren't even sliding, but coming in at me with rolling blocks. I got tired of it. I knew I had to retaliate. Mike Andrews was coming in at me one time and I just dropped down a little bit lower and threw and hit his helmet with the ball. I could have hit him in the face if I had wanted to. But I just wanted guys to know that they couldn't bully me. I think word got around that I wasn't going to accept it.

I just *had* to show Rigney I could stay in there at second. At one point in mid-season, there was a double-play ground ball to third. I was determined not to shy away at second. Sal Bando of Oakland came sliding in. He could have torn me up, but he slid away from me. And I made the double play. He dusted himself off and said, "Rod, you could've gotten hurt." I said, "I know, Sal, and thanks." The next day at the batting cage I saw him and told him the story. "I know what you're going through," he said, "but don't get yourself hurt just to prove something to someone."

Shortly after, there was another double-play ball in a close game. I knew we needed it to win the game. I took my chances and made the play. Rigney didn't say a word about it.

The fear about my knee slowly dissolved. Sometimes I'd still back out at second, but more and more I'd stay in.

I also got my hitting act together and wound up the season with a .307 average, fifth best in the league. I had kept my promise to Rigney when I was at .227 that I'd get into the top ten. That was some consolation in 1971; but the year was disappointing and frustrating in many ways—especially the team's performance. We dropped from the division leader of two straight seasons to fifth place in the six-team division.

I again went down to winter ball after the season and began to rebuild my confidence around second even more.

The native players aren't as aggressive as the players in the States. They don't come into second as fiercely as they do in the major leagues. So I slowly began to get my mind off the runner. Meanwhile, the muscles in my leg were getting stronger. These two factors particularly helped me overcome my fears around second base when the 1972 season began.

I realize now how good a job Dr. O'Phelan had done with the operation on my knee. There are guys who never come back after ligament operations. Or their knees are so weak they have chronic problems. I didn't even wear a brace on my leg. When your leg is taped, it's as if one side of your body were top-heavy. I didn't want any limited action.

By the start of the 1972 season, I was no longer playing with a constant throb. There were a couple of times I almost got hit and didn't budge. I said to myself, It's gone. My leg healed perfectly. And today every time I take my uniform off and I look at my leg and see that scar, I thank Dr. O'Phelan for doing one heck of a repair job.

IN WINTER ball during the 1971–72 season, I gained a valuable appreciation of how difficult it is to manage a team of 25 very different individuals, and it had a deep effect on me.

I took over a team in Caracas, Venezuela, and I was forced to see baseball from a whole new angle.

I didn't go down there as a manager. I went down to play; but the team owner had trouble with the original manager and asked me to handle the club until a replacement could be found. Well, we started off winning something like 12 out of 13 games. I was asked to stay on managing.

The team had several players from the States, including Brant Alyea, Graig Nettles, Enos Cabell, Von Joshua, Billy Wynn and Larry Hainey. Most of the American players took winter ball lightly. They would always have an excuse for missing workouts. It didn't make me happy. Meanwhile, the native players cherished the jobs—they needed the money, and they wanted the experience.

I'd already had a few run-ins with the American players because of their lackadaisical attitude. One day Alyea came to the park just when the game was starting. I had a guy in his place. Alyea was mad. I said, "You're supposed to be here at eleven-thirty for batting practice, and you show up at one-thirty. What do you expect?"

Well we're fighting for a spot in the play-offs, and this is a big game. Now we're in a tight situation. Ninth inning. If we score, we could win. Alyea is up, and he's facing a pitcher who has struck him out something like seven of the last eight times he's faced him.

Alyea swings at two pitches as if he's not even trying. I decide to pinch-hit for him, with two strikes. I send in Cesar Gutierrez, and he singles. We win the game.

Well, Alyea was mad as hell. I thought he was going to try to knock me on my rear end. He's telling me what a horse's ass I am and that I'm no manager. I told him that if he didn't like it, we'd be happy to ship him home. We went at it for a couple of days more, but he stayed.

This whole managing experience made me reflect on my past, and how I was always moody with managers and threatening to jump the club. I thought now, Maybe I was wrong all those years. I decided I was never going to give a manager another problem. And I haven't. I've been fined only twice since then. Once, Frank Quilici hit me for $250 because he thought I didn't run out a ground ball. I disagreed. I had a twisted ankle, and I ran the ball out the best I could. The other time, I popped up a ball in Detroit. I thought it was going foul, and I leisurely rounded first base. But the wind blew it fair, and I was thrown out at second. I should have been running harder. When I got back to the bench, I walked over to Mauch and said, "I'm fining myself a hundred dollars—it was a stupid play." He said, "I thought you would do that, Pro." That's his nickname for me, "Pro." His attitude is such that he makes you want to play really hard for him. He gives a player respect and has a way of making a player feel better about himself; I guess calling a man "Pro" is one of the ways.

# Chapter VII

WHEN I got hurt in June of 1970, the Twins brought up Danny Thompson from the minors to replace me. He did a good job. He batted only .219, but he got on base, and he was dependable in the field. The next season he was a utility infielder. Danny became the regular shortstop when the Twins traded Cardenas before the 1972 season.

I would miss. Leo. He was a good ballplayer and one of the most unusual guys I'd ever known. Leo had some very odd ways. If he was in a slump—say, he'd gone 0-for-10 at bat—he'd walk around the dugout and holler in Spanish, "Untie me! Let me go!" Leo believed in black magic, and he thought that his closest Latin friends on the team—Oliva, Tovar and I—had worked some magic to bind his arms so that he couldn't hit.

I wasn't sure what to make of this. Leo was from Cuba, as was Tony, and I wondered if this was something common in Cuba. "No," said Tony, "and don't let it bother you. He'll come out of it." He did. But he was so supersti-tious that if he made an error, he might blame it on the opposing team's shortstop for hexing the shortstop area. I understand that if he was worried about supernatural forces when he went to bed, he'd sleep with the lights on in the room to ward them off.

With Leo gone, I had to adjust to a new double-play partner. Danny was from a small town in Oklahoma and talked with a little twang. He had heavy dark eyebrows and a cleft in his chin like Kirk Douglas. He was a hard-nosed player. We got to know each other's moves really well. We also became friends. People called us "Salt and Pepper." We'd sometimes turn three or four double plays in a game. We were helping pitchers out of jams and contributing to the club. Guys said, "If it wasn't for Salt and Pepper to-night, we wouldn't have won the game." Stuff like that. Made me feel good.

Danny helped me a great deal to feel comfortable at sec-ond base again after my injury. He gave me the ball well on the double-play toss. He asked me where I wanted the throw and how much should be on it. His throws were almost always at the chest, just where they should be. In-stead of worrying about where the ball is going to be and thinking about the runner coming down from first, I could concentrate on getting rid of the ball quickly because I could count on Danny's throw being clean. We practiced together a lot. Even in infield practice, if there were two shortstops and two second basemen, we'd never have the other guy. We never split up the combination.

He always seemed concerned about me and would ask about my leg. We didn't discuss my fears, but I thought he had an understanding of what I went through because he had had serious injuries when he was in the minor leagues. One time he collided with a guy and Danny's face was twisted to one side for a few days. He had broken his nose and his jaw in other accidents on the field.

Danny and I would occasionally go to dinner after games on the road. We never really got personal, though. I knew he was religious, and a member of the Fellowship of Christian Athletes, but we just stuck to baseball talk primarily.

He would ask me about hitting. And when he was in a slump he'd ask for advice. He was a right-handed batter and had a habit of dipping his right shoulder and swinging under the ball. He didn't realize he was doing it. I'd point it out to him.

In 1972 Danny had a fine season, playing in 144 games and batting .276. I hit .318 and led the league for the second time in my career. The club moved up to third in the standings, and after the last game of the season, Danny said to me, "Junior, we're going to kick some butt next season."

Like a lot of players, Danny called me "Junior." Harmon gave me that nickname after my first season. He said, "Well, I can't call you 'Rookie' anymore, so I'll call you 'Junior.' "

But Danny was right. Things were looking up. Then one day in early February of 1973, I got a phone call from Danny. "Junior," he said, "I've got something to tell you. I've just got back some reports from the hospital about blood tests I took. They think I've got leukemia."

I couldn't believe it. He told me he had just returned from Rochester and that I was the first player he wanted to call. Danny told me he had gone into the Mayo Clinic for a routine annual physical. The doctors said something looked fishy. They told him to check back in four days. It was a long, long four days, he said. Then he phoned the hospital. He asked the doctor what he had found. He said, "Dan, you've got leukemia."

Danny said, "Thank you."

He told me, "I don't know what in the hell I was thanking him for. My mind was spinning."

When Danny came to spring training for the 1973 season, he seemed awfully brave about it. I really tried to boost him. I'd go out of my way to say good things about him to the press. I told one writer, "Danny's the best shortstop I've ever played with." It was true, too. I said I'd always admired how hard he played. His wife called Marilynn one time and said, "I want you to thank Rod for me for saying what he has about Danny. It means a lot to him now that he's going through this thing."

There were a lot of questions about Danny: How long would he live? How strong would he be? Could he play?

The doctors thought they had a chance to arrest the disease. The diagnosis was "slow" leukemia, and doctors said he could live two years or fifty. They just did not know. Nor did they know the effects the disease would have on Danny as a ballplayer.

He never showed any signs of being sick on the field. That's what amazed me. I used to look at him and say, Jeez, the guy doesn't know if he'll be alive tomorrow and he's out here giving everything he's got. If I had a hero in those days, it was Danny.

In the locker room, you'd look at his arms and they were black-and-blue and puffy from the shots he took. It was a miserable sight. His eyes looked tired. Sometimes you'd see him throwing up. Occasionally he'd run a fever.

All this plus the worry had to take its toll during that 1973 season. He eventually lost his starting position. He was naturally unhappy about it and felt he ought to be playing. His batting average fell to .225, and he played in only 99 games.

The following season was better. He started more frequently and moved his average up to .250. By 1975 he was hitting .270 and appeared to be on the way to full recovery. Yet Quilici and Calvin Griffith spoke about getting shortstop help. This didn't get Danny down. Oh, he grumbled about not playing enough, and made jokes about it, but on the bench he was still talking it up. He'd do a lot of running in the outfield before games to stay in shape. What was particularly frustrating for him was that he wasn't playing that much and we weren't winning that often.

We'd talk, and he explained the thing about blood counts and leukemia, and he told me he was going to take a special new drug and kidded about being a guinea pig. He spoke about being in God's hands. Religion was more important than ever to him.

Even though Danny was going through these rough times, he always seemed to find the time to encourage me. I won my third batting title with a .350 average in 1973 and my fourth the following season with .364, and Danny was there cheering for me just as he had a few seasons back when we were the ''Salt and Pepper'' combination.

Danny told me he was writing a book with Bob Fowler of the *Minneapolis Star*. It was a diary about the 1975 season. That winter, the book came out. I was shocked.

In the book, entitled *E-6: The Diary of a Major League Shortstop* (E-6 is the baseball scorer's designation for error on the shortstop), Danny said:

> Rod Carew has been in and out of the lineup with an assortment of leg injuries since the season started. But no one on the club really believes he is really hurting. They think he's still pouting because he lost his arbitration case.
>
> . . . He wanted $140,000 because he had won four batting titles—three of them in a row—and had been an All-Star selection eight straight years. But he lost and had to settle for $125,000 [actually $120,000].
>
> I don't feel sorry for Carew. His raise, $35,000, is more than my entire salary.
>
> His attitude pisses me off.

Danny also accused me of not giving 100 percent every day.

In the four seasons that Danny and I played together, he never, *never* gave me any hint that he felt this way. I don't know if Danny was persuaded that the book would sell more by having some controversy; he also took some shots at Quilici and Calvin Griffith.

Funny thing, but in the season he wrote about, the one in which I was "always taking myself out of the lineup," according to Danny, I missed only 19 of the team's 162 games.

At one point during that 1975 season, I pulled a hamstring muscle and my legs were killing me. I wasn't running well, and I was frustrated. It was getting me down. My brother-in-law, Stu Kloner, told me about a friend who is a hypnotist. He thought the man could help relax me.

The hypnotist's name is Harvey Misel. He had worked with athletes before, and he had taught hypnosis at colleges and hospitals. I did have a pulled muscle. And when I ran I'd start to pull up even before the muscle began to hurt. He thought I ought to run and stretch the muscle to strengthen it. I told him I was afraid to. So through hypnosis he induced me not to worry about the pain. It turned out that the pain wasn't so awful, and my leg did get better as I ran with my normal stride. The club went into Milwaukee that weekend, and I had a good series. I stole a couple of bases, and I didn't feel the ache in my leg. The hypnotist also had put me into a posthypnotic condition in which I could sit on the bench and put myself under hypnosis and take myself out of it whenever I felt I was getting uptight. Some of the players found out about it. I thought they'd be on me for using a crutch, or whatever. Next thing I know, we have about 15 guys going to see the guy.

This "jaking" thing has plagued me my entire career. Some players, Danny obviously among them, felt I could have played when I didn't. But I still will not risk injury if I feel I might do harm to myself. And I feel I'm the best judge of that. If I believe I can't run right and I can't give 100 percent, I won't play. I don't think anyone should. I'm not going to go through the motions.

Danny, however, did say some very nice things about me in his book. I was having an unbelievable year at the plate and hitting over .400 into June and wound up with a .359

batting average for my fifth batting title. Danny spoke glow-
ingly about that. He also said that I had "a good personality
. . . a great sense of humor, and is very pleasant when he's
not in one of his moods."

It's true that I was still a moody guy. I accept that. And
of course I'll accept his compliments. But overall, I thought
Danny was grossly unfair. I was hurt. I felt betrayed by a
friend. I was still in a state of shock when, soon after the
book appeared, he called. He invited me to an autographing
session for the book. He said, "I know there are some
things in the book that might be upsetting for you."

I said, "Danny, I thought the book was supposed to be
about you and the season."

"Well," he said, "some things got in there. But I also
said some good things about you."

I thanked him for that, but said I just couldn't attend that
autographing session because I was unhappy about his
book.

When we went to camp the following spring, 1976, everybody was looking for a confrontation. One of the guys in
the Twins' public relations office told me, "Man, everybody's just waiting to see what's going to happen between
you and Thompson."

In Orlando I saw Danny in the locker room. I didn't want
this thing hanging. He was getting dressed and I was already dressed. I walked over and said, "I'd like to talk to
you."

He said okay. He looked apprehensive, as if maybe I
were going to punch him in the mouth.

"When you get dressed I'll meet you on the field," I
said.

I met him down the first-base line by the fence. Everybody was looking to see what was going to happen.

"I thought we were friends," I said. "And so I just want
to clear the air. I have no hard feelings. You took your shot
and it's over and done with."

He said he was sorry that it happened but he couldn't do anything about it now.

I said, "We're teammates, and let's just play and try to win."

We shook hands.

Gene Mauch had now replaced Quilici as the manager of the Twins. Mauch restored Danny as the regular shortstop. Danny did not sign a contract, though, because he had been bucking for a raise, and Calvin had been bucking just as hard not to give him what he wanted. Calvin was also having contract squabbles with Bert Blyleven, the pitcher. In June, Calvin traded the pair to Texas.

Danny and I had worked out an amicable relationship, although I can't say that I was sad to see him go.

When Danny was with the Rangers and he'd get on base, I'd kid him: "If there's a pickoff, I'm going to tag you extra hard." And when I saw him in the batting cage, I needled him: "You're still dipping your back shoulder." He'd call me "Junior" and would kid me about something or other.

I had asked him how he felt, and he said fine. He said he had lost some weight—10 to 15 pounds—but blamed it on the hot Texas weather.

In November I went on a tour of U.S. Army bases in Germany, Holland and Belgium with three other players, Paul Blair, Richie Hebner and Bill Singer, and Tom Mee, the Twins' public relations director. We showed the troops films of the 1976 All-Star game and talked baseball, and we saw the sights.

I returned in early December. While I was at a hockey game in St. Paul, one of the TV guys came down to my seat and said, "Rod, we just got the news. Danny just died." He was 29 years old.

The reporter wanted a quote. What was I going to say? I told him Danny had had a lot of courage and I respected him as an athlete. I said he was a hell of a guy. I said it was a shock that he died because everyone thought he was getting better. I didn't know he had been back in the hospital. At least I'm comforted that he died knowing I didn't hold a grudge against him. His dad knew it, too. Mr. Thompson came to see games in Kansas City, since he didn't live far from there. He was alongside the dugout one day in the spring of 1977 and I said hello to him.

"I don't want you to think that Danny and I were no longer friends because of his book," I said.

Mr. Thompson said he knew that, that Danny had told him that. His father said he appreciated it.

I had not gone to Danny's funeral. It was in Oklahoma and I'm just not one for funerals. I didn't want to see a viewing of Danny. I wanted to remember him looking healthy. I know how this sickness can deteriorate a person.

Steve Braun was a pallbearer at Danny's funeral. In the spring Steve told me a story Danny's father had told him. Danny was in an oxygen tent and his father was about to leave. Danny waved to him and pointed upstairs. Danny's father learned that Danny died a few minutes later.

I've thought a lot about why Danny wrote what he did about me. I just couldn't justify it. I asked Tony Oliva about it, and he said, "Rod, you know you read a lot of stuff about Boston players saying that Carl Yastrzemski dogs it. Did you ever see Carl Yastrzemski play? He gives a hundred and fifty percent all the time. So why do players say the things they do about him? He makes too much money. Jealousy. It has to be." That's Tony's opinion.

Bob Fowler, Danny's collaborator on the book, said Danny wrote that stuff about me in order to prod me to do better. He said that that was Danny's missionary spirit in action.

I asked Dick Lurie. Dick is a man who has handled my business affairs and has negotiated my contract. He performed the same service for Danny. Dick was a friend of Danny's, as he is of mine. I asked Dick what he thought.

"Much of Danny's views have to do with his background," Dick said to me. "He was a boy from a little town in Oklahoma, a town called Carpon. That culture and sub-culture may have been best described in *The Grapes of Wrath*. The dust-bowl environment. Here is a very deeply religious man, very committed to Christ and all things that overtly represented the White Anglo-Saxon Protestant environment. There was in his mind, I believe, a strong distinction between the white Protestants of the world and those who were not—primarily those who were black. Although I think Danny felt very comfortable with blacks on the field as equals, he probably would have described them as separate but equal off the field. I believe this is so even though he and another black, Larry Hisle, roomed together on the road.

"When a black then marries a Jewish girl, that again went against the grain of the dust-bowl philosophy: it's immoral in some fashion; intermarriage should never happen. It couldn't happen in the environment that he was used to—that is, small-town Southwestern Methodist. I don't believe Danny consciously realized all this. But I believe that subconsciously Danny was making these moral judgments."

I recall racial jokes that Danny and I shared, and they never bothered me. I know a guy like Maury Wills always shrank from racial jokes. He said that they invariably wind up getting serious. It may be so, but it just didn't bother me. A guy would fire a remark at you, you'd fire one back. A Polack remark, or a Jew remark, or Italian remark. There's a locker-room mentality that in many cases allows you to accept this stuff. But I have seen guys go too far and get mad.

And we could poke fun at ourselves. Before one game, I said to Eric Soderholm, "Eric, when you go to bat today, you're going to get a standing ovation."

He asked why.

"Because you're going to be the first white guy they introduce."

It was true. The top of our batting order had me, Lyman Bostock, Larry Hisle, Bobby Darwin and Tony, followed by our white guys—Eric, Steve Braun, Danny and Glenn Borgmann.

If you can joke about something, I find that with goodwill on both sides you can relieve pressure.

Danny and I joked along these lines. And the "Salt and Pepper" thing seemed a natural lead-in to it. There never seemed to me to be any underlying tension in him toward me. Maybe there was—and maybe there wasn't.

As for not giving 100 percent on the field, I'd like to quote Ted Williams from a *Sports Illustrated* article in 1977. Williams said:

> When I first saw Carew in the late '60s . . . he was a little too lackadaisical to suit me. He still *looks* lackadaisical. It's his style. He's so smooth he seems to be doing it without trying. Some guys—Pete Rose is one, and I put myself in this category—have to snort and fume to get everything going. Carew doesn't.

When Danny said I was disturbed by the arbitration decision on my contract in the winter of 1974, he was absolutely right. I sat in on the proceedings. And when I left, I was shaken right down to my big toe. The arguments used by the Twins' negotiators to support their case were unfair, in my estimation, and almost vicious.

And yet by the time I arrived for spring training in 1975, I had resolved a lot of my bitterness and disappointment.

ARBITRATION IS a brand-new thing in baseball. And it's not that old a procedure in labor circles, period. It has been only in the last few years that players have been able to get a larger and fairer slice of the economic pie. Until very recently, baseball teams were run by the reserve clause. A player was bound to that team and that team only until he was traded, sent down to the minors or given his outright release. Now a player can play out his option and make a deal for himself with another team. If a player is good enough, many teams bid for his services. That's how you get the multimillion-dollar salaries paid to players such as Reggie Jackson, Catfish Hunter and Larry Hisle. Also, because of the fight put up by the players' union, led by executive director Marvin Miller, when a player believes he is being unfairly paid, he can seek an arbitration hearing. The independent arbitrator is chosen out of a hat from names given by the American Arbitration Association. The arbitrator sits and listens to the time-limited arguments of each side. Then he and he alone makes the decision, which is binding on both parties. This was a tremendous step for ballplayers.

In the old days—up to the early '70s, in fact—a player's only recourse was to hold out. And since players generally loved to play ball, and generally were making more money than they could in any other occupation, they buckled under. The owners knew the player eventually would.

A lot of the greatest players were holdouts. Walter Johnson was a holdout. Joe DiMaggio was a holdout. But each surrendered before the season began. An old-time Hall-of-Famer named Edd Roush led the league in hitting one year, but didn't hit as high as he had the season before, and the owner cut his salary. He held out.

When Curt Flood in 1969 said that he was a "slave" because he couldn't decide his own baseball fate, even though he was making $90,000 a year, some people laughed at him. A $90,000 slave? The fact is, Flood on the open market might have earned even more than the amount he was making.

Well, *I* was earning $90,000. I thought I deserved

$140,000 a year. The Twins offered $100,000. Later, they raised it to $120,000. I looked around and saw that players like Yaz, Reggie, Pete Rose, Tom Seaver—the other outstanding players in the game—were getting in the neighborhood of $140,000 or more. I thought I was at least equal to them in ability, performance and value to the club.

When all these changes came about in player–management relations, some players hired representatives to negotiate their contracts. Club executives were business professionals; ballplayers were ballplayers. It was an unfair advantage. Dick Lurie is a certified public accountant and was doing tax work for some ballplayers. They asked him to represent them. He did, and did it well. I heard about him and hired him.

Dick Lurie and I decided to go to arbitration. If we won, I'd get $140,000. If we lost, I'd get $120,000.

Each side made its case. Dick Lurie and his partner, a lawyer named Malin Greenberg, prepared skillfully. Clark Griffith, Calvin's son and the Twins' vice-president, and George Brophy, then head of the Twins' farm system, gave the ball club's side. The proceedings were held in a conference room in Chicago.

I sat through the whole thing and never said a word.

We presented our case first. Dick pointed out that I had accomplished spectacular batting feats, including leading the league in batting in four of my eight seasons.

The Twins' rebuttal was that I was just a singles hitter. They said I didn't hit home runs and I didn't drive in 100 runs a season, and I didn't lead the Twins to a pennant. I said to myself, Who am I? Superman? I am one man among 25—one person can't lead a team to a pennant. Baseball isn't that kind of game. Not for 162 games a year.

And I *hadn't* hit many home runs. In 1974 I hit three homers and the year before six. In fact, in 1972, when I hit .318, I became the first modern player to lead the league in hitting and not get even *one* home run.

My RBI numbers were not impressive either. The most I had in any one season up to then was 62. In 1974 I had 55.

Our argument was that I was a player to be compared not to the sluggers, of course, but to the Pete Roses and Joe Morgans. I was a guy who batted second in the order, where RBI's are relatively hard to come by, and my game was to get on base, then steal and create some action so that guys lower in the order could drive me in. That was my particular job, and that was what managers asked me to do.

Griffith and Brophy also criticized me for having led the league with 33 errors at second base in 1974. Our argument was that I covered much more ground than most other second basemen and got to a lot more balls, some of which I couldn't hang on to and which were then scored as errors.

Arguments went back and forth. The longer they did, the hotter I got. I felt the Twins were picking on everything bad to bring up. Of course, my side picked on everything good. We broke for lunch; arguments resumed afterward and then ended in late afternoon.

I came out sick to my stomach. I couldn't believe what the Twins had said. From what I heard, I realized that the arbitrator, John Killingsworth, knew little about baseball. For example, at one point we mentioned sacrifice hits, and Mr. Killingsworth stopped the proceedings to ask what a "sacrifice hit" was.

A few days later, I learned that Mr. Killingsworth ruled against us.

My first reaction was one of deep resentment toward the Twins. Then I thought, But that's business; that's like any business. You try to get a guy to work as cheaply as possible. Why not? Why pay more if you can get him for less? The Twins did all they could in that vein, and I really shouldn't take it personally. But to convince my heart of that was a tough proposition.

Once you get on the field, though, your pride in performance overcomes the off-the-field resentment. At least, it does for me.

I'd like to think my 1975 statistics—the season after my arbitration—prove it. I had led the league in batting again and, coincidentally, I had a career high up to that point of 80 runs batted in. I also had a career high of 14 home runs. I truly wasn't trying to hit homers. The ball was just jumping out of the park.

# Chapter VIII

I DON'T know if hitting a baseball is the single hardest thing to do in sports—as Ted Williams insists—but I know it's not easy.

Consider this: A bat at its widest is 3¾ inches in diameter; some pitchers throw the ball more than 90 miles an hour; and the distance from the pitching rubber to home plate is 60 feet 6 inches. This means the batter has two-thirds of a second in which to uncoil and get good wood and full body into the pitch. And not all pitches come straight in—they dip, float, soar and drop. The best batters in the game hit safely only three times out of ten. The all-time best batters for average succeeded four times out of ten: Ty Cobb, Joe Jackson, Nap Lajoie, George Sisler, Rogers Hornsby, Harry Heilmann, Bill Terry and Ted Williams. They are the .400 hitters. Only eight of them. Amazing when you realize that some 6,000 men have tried to earn their living by hitting a baseball in the big leagues.

Hitting begins even before you get to the park. I've driven to the park and thought about who I'm facing in the game, what kind of stuff he has. If I'm not going well at the plate, I'll think about bunting to get out of a slump. I like to envision the ball I hit. I see it taking a hop and going between the outfielders. And I'm taking off and going around first base, going into second, and then around and into third. I can picture those things in my mind.

It's the greatest feeling in the world to be going out to the ball park every day and knowing you're going to get a couple of hits. *Thinking* it, anyway. God, now I can't wait to get there.

And I look forward to facing the best pitchers. They're doing their best to get me out and I'm doing my best to disappoint them. The challenge is everything. I have the confidence to think I'll win.

I have the greatest respect for my bats. I use a 34½-length, 32-ounce bat tooled from ash. The top is as wide as they make it, and the handle is as narrow as I can get it. For me, it provides a combination of power and whippy action. Up until the spring of 1970, I had used bats as heavy as 36 ounces, and choked up. But in Lakeland, Florida, one day in the spring of 1970 I was standing by the batting cage before a game with the Tigers. Al Kaline had just finished hitting, and I asked to see his bat. I used to hear stories that Kaline's bat would *bend*. And it looked that way when he hit. I wondered if his bat were made of a different kind of wood from other bats. I picked up Kaline's bat and saw that it had a very thin handle and a larger-than-average barrel. It was also light—32 ounces. It really felt comfortable in my hands. I had been using a heavier bat with a thicker handle. I asked Kaline why he used this style bat; he said simply because it was comfortable. This bat felt more comfortable than the one I was using. I began to order bats like it from Louisville Slugger. I still use that model.

Funny thing is, some guys can't swing a bat with a thin

handle and a big barrel. Oliva, Killebrew, Allison—they all tried my bat, but they weren't comfortable with it. To each his own.

I can't stand a dirty bat. We use pine tar for a better grip. When the pine tar accumulates on my bat, I rub it off with alcohol. I don't even like my bat to fall into the dirt. I'm always wiping it off. Some guys don't mind. I can't understand how they can get a good feel for the wood. I see some guys banging their bat against the dugout steps after they make an out. That bruises the bat. I couldn't do that. I place my bat gently back in the rack. I baby my bats— they're how I make my living.

I also lock my bats in a closet in the Twins' clubhouse. The closet is next to a sauna. I think the heat from the sauna bakes out the bad or weak wood in a bat. I used to have a problem of bats' splintering. I don't anymore, and I credit that to the baking.

Most players are told, Get one stance and don't fool around with others unless you're in a slump. I've got at least *five* stances. Dick Williams, when he was the Angels' manager, said I had twenty different stances and that it was like pitching to five different guys every night. I've learned to change my stance depending on the pitcher. With fastball pitchers, I try to stay as far back in the box as possible. It gives me a chance to see the ball a split second longer. With breaking-ball pitchers, I open my stance. That is, more of my body is facing the pitcher. I'm fooled less that way. I also open my stance more to lefties than to righties. I feel I can watch their delivery more closely that way. If a guy likes to jam me and I have trouble handling it, why not open up a little bit so that I can get a better view of the ball and start my hands and hips going more quickly?

Now, take Frank Tanana. He's a lefty, and he runs everything inside on me. He tries to jam me with fastballs. So I open my stance and face him a little more; then I can pick up his pitches better. I never try to pull the ball on him; I try to hit the ball up the middle. Same with Vida

Blue, another lefty, who throws second fastest to Nolan Ryan. Steve Mingori has a good slider and screwball and doesn't throw hard. So I really don't want to overswing at him. I just lean back a little and wait as long as I can on the pitch.

I'm always adjusting. My batting against Nolan Ryan is an example. Nolan fires a great fastball, and it's coming in and the next thing you know it's rising. On days I face Nolan, I hit from a crouch. I crouch on Nolan because I think I take away some of his effectiveness by giving him a lower strike zone to throw at. His fastball isn't going to do as much down low as it would higher up. I do the same with Jim Palmer. On days when I know those guys are pitching, I'm in the batting cage early practicing hitting from a crouch.

No matter how well or poorly I'm hitting, I always take extra batting practice. Sometimes I get a base hit on a particular pitch and I don't feel right about it; maybe I didn't hit it with the meat of the bat. And then maybe I'm not hitting consistently hard to left. Whatever, I ask Tony or Don McMahon or Karl Kuehl, one of the coaches, to throw some extra batting practice to me and keep the ball where I think I'm having some trouble—say, low outside corner. Batting practice for a lot of guys is just hitting the ball into the seats. Then they get into a game situation in which they have to do something, and they can't do it. If there's one single reason for the success I've enjoyed, I think it's due to my always trying to be prepared.

The key to hitting is comfort. You can't be uncomfortable in the batter's box. You've got to be at home there. It starts with getting a bat that feels good to you. Use a bat you can swing and not one that swings you. I grip the bat in my fingers. I think I can handle the bat better that way. Some guys lodge it in their palms, which creates a little bit of dead action that causes them to tense their muscles. It's because of this that the upper part of the body tenses up.

I know beforehand what kind of pitches this pitcher likes

to throw. I know his motion, and his velocity. So I'm making adjustments in my mind. I don't follow his entire pitching motion. My eyes aren't shifting around. I concentrate on the point of release, that chute, and no other place in the ball park. That's where the ball is coming from. The guy's not throwing the ball from his waist, even though he may start his motion from there.

I'm not a guess hitter. Some guys are. I'm not deciding beforehand whether the pitch will be a fastball or curve or what. I take what comes. After so many years of hitting a baseball, I can now usually tell when it leaves his hand what kind of pitch it is by the rotation of the seams. Most hitters eventually pick this ability up. My concentration is good. I block out all other thoughts. I just think about that ball.

I'm not one to take a lot of pitches. I'm not waiting around for the perfect pitch. Once you walk up to home plate and start taking pitches, too many pitches, you're going to lose your aggressiveness. I do, anyway.

If the first pitch is around the plate and I'm confident I can handle it, I'm swinging. That's one of the bad things today with kids in the Little League programs. Coaches tell them, Walk up there and get a good pitch to hit. What is a good pitch? The pitch might be out of the strike zone, but it's a good pitch for you if you feel you can hit it. Like the saying—different strokes for different folks.

Clemente used to hit balls that were practically in the dirt. Who used to tell Clemente what a good pitch was? Or Oliva? Or Yogi Berra? Sure, these guys were exceptional hitters, but they were comfortable at the plate and eager to hit. To me, that's what hitting is all about.

I'm watching the ball all the way in. I think I rarely see the ball actually hit the bat, but I'm looking at the point of contact. My head's not turned away looking to the outfield fences.

If you pull your head away, I think you'd be opening

your body too quickly. Your hips have to be opening just before you make the contact. It's how you get your power. But the timing must be just right. Another thing I found: Relaxed legs are essential to good hitting. You can't hit with stiff legs.

I stride into the ball, and I keep the bat back as long as possible. I'm practically hitting with my hips. Then I try to meet the ball without trying to overpower it. Yet you've got to be aggressive in the follow-through. That accelerates power.

I hold my bat in different positions with different stances. If there's a good fastball pitcher, I might hold my bat relatively horizontal, to get a better whip action. If I'm facing a guy with slower stuff, I'll keep my bat more vertical, to add power. Sometimes I'll hold my bat at an upright angle. It all depends on the situation. I stay flexible.

I also like to keep my hands loose on the bat until the point of contact. Some guys are squeezing the bat into sawdust while waiting for the pitch. My hands are loose; I think it relaxes my mind and body and allows for total concentration on the pitcher.

I begin to hold the bat tighter as I begin to step into the ball. And I squeeze harder as my swing speeds up. When I hit the ball and then follow through, my hands are *firm* on the bat.

EVERYONE TALKS about Nolan Ryan's fastball, and so do I. But he's got a helluva curve ball, too. It's that combination which makes him so effective. But that fastball! Nolan is one of the few guys who really overpower a hitter. He's blown me away, where I couldn't get my bat around on the ball. He simply amazes me—he's the only pitcher who throws a pitch 100 miles per hour in the first inning, and then seven or eight innings later is throwing it *105* miles an hour. He actually gets stronger as the game wears on. Yet he's one of the guys I've hit well in my career. He could be throwing really hard one day and I'm hitting him. Another day he could be throwing equally hard and I won't hit him. I cannot explain it.

I've had pretty fair success with another pitcher who gives hitters trouble. That's Luis Tiant. A lot of hitters are up there and watching all of Tiant's weird bodily contortions. He twists and twirls and dips and spins when he goes through his motion. Some guys are watching his arms and legs flying all around. Dean Chance pitched that way too. Chance used to turn all the way around and show a hitter his back. Guys would be watching his back. What you've got to watch is his point of release. Concentrate on that. Tiant has two points of release. Three-quarters overhand and sidearm. I watch those spots and nowhere else. When I'm on the on-deck circle, then I can appreciate Tiant's contortions. But not when I'm facing him at bat.

Another guy who could be distracting for a batter is Mark Fidrych, the famous "Bird." He's crawling around on the pitcher's mound smoothing the dirt, or he's talking to the ball, or he's tugging at his blond curls. Some guys might have had a tendency to laugh at him and not take him too seriously. But he proved that he can hum that ball. And he's got excellent control. He's always low with his pitches. Rarely does he come above the belt.

All those antics he performs *are* Mark Fidrych. He's for real. I remember when he was hurt and doing television color commentary. I saw him at the batting cage before a game. I asked how he was doing on the tube and he said, "Pretty good, Rod, except I can't stop saying 'Goddamn' on the air or the four-letter words I normally use."

Mark, his teammate Ron LeFlore and I took a cab together to the Philadelphia ballpark for the 1977 All-Star game. Mark's in the front seat and he's talking to the meter. "Don't be clickin' so fast. We don't make a helluva lot of money." A girl walks by and she catches Mark's eye. He lets out a howl of appreciation. Then he's back talking to the meter. When we get out of the cab and go to pay, Mark says to the driver, "Hey, that's too expensive!" It was only about $2.50. Mark slaps the meter, gives the driver a nice tip and then bounces into the crowd.

LeFlore turns to me, and he's laughing. "Well, Rod," he said to me, "that's the Bird in action."

Jim Palmer of Baltimore is the quiet type on the mound. Now, a Nolan Ryan throws hard, and it looks as if he's throwing hard because he puts so much power into his motion. This is in contrast to Palmer. Palmer is what we call "sneaky fast." From the bench, Jim looks so easy to hit. He's tall—six feet three—and he's got a long, easy motion. Very fluid. Everything comes straight overhand. It doesn't look as if he's throwing hard at all. But then he releases the ball and—*bang*—it's jumping right on top of you. Palmer has great stuff. His fastball has excellent velocity and cuts away from the hitter, and he's also got an off-speed curve ball and a fine fast curve.

Some pitchers have fastballs that rise, like Ryan, or cut away, like Palmer. But a pitcher like Bert Blyleven has a straight fastball. It's fast, but it comes in without much movement up or down, so it's somewhat easier to hit. He's also got a super curve ball. I played with Bert for five years, and enjoyed it. I liked his attitude. If a player makes an error or mistake behind him, Bert won't give him a nasty look, the way some pitchers will. "Hey," he'll say, "you'll get a hit and win a game for me."

One of the hardest pitches to hit is a good knuckleball. The best I've ever seen was Hoyt Wilhelm's. It used to hop and jump all over the place as it came toward the plate. He once threw one to Tony Oliva that just before it got to the plate was three feet over Tony's head. Suddenly it dropped across the strike zone into the catcher's mitt. It struck Oliva out. He couldn't believe that pitch and talks about it to this day.

Another good knuckleball pitcher is Wilbur Wood of the White Sox. A lot of guys will try to overpower the knuckleball. I just wait as long as I can and then flick at the pitch with strong wrist action. I'll often go to the opposite field off Wilbur. Another thing about him, sometimes when he's two or three balls behind you, he'll try to sneak a fastball or slider by you. Some guys always expect the knuckler from Wilbur. But I don't.

One of the best sliders in baseball is thrown by Sparky Lyle, the relief pitcher for the Yankees, who always has a chaw as big as a baseball in his cheek. Well, you know that when he comes into a game he's going to tell the catcher to put those three fingers down. That's the signal for the slider. The slider curves sharply to the side, as opposed to a curve ball, which *drops* down and away when it reaches the plate. The slider also has more velocity than a curve. Sparky has an odd way of throwing. He releases the ball with a stiff wrist, almost as if he's slinging it. You wonder how he gets mustard on the pitch— but he does.

In my earlier years in the league, one of the best sliders was thrown by Mickey Lolich. That beer belly of his never seemed to get in his way when he was on the mound. He was a smart pitcher, and he had a good fastball, too. But I always marveled at how well this chubby guy bounced off the mound after bunts or taps. I always thought that the fatter he got the faster he got. He seemed to defy every law of nature.

For a variety of reasons, some pitchers believe that they are obligated to throw at a hitter. After I stole home on Gaylord Perry a few years ago, I saw him nodding his head toward me when I got back to the dugout. He took my steal as a personal insult—that I had tried to show him up. It wasn't true, because I was doing my job and trying to win. Well, next time up, Perry on the first pitch knocks me down. On the next pitch, I swing and miss and let the bat fly out toward the mound. It didn't hit him, but it was close. I was sending him a message. Perry is the only pitcher who has consistently knocked me down.

Frank Tanana is another pitcher who seems to be trying to intimidate a hitter by throwing close. His teammate Nolan Ryan, on the other hand, doesn't. Funny thing, people *think* Ryan tries to brush back hitters, but I've never seen him throw intentionally at a batter.

Vida Blue is another pitcher who won't throw at a hitter. You can hit Vida all day, and he'll challenge you all day. That is, he'll be throwing his best pitches around the plate and challenging you to hit one. And if you do, he'll just tip his hat, as if to say, "You've got my respect." I don't care how hard he's getting hit, Vida never beefs. He gets the ball and he's firing.

There are occasions when a pitcher will throw at a batter as a form of protection for his own hitters. Several years ago, Juan Marichal of the Giants did this when he was pitching against the Dodgers. Apparently, Don Drysdale had been trying to intimidate Giant hitters like Willie Mays, Willie McCovey and Orlando Cepeda. So Marichal knocked down some Dodgers. It touched off a big free-for-all. But all the players—on both sides of the field—respected Marichal. I know this because one of those involved, John Roseboro, told me this story when he came to the Twins. Ballplayers respect the pitcher who will protect his hitters in this way. Your hitters have to be loose when they get up to the plate, and not be concerned with hitting the deck every other pitch.

Of course, no pitcher likes to see a hitter come up to the plate and start digging in deep. I've seen hitters go up to the plate and start stomping in the dirt like bulls. I don't dig in on anybody. I like to walk up to the plate very lightly. I don't let them hear anything. I'd just as soon not let anyone know I'm around. I try to cover up the holes other guys have dug. I like a flat surface. I don't want my back foot, for example, lower than my right foot; then it's as if you were hitting on a hill.

Besides my unorthodox theory of stances, I also have an unusual bunting style. I hold the bat with a swinging grip. My hands are at the handle and the bat is parallel to the ground. Most guys bunt with their hands choked up or several inches apart, and the bat is almost perpendicular to the ground. I also bunt with the bat in front of me, rather than to the side or in foul territory.

My style gives me excellent control. I have confidence that I can drop a ball down anytime at an imaginary spot on the turf, about 5 or 6 feet up the line, and beat it out for a hit.

The ball I bunt has a spin on it, and sometimes it comes backward. Tony Oliva says I have a string on my ball. Maybe it's the angle at which I'm holding the bat. I'm not sure. But it does spin. I remember once when Aurelio Rodriguez was at third for Detroit and I bunted. As he was coming in for the ball, the ball started backing up. He couldn't believe it. I bunted one time against Ken McMullen and the ball stopped dead. The second time it did the same thing. So he moved in closer. The third time the ball took a spin backward. He just threw his glove into the air in frustration.

Another thing I do differently is that when I bunt I start to run with my back foot. Most guys start off running with the foot that's closer to first base. I think you get a better push-off with the back foot.

Sandy Valdespino showed me these tricks when I was a rookie. I practice bunting at least forty-five minutes a day during spring training, and I practice during the season, too. It can get boring, but it's an important part of my game. It's part of my arsenal. I get between 20 and 25 hits a season on bunts.

I know I can do so many things with the bat. I know they can't defense me. And I don't let other clubs throw me off my game by shifting fielders around. I think that if I hit the ball hard, I'll get my share of hits.

As a hitter in the major leagues, I've won seven batting titles, six in seven years, from 1972 to 1978. It has been pointed out that when I won my titles, I won them by consistently larger margins than anyone in history except Rogers Hornsby. In 1977 when I hit .388, it was 50 points higher than the next-best average in baseball, Dave Parker's .338, which led the National League. That's the widest margin between hitters ever in the big leagues. That broke the record set in 1901 by Napoleon Lajoie, who hit 46 points higher than the next-best hitter in the major leagues that season.

The weirdest batting race I was ever in was in 1976, and it wasn't weird because I lost it. That was the season George Brett and Hal McRae and I each had a chance to win it going into the final weekend of the season. George and Hal are with Kansas City. It happened that we were playing the Royals in the final three games. I was a couple of percentage points behind them. McRae was hitting .333 and Brett was .328. My average was .325.

Gene Mauch told me he figured that if I went 7-for-12 and if our pitchers held Brett and McRae, I'd win it.

Before the first game, someone from the Royals' front office told me that this was going to be a race to the wire, and they wanted to bring in a special scorer to make sure everything went right. That really disappointed me. I said, "What do you need a special scorer for? Whoever wins it, wins it."

Special scorer or not, some odd things happened. One time Brett hit a ball to Roy Smalley, our shortstop, which, it seemed to me, Roy booted for an error. The scorer gave Brett a hit. Another time, Brett hit one to right field. Danny Ford ran in and the ball went over his head for extra bases.

Brett was getting his hits, so was McRae, and so was I. Since they were ahead of me to begin with, they stayed that way. In the seventh inning of the final game, Brett doubled and McRae singled. Hal was on first base. He was a fraction of a point ahead of Brett. He turned to me and said, "Well, I guess the pressure's on George now. If he doesn't get a hit next time up, I'm going to take myself out of the game." I looked at him and said, "Come on, you don't want to win it that way. If you're going to win it, win it swinging." He didn't say anything. In the ninth, Brett hit a fly ball to Steve Brye, our left fielder. Brye backed up and the ball fell in *front* of him. Steve's a good outfielder, and I've seen him make catches running in and sliding and leaping against the wall. But the ball dropped. I couldn't believe it. My first thought—and I still feel it's true—was that Steve lost the ball in the sun. Well, Gene came out ranting and raving. He didn't know what had happened.

Now, McRae gets another time up. Brett is now ahead in average. McRae needs a hit; he grounds out. After running out his ground ball, the people are giving him a standing ovation. All of a sudden he's giving Gene the finger. I'm thinking, What's going on? Then McRae starts walking toward Gene, and Gene comes out of the dugout. Now they're holding McRae back. He's saying that Mauch dislikes him and let Brett get a hit his last time up.

Gene is practically in tears now. He called Cookie Rojas over. Cookie is the Royals' second baseman. Cookie had played for Gene in Philadelphia.

"Cookie," Gene said, "do you think I would have done something like that?"

In front of everybody, Cookie said, "No, Gene, I don't."

"That's all I need to know," said Gene. "I'm satisfied."

After the game, Brett said he was sorry that it had ended that way and he suggested that McRae should share the batting title with him. That was too bad. It's a shame Brett had to feel guilty. Here's a kid who had swung the bat well all year. Why should he feel that something was given to him on the final day of the season?

Brett finished at .333, McRae .332. I followed with .331. It was an exciting way to end the season—though I would have preferred a slight alteration in the result.

Some people have wondered if exceptional batters possess exceptional physical characteristics. Some do. Williams' eyesight was supposed to be so remarkable he could read a license plate a block away. Cobb's wrists were so quick it was claimed he could pick a pitch out of the catcher's glove and hit it for a single. Ruth's strength was legendary.

My eyesight is good, 20/15, but a lot of people have eyesight that good or better. I'm strong for my size, and I lift weights to increase my strength—I curl a 13-pound metal bar a great deal during the season. But there certainly are people much stronger. I've got excellent hand–eye coordination in things other than hitting. I'm good in Ping-Pong and have picked up tennis quickly. I also was a decent volleyball and basketball player in high school.

But nobody has ever had more desire than I. I practice a tremendous amount. I take so much more batting practice than most guys, it's unbelievable. We've got guys on the Twins that hit .200 and .220 and you have to beg these guys to go out there and take batting practice.

If it's raining and there's no batting practice scheduled, I might grab a bag of balls and go to the batting cage anyway and have someone just toss up balls easy so that I can swing and loosen up. Then I chase the balls.

Baseball was in my family. My uncles played it well. So did my brother. My sisters and father played it. Eric had a fine reputation as a pitcher in Panama. When my mother was in grade school, she was a good softball pitcher, she told me. All I know is, her front teeth are false, compliments of a line drive. I guess I inherited my fielding from her.

My uncle Mr. French said that when I was a little boy I was a natural ballplayer. I always felt I was gifted. From the time I was a kid, I thought God gave me the gift to hit a baseball better than other guys. I took advantage of that gift by working. By putting in extra time and trying to refine that gift. I felt that if I had the ability, why should I just take it for granted? Why should I not go out there and work more and try to improve to become even better?

That's my way of expressing my thanks.

# Chapter IX

A WOMAN acquaintance once said to Marilynn's mother, "It's one thing for Marilynn and Rod to be married—but how can they have children?" If I had known the lady, I would have sent her a biology book. Marilynn and I had no unique tricks up our sleeve; we kept to the tried and true.

What the woman implied, of course, was that the child of a black–white marriage will have a lot of problems, more than one who is straight black or straight white. Marilynn and I discussed that. We felt that if children have love and the feeling of security in their home, then they will have as great a foundation as any human being needs.

Charryse was born in 1973; Stephanie came in 1975, and Michelle in 1977.

Each was as thrilling for me as the next. To go to the hospital and feel the tension, and the nurses coming in and telling you, "Mr. Carew, it's a daughter. She's beautiful."

Each one. The excitement of all the people coming to look. And then the kids growing up. Loving them.

My basic concern when the kids are young is to spend as much time as I can with them and teach them about loving people and liking people and not to worry about the color of their skin. They're going to have their problems. I'm going to make sure they know that no matter what happens, their parents are going to be there to help them through.

When Charryse was only 3 years old she was conscious of color. She looked at Marilynn one time and said, "Daddy's black and I'm black and Stephanie is black, but you're white, Mommy." They're a kind of tan, I'd say. Not really black. But Charryse was making an observation, not a judgment.

A niece of mine had a little friend who, when Charryse was born, asked if the baby was polka-dot. Kids as well as adults are concerned with color. This is something we have to confront.

There are people with narrow minds out there, but you can't live your life worrying about what those people think.

I want to give my kids a sense of well-being. Then they'll be able to handle almost anything. I want to create some happiness for them, because I didn't have a lot of happiness in my home when I was a kid. My mother loved me, but my father never expressed any warmth or love.

I want my kids to learn to love. I can't leave the house unless I kiss my kids and tell them I love them. I can't leave the house and tell them I'm going to be gone too long. I always try to tell them I'm going to be right back. If I say I'm going to be gone for a couple of days, they get a frown on their face as if I were walking out of their lives. It kills me. I want them to know I'm coming back soon.

When Charryse first started going to the airport with us as I was departing on a road trip, it was rough. It was a new experience for me to watch this little girl cry as much as she did when I got out of the car. I felt I was breaking her heart. Now, here's a little girl who all of a sudden came into Daddy's life and she's there with Daddy playing all the time and then I have to pick up and go away for a week or ten days.

When Charryse was born, I couldn't wait for her to walk because I dreamed of going into a big department store and playing hide-and-seek with her between the clothes racks. I wanted to put her on my shoulders and go for walks and take her on swings. Just enjoy her. I know that she's going to grow up and have her friends. A big day for me now is to take her for an ice cream. I'm the big man in her life. I want to enjoy it while it lasts.

I can also get upset with the kids. I'll pinch their ear—and then turn around and do something nice. Be strict, and then spoil them, because I just couldn't sit and watch them—see that frown on their face or tears in their eyes.

Not long ago the family was sitting at the dinner table and Charryse didn't want to eat. She was playing with her food. I told her to leave the table and go to her room because she shouldn't disturb our dinner. She got up and gave me a long face as if she were going to cry and walked out of the room.

A few minutes later I went to see her.

"Charryse," I said, "do you know why Daddy sent you to your room?"

She said, "Uh-huh."

"Do you know you're supposed to be eating at the dinner table and not playing around?"

So this 4-year-old girl looks up and says, "Yeah, I got that."

*Yeah, I got that.* It bowled me over. I hugged her and said, "I love you. When you get ready to eat like a lady, you can come out and join us." She soon came out and said she was ready to eat like a lady.

When I'm on the road, I call home every day. Sometimes twice a day. I always talk to the kids.

I'll never scream at the kids, but I might raise my voice. When they scatter my record albums all over the den floor, I want them to know that I am not overjoyed. But I don't want them to fear me or dislike me the way I did my father. And that's also why I try to treat all the kids equally. I mean, if I hug one, I hug them all.

The kids are growing up Jewish. Marilynn and I decided on that before we were married. It was never a problem. We knew Marilynn would be spending most of the time with the kids, so she would be most comfortable, of course, bringing them up Jewish.

When Charryse was old enough, she went to Jewish nursery school. One day she surprised us before dinner by saying a prayer in Hebrew. It was fantastic.

I grew up an Episcopalian. At least, that was the church I went to, when I had the clothes to go to church as a kid. I was never really very religious, though. My mother is. She always talks about God, always thanks God for everything. Now my family at home is Jewish. And I've felt that I want to learn more about it, and that when the kids come to me with questions about Judaism I can answer them. I think it's important that I can do that. So I have decided that one day—I'm not sure whether it will be soon or not— I will convert to Judaism. Marilynn says she doesn't care whether I do or not. She respects the fact that I grew up Episcopalian, and that if I want to remain that way, fine with her. But the closer the family becomes, the more I feel I do not want to have a split home.

I've spoken with rabbis, and I've read a great deal of Jewish literature. On Yom Kippur, the highest Jewish holiday, the tradition is to fast. I haven't gotten that far yet. But if we have a game that falls on Yom Kippur, as we did in 1977, I don't play, out of respect for my family. On Passover, I do follow the tradition of eating no bread or other flour products.

I like the Jewish religion because it seems to afford freedom of choice and thought. Some religions are so restrictive. In Judaism, you do what your conscience tells you to do within a broad set of rules.

I hear about a lot of people getting involved with Christianity now—"Born-Again Christians" and others who are giving themselves to God in order to be saved. It's nothing of that sort with me in regard to Judaism. I'm looking for something that's going to help keep our family as one.

The parallels between the black experience in history and the Jews in history are remarkable. Each was persecuted as a minority. They were beaten, hanged, kept in chains. Each showed courage and struggled to better themselves against tremendous odds.

I'd like my girls to know the history of each group. Black heritage will be as important as anything else to them, I hope. They'll learn that in due time.

Right now, it seems that the only pressures my daughter Charryse feels in the outside world—and for her now that's nursery school—concern her father as a baseball player. One day she came home and said, "Daddy, everybody in school knows that you're a baseball player."

I said, "How do they know that?"

"Because I told them. I told every one."

I asked, "Did you say I was a good one or a bad one?"

"I said, 'He's the best baseball player I ever did see.' "

Now, that's love.

THE ADULATION that a major-league baseball player receives can inflate his head. Your name is in headlines. Television cameras follow you. People seek your autograph. Women send you nude picture of themselves or sit in the stands blowing you kisses—women want to meet you. It's easy to quickly believe that you are the center of the universe.

The reverse of the coin is the great amount of travel; the

long days of loneliness on the road; the demands of the public—the boos—and the insecurities that they can produce. For a family man, the problems are compounded. Marilynn and I have had our share.

The first years of our marriage were hard for both of us to deal with in this regard. It was hard for Marilynn to handle the fact I traveled a lot, that there are a lot of women out there. The phone calls that I used to get in my bachelor apartment didn't stop just because I got married. Some women don't care whether you're married or not.

Women have stuck their phone numbers in my pocket, and called on the phone in my hotel room. They've knocked at my door—they've done this with Marilynn in the room. She was infuriated, and rightly so.

I know of few men, though, who have not been tempted by this attention. One famous baseball player I know had been married briefly when he made a road trip with the club. His bride missed him and decided to surprise him. She flew to where he was and went up to his hotel room. It was some surprise. They were divorced shortly after.

One time, a girl knocked on another player's hotel-room door. She said she wanted to meet him. He let her in and right away she's screaming rape. A ballplayer has to be very careful.

I won't tell you that I haven't gone out when I've been on the road. I would be lying. The fact that I have has been the source of more friction in our marriage than almost anything else.

The strange world of the baseball player on the road was something I had to learn to deal with if my marriage was going to survive—and I wanted it to. Marriage is a two-way street, of course. And so my problems became Marilynn's problems. This is how she has tried to handle them:

MARILYNN: *When I fell in love with Rod, I had him right up there on a pedestal. There was nothing that could touch* him. Like my father. I came from a world in which my father protected his poor little darling. If anything happened to her, come to Daddy. So to think that Rod would deceive me in any way was inconceivable.

He always bought me gifts, always bought me flowers. Roses. Red roses. And he'd send me a card from on the road and tell me he loved me. He'd call every day. He can be so tender, so warm.

But I've learned that if a woman, knowing the position these guys are in, thinks that they are true blue, she's either naive or stupid. I was young. If there's a saint out there, I want to meet him. I think that's the difference between my being 20 and being 32. I know now that there is no perfect man and I can't expect Rod to be perfect. What I have, I've learned to accept. I couldn't at first. It was torture to think that he was with other women. I told Rod that I share him with the public. He's not totally mine anyway; I have to share him with everyone out there. I don't want to share a bed too.

In the early years, I wasn't sure of my ground. I mean, there were a lot of pretty women chasing him. Pretty models. They're six feet tall. I'm five-one. I'm a little chubby, and I bite my nails. It affected me when Rod said things like "Oh, Marilynn, why don't you wear sweaters like she does?" or "Why don't you have your hair cut like that person?" Then when I did, he'd say he liked me better the other way. I was very insecure. So then, everything he did I really blew out of proportion.

Many times he wouldn't come home right after a game. He'd come home late. Where were you? Why didn't you call? The third degree. He wouldn't say anything. A dentist couldn't pull anything out of that mouth. It drove me bananas. It was like when he was a boy. His mother would ask him where he'd been and he wouldn't answer. She told me that. I used to call her. What is it? Why is he that way? I knew only sketchy things about his father. Rod wouldn't tell me about him, but I imagined horrible things. I said to

Olga, *"What happened to Rod when he was a child? What did that man do to Rod that he should be this way?"*

I'd raise my voice at Rod. He'd say, *"Talk softly. Screaming and cussing remind me of how my father acted. I can't stand it."* He'd walk out. He'd get in his car and drive away. Later, he'd tell me he sat in a movie theater, and I didn't believe him. It didn't make sense to me—until I got to know the man.

We had many fights, bitter ones. Rod packed his bags and left a hundred times. Two hundred times. But he'd always come back. Sometimes he'd get as far as Highway 12, a few blocks from the house, and call. He'd make an excuse, like he remembered he had to do something for the kids—some kind of excuse.

Rod would not talk about his problems at all. When something happened at the park, he'd come home and wouldn't discuss it. I nagged him: You must talk; we must communicate. At first, he'd come home and not say anything and, with my insecurities, I assumed I had displeased him. He was wrong not to talk more. And I was wrong not to be more understanding of his situation. After all, he's in the limelight; he has to put forth his effort every day or else thousands and millions of people aren't going to like him. How would we react to that? To be thrown in the center of a ring and told, *"Today we're going to like you and tomorrow we're not. You've got to perform continuously. And to perform up to our expectations. All the time."* All the time. Don't ever let down. You have the whole nation to account to. The pressure could be unbearable.

You would have to live with someone to understand the fantastic frustrations for someone in that kind of life. I knew that it wasn't a woman at the core of the problem every time: the team is losing, the players said you didn't do the job, the reporters are on your back, the traveling, and you get to the hotel and your bags aren't there. They lose your suitcase. The boos. Oh! Zero-for-four. An error.

*The manager didn't compliment you when you did well. The constant pressure. Then the kid's got a fractured skull at home, right? The wife's not happy: Where were you? . . . It was very hard for Rod as well to adjust—to come home and play patty-cake with the kids after he went 0-for-5.*

*I couldn't blame him, so I tried to learn. Still, I would invite a couple over for Saturday night and I was never sure whether Rod would be there. If he was in a mood, he'd go away. On Saturday afternoon if the sun came out the wrong side, he wouldn't be there that night. So I would have to explain to these people, to cover up for him. He wouldn't tell me what was wrong. I screamed at him, "You shmuck. Talk!"*

*And I was learning that even if Rod were the perfect person I once imagined he was, the life of a baseball wife could be terribly trying anyway.*

*You worry about being traded and picking up and making a whole new home some place else. The best and worst get traded. You watch him play and you know any minute you could see your husband get hurt. I did not see him get smashed up with that knee injury in 1970, but I have seen him taken out for injuries, such as twisted ankles. I think I was in more pain than he was.*

*Of course, if you complained to anybody, they'd say, "What do you have to complain about? You get to go to Florida for six weeks in the winter. Your husband makes a good salary. You got a parking place at the ball park. What's your beef, lady?" Sometimes it was that my husband works nights. Sometimes it was just a day off on the road. That fries me. They should save all their days off for when they're home. Oh, and the thing that galled me so much: whenever we'd have a fight, he'd go 3-for-5, 4-for-4. It used to make me so mad. But he's such a professional that no matter what mood he's in, he will go out there and do the best he possibly can.*

*People will never understand the loneliness of this life. I know that I just could never have done it when I was 20. I remember when Danny Walton's wife, Jill, had a baby. Danny was on the road with the Twins. I was in the labor room as the father. Imagine that! Jill had no family there. Her family was somewhere in California or Oklahoma, or whatever. Not in Minnesota. But we happened to like each other, and I had opened up my home to her because I figured, Aw, that girl's by herself. Husband's off in Texas playing ball. And so here I am in the labor room with her. She accepted her husband's being away at a time like that. I don't think I could have.*

*Another thing is, some people don't think I'm a person. That is, they think I'm just Rod Carew's wife. A reporter once asked me, "How does it feel to be in Rod's shadow?" Like I'm nobody because Rod's got a name and I'm just supposed to be following. I said to him, "I do what I do as well as he does." I don't think I'm belittled or anything else because I'm doing my thing. Being a mother. Being a housewife. There aren't a lot of women that do the job I do—keeping my house and raising my family. I can go 5-for-5 too. And if my pound cake doesn't come out, then I go 4-for-5. I don't know if I excel to the extent Rod does, but Rod is an artist, a truly sensitive artist. I compare him in temperament to someone like Van Gogh. I really do— the effort he puts into his work, the dedication, the love. But I do my job well, so I'm not dissatisfied being a housewife and mother, not being a career woman. I was raised to do this. I was conditioned, as a lot of women are. I can't break that conditioning, and I haven't wanted to because I enjoy what I'm doing. There are times when I want to throw in the towel—I'm sure Rod gets discouraged and he wants to do the same thing. Please, if I wash another floor, I'm going to go crazy. Or another diaper. But percentwise, I'm doing what I want to do.*

*For all this, I still did not want to be just the wife sitting home taking care of babies. I wanted to be a part of his*

*life, and when he didn't share it with me, it frustrated and
angered me. We quarreled.*

*He'd leave. I said, "Go, leave me alone." All the while
I'm crying and thinking, The bastard. He's breaking my
heart. He knows it. How can he leave? And I'm saying,
"Go." And through all this, even when he was, like, cold
. . . he* can *be cold, yet there's always something soft. You
know he's hurting even when he's trying to cover up. It's
things you can't even put into words because you can see a
man who's trying to be cool, but he knows that he's a
shnook; you've got to know the man to know that. Like men
put on airs or whatever. But I didn't understand until I
really got to know him that even when he was just plain
mean and cold and nasty, he was hurting inside.*

*He would tell me, "Listen, I'm always coming home to
you. I'm not coming home to anybody else. I love you and
I'm not ever going to leave you for another woman." I
couldn't say, "Oh, well, that's fine." I still wanted to know
where he had been, and why that woman called here. Or
whatever.*

*All this time—about five years—my friends and family
often took Rod's side. Or at least sympathized with him.
They defended me too, and I knew that I had their heart
and their shoulder, but they tried to give me some perspective.*

*My mother would say, "Aw, let him alone. Don't pick on
him; you're being too sensitive." She thought I might be
imagining more than there really was. She would protect
him, make it more difficult for me. I didn't want to protect
him. I just wanted to slap him—Wake up!*

*Rod had always been a challenge for me. I thought he
was complex, and I enjoyed trying to figure him out. One
night, when we were dating, we went to a club. I knew the
piano player. I said hello to him, and Rod got mad and
walked out. But, look, a person can take just so much of
this complexity—this nuttiness.*

*My mother would say the same things my dad did about*

*Rod. My dad died in 1975. He used to rave about Rod, that he was such a good person. Rod was so nice to him—little things; just the way he sat and listened to my father. I thought my father had so much wisdom. I wondered, What does Dad see in Rod? What am I not seeing in Rod that he sees? I'm crying at night, and my mother's saying, "Give him another chance. He loves you." What am I not seeing?*

*Well, he was wonderful with the kids. And some of our most beautiful moments now are with the kids. A special moment for me is when I'm in the kitchen cooking and I hear Rod in the family room playing with the kids or reading to them. I just love that. Rod would tell me, "My main concern is that I want to make you and the kids happy." He's a good provider. We really have a good relationship. Rod and I enjoy a lot of the same things together. Even TV programs. We both even like to watch* Kojak—*those kinds of things: simple things that other people might hassle about. We both like to eat meat. The everyday shtick we don't have to deal with. We're really not materialistic. Rod will buy an expensive watch, or he'll buy me a necklace with his baseball number, number 29, in diamonds. But he'll go to a coffee shop and order a side dish of tomatoes, and if they're a few cents more than he normally pays, he'll cancel the order. And me, I don't think there will ever come a time when I'm not going to look for Hi-C fruit drink at 39 cents a can. And Rod and I laugh a lot together. We enjoy each other's company. There's often a lot of warmth and love between us.*

*So that's the other side, that's why I stayed. But then, boom—a bad day. The sky would fall. Rod was mad about something. Was it me? I decided, This is crazy. Who needs this crap? People bothering you, your life's not your own, and I have to worry about his moods . . . what's this all about?*

*I was ready to leave many times. I had gotten so tired of the whole thing. I had given him every opportunity to leave. There was never a time when I said, "I will never let your kids see you. . . ." You know the threats women give when you're going to split up, right? I will not take him for every dime he's worth. I said, "Where are we going? Let's not hurt each other. If you want something and you're not getting it here, then go get it somewhere else." I wasn't sure Rod took me seriously. And one day in the spring of 1976 he didn't come right home after a game. I didn't hear from him. He didn't come home until late. I didn't let him in the house. I had packed his suitcase and dumped it on the doorstep. I called my sister-in-law, Arlene, and told her I was going to leave him. She said, "Now, just hold on a minute." This was 11:30 on a weeknight. She said, "Just hold on a minute," and she meant it literally because her other phone was ringing. She went to answer it and it was Rod, she told me later. He said, "Would you please come to the Lincoln Delicatessen and meet me?" Arlene came back and said to me she had to hang up. She went to meet Rod. He said, "I don't know why I do what I do, but I love her."*

*I guess Rod was feeling a lot of pressure at home and in his professional life. This was a rough period for him. There was the Danny Thompson episode. The team was losing. But I had my own problems. We all do. And I had had them up to my eyeballs.*

*Well, he came back the next day and I let him in. He wanted to talk. I remember he said, "I don't want to leave. I think I'd be giving up a lot, and for what? To go out there and get what? End up with what?"*

*I said, "A baby." He said, "Great line, Marilynn. There just aren't enough comedians in the world, right?"*

*Arlene suggested we see a marriage counselor. I went first. Bob was his name. He suggested that I find interests outside of my home and Rod. He said that I shouldn't be so possessive, that if Rod has a bad day and is in a bad mood, no reason I should be too. He told me to give Rod breathing room. I tried. I started letting up.*

*Rod went to see the counselor too. He said he liked him,*

*found him easy to talk to. But when Bob began delving into Rod's father, Rod stopped seeing him.*

*Things got better between Rod and me, but they were still rocky. I wasn't sure we were going to stay married, and I decided that I didn't want to have any more children. Even if I married again, I didn't want to have anyone else's children but Rod's. And Rod had been insistent since Stephanie, our second, that he didn't want any more children. So I made an appointment on a Monday to see a doctor on Wednesday to have an operation that would eliminate the chance for another pregnancy. I told Rod.*

*On Tuesday afternoon he comes into the kitchen and says, "Sit down at the table." I said, "What?" He said, "I don't want you to have that operation." I said, "Why not?" "Because," he said, "I'd like to have another child." He said he had talked it over with Don Knutson, his best friend. He said he had thought about it for two days. "Marilynn, I think I've done a lot of growing up in the last two days," he said. And it was unbelievable the change that took place. He became more open and less temperamental in the last year than he had in the previous six. He even began to discuss his father! Rod seven years ago and Rod today is not the same Rod. Just twelve hundred times over. He's a different person. It seemed like close to overnight. All of a sudden you wake up and he's willing to talk.*

*One day he came home and said, "Guess what happened at the ball park today." I almost fainted. There was a minor incident with Rod and Larry Hisle, something about Rod not wanting to pose for a picture with Larry. I knew about it the night before it hit the papers. That was just about a first between us.*

*Another day Rod came home and said, "I'll take the girls away this afternoon; why don't you take the afternoon off?"*

*And if he's not coming home right away, he'll call and*

*say, "I'll be home a little late, honey." I can accept that.*
*Before, there might not have been a phone call at all.*

*We went to the 1977 All-Star game in New York with my*
*brother Don and Arlene. Now, if anyone was going to lose*
*his temper, it should have been Rod. Oh, goodness! It was*
*outrageous! People were climbing all over him. Hanging*
*from the rafters waiting for him. The .400 hitter. We*
*couldn't get out to get a cup of coffee. We couldn't sit*
*down. You couldn't get into a restaurant. We finally found*
*a Japanese restaurant with seaweed that cost $50. It was*
*the worst food we ever ate, but the funniest meal we ever*
*had. Nobody bothered Rod, because they were all Japa-*
*nese and I honestly don't think they could speak a word of*
*English, and it was so quiet and pleasant. But at that time,*
*the pressure was at a high point. We went into the hotel for*
*the All-Star luncheon. Don had to be Rod's bodyguard.*
*The pushing, the shoving! Rod took it all gracefully. Be-*
*fore, Rod wouldn't have gone to the luncheon. He would*
*have locked the door and stayed in his room.*

*But we've both changed. He doesn't run away anymore,*
*and I've stopped nagging him about where he's been or*
*where he's going. I mean, there's no "first-degree" ques-*
*tioning, which was his phrase. None of that. And I've got*
*to the point in our relationship, I don't try to control him*
*the way I once wanted to. Whether I bitch or complain or*
*cry, he's going to do what he wants to do. It took me six*
*years to get myself together: See here now, just because*
*you're not so sure of yourself, don't blame him. But he*
*knows I will not tolerate unfaithfulness. In the last two*
*years, we've gotten it together where I feel secure that I*
*know Rodney needs me. Rod loves me. I couldn't say that*
*before. I wasn't sure. Now, when I get a card from him*
*when he's away, one of those funny cards, he writes how*
*much he needs his family and misses us. I believe him. He*
*signed one once, "Your hubby." I loved it. You know,*
*everyone has something that they have to deal with. I feel*

*Rod and I have enough together that we can deal with these things, and we have. We've proved it. When we got married, everyone was looking for Rod Carew and Marilynn Levy not to make it because the black and white aren't going to make it. They're sure of it, right? I said, You know what? If they're right, I'll go and tell them, "You were right." If that's what they want to hear.*

*If something happened between Rod and me, I could never convince the world that race had nothing to do with it. Oh, maybe deep down somewhere you might get into the difference in childhood environment. But that's too heavy, too remote for me, and for Rod. We've never had an argument or a confrontation or a difference over race or religion. We empathize with each other, and with the history of persecution of both the Jews and the blacks. Even in our most heated arguments, we have never called each other a racial name. We've called each other* names, *but never one about being Jewish or black.*

*We aren't political people, so no arguments about politics. We both have super families and we get along beautifully with them. No, if our marriage ever dissolved, it would have more to do with the problems all other marriages suffer through—everything from jealousy to who's going to change the kids' diapers.*

*But right now, we're just two human beings—a man and a woman—living in a Minneapolis suburb—trying as best we can to mesh our lives together.*


As Marilynn says, a change did come over me in the last couple of years. I think the idea that Marilynn seriously considered breaking up the marriage jolted me. I had taken my situation for granted, and Marilynn was getting the short end of the stick.

I had another realization. In some ways I was duplicating my father. He had treated my mother terribly, and I had hated it. Now I was causing Marilynn anguish. I did not like that in me at all. It was a shock to fully understand that.

And after seven years of marriage, I came to appreciate something else. I learned that in the end a man really has only his family to rely on. The public is fickle, and those people can turn against you as easily as they are for you today. Win or lose, hit or strikeout, Marilynn and the kids are behind me. That is the most important thing in my life.

# Chapter X

THE WHOLE family piled into the Mercedes and drove down to spring training in February, 1977. Marilynn and I up front; in the back seat, the two kids and my mother-in-law, who lives with us. In the past, I've been hassled by white cops when they've seen me driving a nice car with an attractive white woman. They think you've got to be a pimp. Hell, just a black guy in an expensive car is hassled. And now I was going to be driving through the South. I placed a tape recorder under the seat, just in case. If there was to be trouble, I was going to have proof and do something about it. Absolutely nothing happened.

We stopped at a few hotels overnight. Marilynn always checks in, to avoid having the clerk tell me the hotel is filled. For meals, we order room service.

I thought the kids would get restless and begin to squabble. But they sat quietly in the back and colored in their drawing books.

I felt at peace with myself and with Marilynn, after all that we've been through.

I thought about the season coming up, and looked forward to it. I thought the team was strong and might have a shot at the pennant. The season before, we had finished just five games behind Kansas City, the division leader. I was healthy, in my prime and confident. I don't believe in setting goals for yourself, because I think all you're going to do is put more pressure on yourself. I was just gearing myself up to work hard and go into the season fit and with a running start.

When we pulled up in front of our apartment complex in Orlando, Marilynn stepped out of the car and found a $5 bill. We walked across to the apartment—which was, coincidentally, number 29, my uniform number.

"This has got to be a good year for us," Marilynn said.

It started getting even better that night. Nine months later to the day, our third daughter, Michelle, was born.

In camp the next morning, I went in to say hello to Gene Mauch, who was now in his second year as manager. Mauch has my respect. Mauch is not one step ahead of most other managers during a game, he's two and three steps ahead of them.

I was playing first base now, and had been since the last few weeks of the 1975 season. I had been moved there, I was told, because it could prolong my career a few years. The chance of injury is decreased at first base—you don't have the guys barreling into you to try to break up the double play as you do at second base. And I guess that was of some concern, although I had stopped being fearful of it. Also, I was still making too many errors, mostly on throws.

When Mauch joined the Twins, he worked with me a great deal at first base. He showed me how to smother the ball with my glove when the throw is in the dirt, and explained how to hold a runner on.

Gene said, "You can be a good fielding first baseman if

you want to be." It gave me the best feeling I've ever had about my fielding. He told me he thought I could win the Golden Glove for fielding excellence. After that, the guys started calling me "Golden Glove." It was a welcome change from years past.

Somehow, I had felt open to him from the start. In our first meeting in the spring of 1976, I said to him, "Gene, I've been a problem to a bunch of managers. I just want to tell you that I've grown up in the last few years. All I want to do is go out there and play for you and give one hundred percent."

He said, "I'm glad that you're honest with me. I knew about it and wanted to hear it from your lips."

I couldn't wait for the season to start. And when it did, I almost wished it hadn't. After the first two games I had four hits in nine times at bat, but suddenly I went into a tailspin. I went 2-for-19. It was one of the worst starts of my career. I was getting good wood on the ball, but it was a line drive right into the shortstop's glove, or the center fielder made a shoestring catch. Nothing dropped. What can you do? I tried to keep my cool.

Just as suddenly, the hits started falling. I go 10-for-15. I'm getting a hit or two every game. We're going up and back with Chicago and Oakland and Kansas City for first place in the West. We go to play the Texas Rangers. Toby Harrah is the third baseman, and he's baiting me that I can't bunt off him. I bunt down third and beat it out.

The next day, he's baiting me again. He said, "I'm moving in closer. I dare you to bunt on me now." I lay one down and leg it out. I'm on first and laughing, and I look over at him. He looks back with this helpless expression, and then tips his cap.

We're home and playing Seattle. I get to third base. Frank MacCormack is pitching. He's a young six-foot-four right-hander with one of these slow, easy motions. And he's wild, throwing the ball all over the place. Just my style for stealing home. I had said that I would never do it again. I'm getting older now and the injury risk is greater, and pitchers usually use a stretch when I'm on third. But MacCormack wound up and his style was so tempting that I couldn't resist. I lit out. MacCormack made a perfect pitch, his only one in about five innings, and I was nailed. The law of averages caught up with me; it was the third time in eighteen tries to steal home that I had been caught.

The next day or so, Davey Lopes of the Dodgers comes out with a statement that only amateurs try to steal home. He assumed I was trying to embarrass Seattle. I thought that only an amateur would make a remark like that. You steal home to disrupt a pitcher's concentration and to try to win a ball game. You don't do it to try to embarrass another team. Lopes was wrong.

Anyway, on that last attempt, I slid into the catcher's shin guards pretty hard, and I banged up my legs and my ankle looked pretty bad. I said to myself, I don't know if I'll ever try it again.

By the end of April I'm hitting .349. Detroit comes to town. It's a Saturday-afternoon game, and we jump on Dave Roberts, a six-foot-three southpaw. We're ahead 4–1 in the second inning. We have men on first and second when I come up.

In the first inning Hisle had homered, and I followed with a bunt single. I don't know if there's an unwritten law in baseball that after a guy hits a home run you're not supposed to bunt. If there is, it's the pitchers who tried to circulate it. A hitter's going to do whatever he can to get on base at any time. Maybe Roberts felt I tried to pour salt in his wound. Whatever, in my next time up, the first pitch Roberts throws hits me square in the back. I know Roberts isn't that kind of scatter-armed pitcher. He's a control pitcher. If he had thrown a ball to brush me back, it wouldn't have bothered me. But when he throws it *behind* me—I'm going to let him know he can't try to intimidate

me. What can a batter do? You throw your bat at him,
you're suspended. The next-best thing is to go out there
and let him know that I wasn't going to accept that crap. I
don't want anybody trying to hurt me. He could have broken my ribs, punctured my lungs—who knows? I went
right out to the mound after him. I threw several punches.
I landed a couple on his chest. He wasn't swinging back. I
didn't know why, and didn't care. Baseball fights are usually considered funny things. We're not boxers, and you
see the pictures of baseball guys swinging wild windmill
shots and they're ripping each other's uniforms. Maybe
even pulling hair. I didn't know how I looked. I was boiling.
Everyone came off the bench and pulled us apart.

I was thrown out of the game. It was only the third time
I've ever been ejected. Once was after I argued on a close
play when I was in the field; another time I was on the
bench and I flipped a towel into the air when I thought I
saw a poor call by Marty Springstead. He walked over and
said, "Carew, you're gone." But I get along with umpires.
I'm not salty with them. I enjoy talking with them. I've had
umpires admit to me that they've blown a pitch or a call. I
respect that. If someone like Nestor Chylak or Ron Luci-
ano or Bill Haller calls a bad pitch a strike, and I turn
around, they'll say, "Well, I blew the call."

Even at first base I've had an umpire say, "I called the
play too soon" or "I was anticipating; I was looking at the
ball and not looking at the whole area." They've told me
they had a bad angle, or weren't in position. I appreciate
that. I've blown a few plays myself.

I got off on the wrong foot with Chylak, though. When I
was a rookie he called a pitch I disagreed with. I started
mouthing off. He said, "Get in there and hit, Rook." I kept
blabbing. Nestor gets really excited. He says, "I'll remember you."

Sometime later, Nestor was umpiring at first base. I hit a
wicked drive down the line and he couldn't get out of the

way. I hit him on the calf, and it hurt him pretty bad. I was concerned. I ran over to him. He appreciated it. We became friends after that.

Some umpires hold grudges. They put it in the back of their minds if they think you tried to humiliate them. And if the pitch is anywhere near the plate, they'll call a strike on you. So you'd better be swinging.

By May 27 I had raised my average to .385, but then went into another nose dive, going 1-for-17. I was still confident. I was meeting the ball well. And now it's the ninth inning of a home game against the Yankees and we're losing 3–2. There are two outs. Sparky Lyle is pitching. Roy Smalley is up, and the count goes to 3 and 2. I'm sitting in the on-deck circle and I'm thinking, Let him walk you, Roy. Don't swing at a bad pitch. I wanted to hit. I could taste it. Roy walked. On a 2-2 count, I lined a hit to left center to win the game.

Now, Sparky is a lefty, and lefties are supposed to give left-handed batters trouble. Some lefties do give me a headache. And I do have a little more trouble with lefties than I do with righties. But so far this season, it hadn't mattered to me who pitched. I remember one game against Toronto. The Blue Jays started with one left-hander and I got a single the first time I faced him. Then Toronto brought in another left-hander and the first pitch he threw I hit for a triple down the first-base line. The next time up, a single to right. Another lefty was in and I tripled to left center. Everything just seemed big. The ball seemed like a grapefruit. I was hitting it hard and just out of reach of the infielders.

Sometimes I would see a shortstop move over a step or two toward third, and then I'd hit the ball a few feet from second base—into the hole he had just created. I was placing it. I felt I could do just about anything up there.

I'm into one hitting streak after another, and by the middle of June I'm up to .388. The Texas Rangers come to town and they announce a managerial switch. They fire

Frank Lucchesi and hire Eddie Stanky. Stanky's a small, intense guy who was famous as a player for kicking the ball out of Phil Rizzuto's glove in a World Series. He was a guy who really wanted to win at any cost. I remember when he was managing the White Sox and when they'd lose to us Stanky would walk from the ball park all the way downtown to his hotel, stewing all the way. That's a ten-mile walk. On the day he takes over, I go 4-for-5 and raise my average to .390. That evening I learn that Stanky quit. But I can't take any credit for it. For the last several years he had been a baseball coach at an Alabama college. He said he was returning to his home in Mobile because he missed his family so much and didn't want to live the life of traveling anymore. I could appreciate that. Those plane rides, and being away from home so much gets very dreary. The Rangers chose Connie Ryan, a coach, to take over as manager.

The next game, I'm at the plate for my second time at bat, after having doubled my first time up. I know they've tried everything on me. Infield playing in, infield deep, outfielders shifted to the right, then to the left. Pitchers throwing me inside, outside, breaking balls, change-ups. Nothing works for them. So now Jim Sundberg, the catcher, says, "Ryan told me to tell you what's coming. He thinks maybe that'll work. He said, 'One fastball coming up.' " I didn't believe him.

I took the pitch. He was right. Fastball.

"What now?" I asked Sundberg.

"Fastball again."

Fastball it was. Right down the pipe. I lined it for a single to center.

Ryan hollers from the dugout, "See, we held him to a single."

I'm 15-for-18 and hitting .395. Now all the talk about .400 is starting up. Speculation in the papers every day. No one since Ted Williams in 1941 has hit over .400. Jimmy Pier-

sall, who was a teammate of Williams', says I can't compare with Ted. Well, I don't think there's any comparison
either. Ted was a swinger and I'm a finesse hitter. But just
to be placed in a category with him was a treat.

It's nearing the end of June and we're still in first place.
Everybody's happy. You want to go to the ball park. The
place is alive. When you're losing, you don't really look
forward to going out as much because it's frustrating. You
play your heart out and then come off the field with an
"L." When you're winning, you want to go out there and
stay out there as long as you can. You *never* want the game
to end.

I don't check the papers daily to see what my average is.
I don't have to. Everybody is telling me. And when you go
into some parks, they flash your average on the scoreboard.

On Sunday afternoon, June 26, we're playing the White
Sox and I'm going into the game batting .396. A good day
puts me over .400. It was one of the most incredible days
of my life. First of all, it was Twins' T-shirt day. And all
the T-shirts they gave out had number 29 on them. When I
heard about it, I was unhappy. I was disturbed that other
players' numbers weren't on some shirts. We had guys who
were having terrific seasons. Bostock was up among the
league leaders in hitting, and Hisle was one of the top RBI
men in the league. Goltz was a winning pitcher, one of the
league's best. Management disagreed with me. They said it
should be my day.

It was a record crowd of 46,963, the largest regular-sea-
son crowd in the history of the Twins.

I went 4-for-5, with a homer, a double, a stolen base,
three runs scored and six runs batted in, and we won.
Every time I got a hit the scoreboard flashed how much I
was hitting, and the people would go crazy. I got four standing ovations. It was great, but a little embarrassing. I kept
taking my hat off and tipping it. I didn't want the other
players to think that I was milking this thing, so at the third

ovation, I just barely took my hat off; at the fourth standing
ovation, I didn't take my cap off at all. The fans wouldn't
sit down; they just stood and clapped and clapped. I was
out on second base and I kept looking around at the infielders and the umpires, and then I finally took my hat off, and
that's the way it was.

I had goose bumps, and I kept thinking that the fans had
finally accepted me, that they'd finally come over on my
side. I had had a few standing ovations before in my career.
Two that I remember. One came when I made a good running catch in foul territory and slid on my fanny; another
came in 1975 when I was awarded the silver bat at home
plate for my fourth consecutive batting title.

But I've been booed. Have I! I remembered 1974, that
bad fielding year at second. I made 33 errors, to lead the
league. Every time I made an error, I wanted to dig a hole
and crawl into it. I felt, Find me a place to hide! Oh, they
were booing and they were booing terribly. Even though I
was hitting—all that time. They still hollered from the
stands, "Get that bum outta there!" I remember when
there was a pop-up I was chasing, and the wind blew it and
I fell to my knees and it tipped my glove and I got an error.
They just booed their lungs out and carried on. After one
of those games, I went in and said to another player, "Man,
it sure would be nice to have a change." A reporter heard
it, and the next day the headlines read: "Rod Carew says
he wants to be traded." After that, the boos kept coming in
long blasts. I'd wake up in bed hearing the boos.

Now they're cheering and cheering, and I love it. Maybe
it was all the national publicity that changed the crowd. Or
maybe the fans were caught up in the excitement of the
achievement. Whatever, I felt no bitterness at all. I was
happy to have the crowd on my side.

I'm hitting .403, and all hell is breaking loose with the
media. *Sports Illustrated* and *Time* magazine are planning
cover stories on me, *TV Guide* is doing a story. So are
*Newsweek* and *People* and *Sport* magazine and *Black*

*Sports.* ABC-TV news is doing a network segment on me. I'm even getting comments on the editorial pages.

The *Washington Star* said: "Rod Carew has gone quietly about his business—of being perhaps the premier hitter in the game and a gentleman journeyman. Thanks Rod, we needed that." So did I. This editorial and another in *The Washington Post* were read into the *Congressional Record.*

I received tons of mail. One of the most moving letters was from Hubert Humphrey. The Minnesota Senator was a sports fan, and we had met several times at the ball park. When Marilynn and I were married he had sent a note congratulating us. Now he was writing from a hospital bed where he was fighting a losing battle with cancer. He said he was checking the box scores every day to see how many hits I had made. My performance was inspiring for him, he said, and it took his mind off his problems.

People are calling my house so frequently that I have to change my number every two weeks. Where do they get the number? I stopped answering the phone. Marilynn would answer it. There was always somebody calling or ringing the doorbell. At times I couldn't even leave the clubhouse; the crush of people waiting for me was gigantic. On the day we had that record crowd, I was lucky to meet up with a professional wrestler I knew. He came up to the clubhouse door and asked me to sign something for his little boy. Then he asked, "How are you going to get through the crowd?" I said, "I don't know. I'm going back into the clubhouse." He said, "Follow me; I'll get you to your car." He was about six-two and weighed 300 pounds. People were screaming, but he certainly cleared the way.

In the midst of all this notoriety, I was running in the outfield at Metropolitan Stadium one day while a camera crew filmed me. I called to Roy Smalley, "Run with me. C'mon over and run with me."

Roy refused. He said they didn't want him in the picture. I said, "I do."

All this publicity was been fine for me. I'd never had it

like this before, but I didn't want to bug my teammates with
it. That's why I wanted Roy to run with me. I wanted the
guys to be as much a part of it as possible. I didn't want
them to think I'm separate or different from them.

Sometimes they'd kid me, "We've got a movie star on
our hands," and on the team bus someone would say,
"Leave a seat for Mr. Carew." But I thought they took the
whole thing well.

I also think the guys liked the added exposure. A lot of
us are conscious of the television camera. Some will go into
the clubhouse after batting practice and shave and comb
their hair. I think one of the funniest guys is Hisle. Hisle
will go in and spend fifteen to twenty minutes getting his
Afro ready and making sure it's all in place. He doesn't put
his hat on until the last minute. He'll always run out to
center field with his hat in his hand. He says he wants all
the beautiful people in Ohio, his home state, to see his face.
Sometimes he would say, "Man, I got to stick close to you,
Carew, because I know the camera's going to be on you."
But a lot of guys do that, primp themselves, especially
when they know the game will be on national television.

I have my own quirks. I usually shave and comb my hair
before a game too. But I always keep my hat on in the field.
I never take my hat off. I've got a complex about it. You
know, when the hat sits on your head and then you take it
off, your hair balloons out. With black guys it really shows
up because of the texture of our hair. It makes it seem as if
you've got a whole mountain on the top.

When I'm in the on-deck circle or if I'm out on base and
somebody makes a last out, I would never take off my
helmet and throw it to the dugout and then put my hat on.
I'd always take my hat out of my pocket first, shake it out
and then with one motion take off the helmet and slip on
my hat.

Another thing, I like my uniform clean. If I go out and I
slide or dive for a ball and the suit gets messy, I go in and I

change. I like my uniform to fit me well. I don't like it
baggy. I don't like it too tight, so that I don't have any
flexibility in it. I make sure that my shoes are clean. I always check myself before I go out.

I was joking with teammates now more than I ever had.
Maybe it was to show them I was *still* one of the boys. At
one time I was so quiet and reserved I had nothing to do
with the pranks around the clubhouse. That changed in my
later years. And now I was into a lot of things. One is
spitting tobacco juice on a guy's shoes. Everyone does it.
Standard operating procedure in the big leagues. But one
afternoon I let fly a glob on Paul Thormodsgard's new white
cleats, and he got ticked. We had some words, and I apologized.

I had one other unpleasant incident with a teammate that
season. *The Sporting News* wanted to take a cover photograph of Larry Hisle and me. He was the league leader in
RBI's, and I was tops in average. I agreed to it, but then
decided that Larry and I shouldn't share a cover. He's
having such a great year, he ought to have a cover to himself. And if they want to do another, I ought to get one for
myself. It got blown up in the papers that I didn't want to
pose with Larry. I immediately explained to him that it
wasn't true, and he told me he knew that, because Bostock
had overheard my conversation with the reporter and told
Larry. It's true I originally agreed to the combined cover
picture. But I can change my mind. *The Sporting News*,
considered the Bible of Baseball, had ignored me for a
cover for a long time. When I turned down the cover, the
*Sporting News* reporter in Minneapolis told me that they'd
never give me another chance to be on the cover. Well, at
the end of the season *The Sporting News* named me Player
of the Year. And I was on the cover—but I still had to
share it. I shared it with Marilynn and my daughters, Charryse and Stephanie.

When things got so hectic during the season that I

thought I was upside down, I'd take my family for a picnic in the afternoon. Minneapolis is great for lakes, and we'd sit beside one of them. I'd play with the kids on swings, and Marilynn and I would take walks. Those were restful moments for me. It gave me a chance to think quietly.

I was happy to be recognized by the country now; I had thought one day it would happen. Henry Aaron was my inspiration for this. For twenty years he was a great player and hitting a ton of home runs and yet playing in the shadow of a lot of players. Then all of a sudden he's tracking down Babe Ruth's home-run record and the world discovers overnight that he's one of the greatest home-run hitters of all time. One day, I thought, people will finally open their eyes to my accomplishments too. As they say, good things come to those who wait.

After Chicago, Milwaukee came to town. In the first game, a rookie pitcher named Sam Hinds is on the mound. I got around to third base. On the first pitch, I was surprised to see him take a windup. I broke up the line and he didn't look. I thought, if he does that again, I've got to go. He did, and I did. I stole home in a breeze. In the series, I go 6-for-9 and my average is .411. We fly into Chicago. And I see Ralph Garr, one of my good friends in baseball. We always talk hitting. So this time we go into the bull pen. Jorge Orta, the White Sox infielder, wants to come along. I have the feeling some of my teammates are looking at us as if to say, "You're helping these guys and then they're going to go out and beat our brains out." I didn't care what they thought. If I can help a guy, why not? We're all in this business to do well, and if someone asks for my advice, I'll talk to him.

Earlier in the season, Roy Smalley told me he had a friend who was an infielder with the A's, and the guy was working hard and was pressing because he wanted to do well. Roy said the guy wondered if I might watch him and make some suggestions. I said sure, so we went out to the

park early the next day. I was able to pick a few things out
that he was doing wrong but hadn't realized. As the season
wore on, Roy told me the guy was doing better and that he
appreciated what I had done. Roy and I have also talked a
lot about hitting. One time Gene asked me, "Do you think
Roy will make a hitter?" I said I did.

I like Roy Smalley. He puts in a hell of an effort. He's a
dependable fielder at short, and he has good bat control.
He's thin, but he has worked with weights diligently to get
stronger, and he's improving all the time. He's Gene
Mauch's nephew; Roy's mother is Gene's sister. His father
is the Roy Smalley who played shortstop for the Cubs,
Braves and Phillies in the 1950s. Since Roy is a relative of
the manager's, he gets a lot of guff from the fans in Minnesota. I know how they can bear down on you. It's distracting and senseless. Roy takes it like a pro.

The White Sox have a young pitcher now named Francisco Barrios. He's fond of knocking me down. But whenever he comes in on me or wings one up by my head, I just
step back in and *bang*, I get a hit. I'm over at first one time
and he calls out in Spanish, "I'm going to get you." I say,
"Go ahead." Next time up, down I go. But I get up and rap
another hit. I'm at first base and I call out, "Now respect
me, Barrios; I'm your father." Jim Spencer's the first baseman, and he's laughing. The next day Barrios comes over
to me behind the batting cage and he's got a big grin. He
says, "Yeah, okay, man, I respect you now."

In Chicago, I aggravated an old back injury. I couldn't
even bend over the following day. I had to wear a corset. I
couldn't swing as hard, but I was still hitting the ball well.
Yet my average dropped a little.

I was scheduled to meet Ted Williams in Milwaukee for
an article *Sports Illustrated* was preparing. He was supposed to analyze me for the magazine. I looked forward to
it. I hadn't seen Ted in a few years, since he quit managing
the Texas Rangers.

The first time I ever saw Ted was at an exhibition game between the Twins and the Washington Senators, the team he was managing then. It was in the spring of my second big-league season. I walked over to him and said, "Pardon me, Mr. Williams, but would you autograph this ball for me?" I gave him a ball and pen.

As I walked away, Williams asked Wayne Terwilliger, one of his coaches, "Who was that guy?"

"That guy," said Terwilliger, "is the All-Star second baseman."

Williams was still the same guy, talking loud and cussing. He's so well meaning that it's actually enjoyable. Ted's a very intelligent person, and he can really get into figuring out angles and degrees of the bat, all those things. Things I never think about. Which isn't to say I'm wrong. Everyone's different.

When I saw him on the field now, I noticed that he'd gotten heavier. You really couldn't call him the Splendid Splinter anymore. But he's got such vitality. He's great to be around. He looked at me and said, in that John Wayne voice, "I want you to go out there and hit .400 so these guys will get off my rear end. I want them to leave me alone so I can stay up in the lakes fishing and not be bothered."

Ted and I talked about what I did when the bat gets heavy as the season progresses. I said I choked up. He said he did too. He also said he used a shorter bat; it gave him more control. He gave me some interesting advice. He said, "If you want to use a shorter bat, switch to one about a half inch shorter, but turn the trademark away from you so that the bat will *seem* longer because you're looking at all wood." I tried it and it worked.


THE PHONE didn't stop ringing. On the road I'd be awakened at 7 in the morning, or 2 at night. I'd go downstairs to the lobby for a newspaper and when I returned there were twenty messages waiting. I began using fake names to register at the hotel.

I got a call and was invited to the White House, to present one of my bats to the President and Vice-President Mondale, whom I had met when he was a Senator from Minnesota.

All of a sudden the Panama Canal thing came up and people wanted me to get involved. Should the United States get out of the Canal Zone? Should it maintain troops there? Should Panama have full control? I'm no politician. I've always felt that I shouldn't get involved in politics. I have my own view, but I'm not going to take sides. I already had enough going on in my life during the season, and I didn't need any added pressure. I know people back home in Panama look upon me as an important figure, but I still want to stay out of politics.

The pressure was beginning to wear on me. It was July, and hot. I much prefer to play in cold weather, strange as it may seem. I'm from the tropics, and most guys from there generally like to play in warm weather because they feel it keeps them looser. Even Williams told me he was that way. But I like to hit in 50-degree weather. I guess it makes me move around more to keep warm. Well, the heat of one afternoon made me woozy, and I had to be taken out of a game.

Perhaps all this confusion around me had something to do with it. I don't know. But I remember that I was losing concentration in the field. Like one time there were two outs and a runner on first. A ground ball was hit to me. All I had to do was step on first for the third out. Instead, I threw to second, thinking I'd get a double play. Another time, I was holding the runner on with two outs and a 3-2 count on the left-handed batter. Normally, I would have been playing back in the infield. The batter singled right past me. If I had been in the correct position, it would have been an out.

On July 11, I dropped under .400 for the first time in two weeks. It was also the day that the *Time* magazine cover story appeared. I was thrilled by it (and it turned out that I'd get something like three thousand of those covers in the mail to autograph).

The following day I learned that I received over 4 million votes from fans for the All-Star team. It was the highest vote total any player had ever received, and it also meant I would be in the American League's starting lineup for the eleventh straight year. When we got the news, Marilynn said she was amazed. She told me, "I didn't think there were four million people in the country who knew who you were."

The reason for the high total, I felt, was that I had created excitement in the way Mark Fidrych had the season before. Everyone was waiting to see how he'd do in his next appearance. For me, it was like that little commercial with the ketchup—you anticipate when it will come out of the bottle. So now it was, Will Rod Carew Hit .400?

The All-Star game was at Yankee Stadium. That was perfect for me. A homecoming. I would take Marilynn, Don and Arlene with me. I'd see my mother, brother and sisters and their families.

I did not expect to see my father. The last time I had laid eyes on him was a few years before at the ball park in New York. I had received a call in the locker room that "someone who says he's your father" was at the ticket window. He wanted to get tickets for the game. I said, "Let him pay."

When I was on the field, I noticed my father in the aisle near the dugout. I didn't want to speak to the man. So when I went from the field I ran right into the dugout. I didn't linger along the railing at all.

A year or so before this, Marilynn and I had come to New York to visit my family. We brought our daughter Charryse with us. Marilynn thought it would be proper to let Eric see his granddaughter. I didn't think so, but I said all right. My brother got in touch with Eric. A meeting was arranged. My mother made a big dinner. He never showed up. I told Marilynn, "Don't do me any more favors with that man."

My thoughts didn't remain very long on him, except to think that I was doing well and that I felt I had triumphed over him.

Now I thought back to my first All-Star game when none of the press cared to speak to me. This time, I'm being deluged. I saw Reggie Jackson. He and I had been friends, and Marilynn and I have had him over to the house for dinner. But I think Reggie has let his fame go to his head. I remember when a bunch of the Twins went to a basketball game in San Francisco one May evening. Reggie was with Oakland then. He strutted into the arena as if he were a king. He didn't pay any attention to us until he had finished his strutting: then he walked over and said hello. We shook our heads.

Now he started telling me about the candy bar being named for him and his big business deals and big Yankee contract.

He said, "Rod, how can you play in Minnesota for peanuts?"

I said, "Reggie, I'm happy living and playing in Minnesota. I don't need all the action you need. I don't need all those material things."

Then I said, "Do you have peace of mind?"

He said, "Well, that's not what it's all about."

Shortly thereafter, I read where he said he thought he was going crazy, what with the pressures of living up to his multimillion-dollar contract in New York, and the problems his mouth had gotten him into.

I had a single off Tom Seaver in three at-bats in the All-Star game. I was 3-for-27 for a .111 average in All-Star competition. It rankles me. I'd like to have done better because it is a showcase event, but it takes me a little while to get to know pitchers. When you see these National League guys just once a year, it's not enough. At least, it isn't for me.

By the end of August, my average has fallen from .401 in mid-July to my season's low of .374. I dropped 27 points in 42 games, and in only 6 of those games did I fail to get a hit. I am learning that hitting .400 is some feat.

I'm feeling tired and hurt. We're going into the sixth month of the season. On September 1, I'm hitting .378. My arms feel like lead. The bat feels as if it weighs a ton. Now I decide to order bats weighing 31 ounces, instead of my usual 32 ounces. Blisters on my hands are so bad I wrap my hands with tape. It's one thing after another now. I sprain my left wrist in a slide. And so I tape that. Every day I use four rolls of tape on my hands. I'm also wearing a corset for my back. Somebody says I ought to be shipped out to a museum and put in the Egyptian mummy section.

I don't want to sit out any games. I feel I can play. I'm not hurt, just achy. I don't like sitting on the bench that much. I always start falling asleep. To me, it's boring sitting in the dugout when I'm in uniform and feel I could be playing. As much as you try to get yourself going, you find yourself dozing. So you go for a tobacco-juice trick on a guy's shoes. Or you run up to the clubhouse and back for water or a soda.

I began hitting again, and my average started to inch up. But the team was sinking. We went from a half game out of first place on August 9 to 9 games out a month later. By the end of September we were 17 games out. We couldn't pick up any runs and we dropped like a bomb. The Royals were on a hot streak and just overpowered everybody. We couldn't keep pace. It was disheartening. I have always dreamed about playing in a World Series, and winning it. Well, my dream would have to wait at least another year.

We went into Kansas City on September 20 and I developed an infection in my arm. I sat out that game. The following day was Yom Kippur, and I sat out that one too.

Gene Mauch told me about a Yom Kippur once in which Sandy Koufax was scheduled to pitch against his team, the Phillies. Gene had a kid pitcher whose turn it was on the mound. When the kid found out that Sandy wouldn't play, he got pumped up and goggle-eyed, "Gee, we don't have to face Koufax today!" He went out and threw a two-hitter.

We had two series left—two home games with Chicago and three games at Milwaukee. I went into those games at .381. I went 3-for-5 and 2-for-3 against the White Sox. The games were played on two beautiful afternoons, cool but sunny. We had several thousand people in the stands. A decent crowd, all things considered. We had created so much excitement in the Twin Cities all season that people had come out to see us in flocks. Even when we fell behind by a lot of runs the fans weren't leaving the ball park until the end of the game. They were still pulling for us and cheering us on. It was frustrating to finish up the way we did. But it really tickled me that on my last time at bat I got a wonderful round of applause and the park organist struck up "Thanks for the Memory."

At Milwaukee, I had 4-for-8 in the first two games. I'm at .386. A good day on Sunday, the last game of the season, would give me a chance at Williams' .388 mark, set in 1957 when he was 40 years old. It's the highest average in baseball since Williams' .406 in '41.

I'm hot now. When I'm like this, I can practically read Lee MacPhail's signature on the baseball as it comes in. I can see virtually every stitch of the ball. The ball seems brighter to me—magnified.

When I'm not going well, I'm usually tired. I'm pulling my head away from the ball. My mind is fogged. My arms and legs ache. I'm seeing only half the ball.

That usually happens to me in the dog days of August. In September it's my pattern to get revived, and I'm back seeing the full rotation of the ball as it comes toward the plate. That's how it was now, at the end of the season.

When I came into the clubhouse at County Stadium before the last game, I was greeted by Jim Ksicinski, the clubhouse man.

"Hi, Mullion," he said. I laughed.

"Mullion" is a common baseball expression meaning "ugly." Jim and I have been friends for several years—despite his honesty.

The field had been muddy because of the rain the day before, and I had asked Jim to have one of his helpers clean my shoes. When he returned, they still had mud on them.

I looked at them. "These are clean shoes?" I asked. He said, "Picky, picky." He went off with the shoes.

It was a strange kind of lonesome day out on the field. Overcast one minute, and then the next minute the sun comes out and creates an awful glare from the red railings around the stadium. During batting practice everything seemed so quiet. The crack of the ball being hit sounded very, very loud.

There couldn't have been more than 1,500 people in the stands. It was probably the smallest crowd I had played before all season. You had the feeling you were in spring training again, and everything was starting over.

When I came up the first time, the organist played the theme song from *Jesus Christ Superstar*. Bill Travers, a rangy lefty fork-baller who is called "the Stork," was on the mound. In the first inning, I laid a bunt down the third-base line and beat it out. Next time up, I grounded out. In the sixth, I singled through the middle. In my last time up, in the eighth inning, the shadows from the light towers were slanting across the field. It's a difficult time in which to pick up the pitches. They come at you from in and out of the shadows. On the first pitch, I lined one off the left-field wall for a single.

We won, and at game's end the organist played "Auld

Lang Syne." It was a bittersweet moment. I knew some guys like Larry Hisle and Lyman Bostock would probably not be back next season. They had played out their options and now were negotiating for bigger contracts with other teams. Calvin did not want to pay them what they were asking. Other guys might be leaving too. There was talk that Gene would go if the team broke up like this. I can't blame him for not wanting to stay aboard a sinking ship. I said for print that I'd want to play for Gene anywhere he went. But I also liked Minnesota. I would be torn. My agent at this time was opening negotiations with Calvin for my contract. I didn't know what my future held either.

In the clubhouse, I was told I had finished with a .388 average, having had 3-for-4.

"Hey, Rodney," Bostock said, straight-faced, "a good hitter would have gone 4-for-4 to pass Williams."

Before the game, Craig Kusick had asked if I'd give his brother-in-law a bat. I called Kusick over and gave him the bat. I had driven in my 100th run—the first time in my career I reached that mark—and I gave the bat that I did it with to Gene. He was surprised to get it. I told him I had appreciated his support.

Someone said I was only eight hits short of hitting .400. It would be so easy for me to pick out eight balls that I'd like to have over again, hard-hit balls that someone made a terrific play on. But I wasn't terribly disappointed at falling short. I knew it was going to be hard to do, especially for my style—I wasn't walking a lot, and to hit .400 you probably have to be more selective with pitches.

A lot of people say how much harder it is to hit today than it was when Williams hit his .400. He did it thirty-seven years ago. There's a lot more travel today, and the use of relief pitchers is greater; gloves are bigger; schedules are longer and more tiring; in night games it's supposed to be more difficult to see the ball.

I don't buy much of that. I imagine train travel was as

rough as jet travel. Although the use of relief pitchers is greater, we have many more teams (26; there used to be 16), and the caliber of play may be diminished, though a counterargument is that the population has grown to balance that. And I prefer hitting at night, even though my lifetime average is slightly better during day ball. But during the day you squint a lot, and then there's a lot of stuff in the air—especially in California—and it burns your eyes. There's the glare of the sun. And in some places the artificial turf smokes up and your legs are burning. Then the perspiration during the day is running down your face. I like nighttime. You're cooler and more relaxed.

Hitting on artificial turf is no problem for me. I thought that it would detract from my bunting because the ball moves faster on artificial turf. And I get a lot of infield hits and bunt hits. But I just don't believe I've been affected by artificial turf.

# Chapter XI

AT THE end of a season, I often think about the day I'm going to have to call it a career.

Some guys that I've played with through the years made relatively smooth adjustments when their playing days ended. Harmon Killebrew is a partner in an insurance company in Boise, Idaho, and also does the color commentary for Twins telecasts. Bob Allison is a district sales manager for Coca-Cola in Minneapolis. Al Worthington, the relief pitcher, and a religious man who used to sign his autograph and add something like Psalm 6, verses 1–5—he coaches the baseball team at a Southern Baptist college. Earl Battey, the catcher, is a counselor at a school for emotionally disturbed youngsters in Dobbs Ferry, New York.

Other guys have had it tougher. Dave Boswell is back in his hometown, Baltimore, and works at a brewery there. His job is to clean out the vats at day's end. He had been

211

invited to the Old-Timers game in 1977, but didn't come. He wanted to bring his wife. The Twins pay for only the player's plane ticket. Dave said he couldn't afford her ticket, so he stayed home.

Zoilo Versalles is a janitor in Minneapolis, and sometimes drops into the clubhouse for a visit.

I remember being struck by one of the players I played with when I was in my early years. He had played his heart out, and all of a sudden he was over the hill. Just so fast. I think he didn't take care of himself the way he should have, and he squandered his wonderful talent. He was the kind of guy who was rarely concerned with anybody else. Then everything began to crumble and he was looking for people to help him. I saw him put people down because he had the world by the tail.

He was always a big spender. He used to buy $200 suits, and he was the type of guy who would go and buy a $30 shirt and get a handkerchief to match the shirt—if he couldn't find one, he'd cut the bottom off the shirt and stick it in his pocket, and then he'd turn around and just throw the shirt away, or give it away. He'd buy a $125 pair of shoes and wear them two or three times and come back to the park and sell them to one of the players for $25 or $30. When he went downhill, he lost everything. A friend of mine told me that the three things that go first are your reflexes, your money and your friends, in that order. That's what happened to this guy. People got off his bandwagon and looked for somebody else's bandwagon to get on.

Now I see him, and it's sad. He's down and out. Nothing flashy about his dress now. I have to think it's nobody's fault but his own. He never looked to the future.

I try to guard against that. I try to pick my friends carefully.

I remember when I first saw the guy I've been talking about I thought, This guy's going to be around for years. But I saw how quickly you can lose it. I'd like to play several more years, until I'm 40.

My whole life has been concentrated on being a baseball player. I think, What am I prepared to do when it's over? I have good people who know about money to advise me. My lawyer, Jerry Simon, and my business representative, Dick Lurie. My house is paid for. I have college scholarship trusts for my three daughters. I think I've provided for my family.

From a business standpoint, I've considered various kinds of restaurants. I've made careful investments. I've saved my money.

But I'd like always to keep involved in some way with baseball. I wouldn't mind working with young players. I think I can help them develop their hitting. I wouldn't want to be a manager. I don't want to get old fast with ulcers. I also thought of sports broadcasting. It's something I want to look into.

For now, my life is still centered on hitting a baseball. I still devote my energies to that.

With enough money in the bank to keep me relatively secure financially, I feel I can make a careful decision when the time comes. I won't have to be rushed into anything.

What's amazing is, I'm the oldest player on my team now. Some of my teammates were in the third grade when I was a rookie with the Twins.

Even though I am the so-called elder statesman of the club, I'm still friendly with many young players, particularly Craig Kusick, Glenn Borgmann, Roy Smalley and Glen Adams. One of my closest friends in the late '70's on the Twins was Danny Ford, the young outfielder from Los Angeles. Danny often pops into my house for a talk, and sometimes a meal. Danny's black, about the same height and weight as I am, and he's got a lot of ability. He's also moody and sometimes overly sensitive. In many ways, I see in Danny the way I was when I was his age—25, 26 years old.

He throws well, he can run and he can hit for power. But when he gets down on himself he won't run out ground balls, or he'll lose concentration at the plate, or he'll come late for batting practice. "Danny," I've told him, "you've got all the talent in the world. You can be a tremendous ballplayer. Don't squander it." Now, he can be a pretty loose kid—I call him "Cool"—and he says to me, "Junior, don't worry about a thing. It's all gonna turn out mellow."

Since he's been with the Twins, his highest average was .280, and his best home-run and RBI production was 20 and 86, respectively. But he can do better. I've thought that as talented as Lyman Bostock and Larry Hisle were, Ford's got even more ability. One day I'd like to see Danny bust out and become one of the big stars of the game. It's where he belongs.

We were sitting on the bench and watching that 1977 Old-Timers game in Bloomington and Danny Ford said, "Oh, you got to get Carew out there." I laughed. But I know, one day soon. . . .

Tony Oliva also played in the Old-Timers game. I thought of how much he's gone through in the last few years.

It was so hard for him to retire. He would talk about what he might do after he did quit—that was the biggest fear he had. He hadn't gone to high school, because he had helped his dad with the family farm. He had no idea what he was capable of doing in the way of a job in America, outside of baseball.

And he had a language barrier. Oh, you can communicate with Tony in English, but you have to listen closely. As hard as he tried to do something about his knee, that's how hard he tried to speak English well. He would take *two* suitcases on the road with him. One had his massaging stuff, and the other had a tape recorder with English lessons. I've seen him sit in the hotel room day after day with a headset plugged into the tape recorder, and he's speaking and listening. But he has never really got over the hump.

Deep down, I think Tony just never wanted to get away from his native tongue. He's not lazy, and he's certainly not dumb. When it comes to money, especially, Tony has no problem whatsoever.

But English fluency bothered him a great deal. He felt it hurt him in that he was missing extra money from speaking engagements and TV commercials. I don't know about the latter. I've seen Minnesota North Star hockey players on TV commercials, and they spoke only French. Black athletes in Minnesota did not get commercials. I speak as well as the white players, and I've never been paid for a TV commercial in Minnesota; but white baseball players with lesser records than mine have.

AFTER the last game of the 1977 season, I flew back to my home in Golden Valley, a few miles outside of Minneapolis. We had bought the house in 1972, and when I was managing down in Venezuela that winter, Marilynn had come back to close the deal on the house. There was a big snowstorm, and we didn't have any equipment to shovel the snow. She was alone. A neighbor across the street was shoveling his driveway. He came over and asked Marilynn if she wanted him to do ours. When I saw him, I thanked him. Right from the start, we were made to feel at home in the neighborhood. I've heard so many stories of a black man moving into an all-white neighborhood and there's trouble. Even a man known to the public. I remember a few years ago when Willie Mays bought a home in an all-white section of San Francisco and there were troubles. It's been nothing but pleasant experiences with neighbors in Golden Valley.

We have a comfortable home—four bedrooms, four baths, a den, a two-car garage—and two dogs. The kids in the neighborhood come over and they know they're welcome. They all used to call me "Mr. Carew." I told them to call me Rod. I love kids. I love having them around.

It's things like this that make me like living in Minnesota. That's not to say there are not problems. There's a hassle with a cop, or someone writes a nasty letter, or I get booed. You can get that anywhere. I think you get less of it in Minnesota. And in the bad winters, it's nothing to see somebody stuck and people stop to help the person. In New York, a woman gets murdered and 38 people look out their windows and then pull down their shades. I think Minnesota is one of the best places for a black man to live in America. But he still has his problems, even if his name is Rod Carew.

I've had some bad experiences with cops, especially. After a game in Met Stadium a few years ago, I'm driving down 35W near my home and going 50 in a 55-mile zone. Two cops in a squad car pull me over. "You know the speed limit, boy? You think you're going to be burning up the road with this fancy car you're driving?"

They asked me for my driver's license. My first instinct was to tell them that I've got my license in my pocket and if they want it to take it out. Among blacks, white police-men have a reputation that as soon as you go into your pocket, they think you're going to pull out a gun. They could jump me and pull out their guns and it's all over.

I told them my doubts. One cop said, "Do it slowly." When he saw my name, he starts shaking his head and says, "Well, Rod, you're nuts for going over the speed limit." I said, "I know I wasn't going over the speed limit. I knew you guys were behind me. And I knew you were going to stop me." They wanted to let me go. I said, "Damn it! Give me a ticket. I don't want any favors." Then I went down to City Hall and was going to lodge a complaint for harass-ment. I told them I wasn't going to be treated like a dog. Nothing came of it. I'm Rod Carew, but the bottom line is still that I'm black. Once, I'd walk away from it. Now I feel I've got to take a stand. I've never been a militant. The black Latin players generally are not militant. I guess most of us are just happy to be here in the States and playing ball. We know that the opportunities don't exist in the Latin countries the way they do here. So we have a tendency to shut our mouths more than American blacks—like we're guests in the country. We get older, though; we change.

From some of these experiences, a black can become justifiably paranoid. In the off season, I jog. But I jog indoors. Someone asked why I don't jog outdoors. I replied, "If someone sees a black guy running, they immediately think he's just stolen something." I was only half joking.

MARILYNN THOUGHT it was cruel that so many people were calling and writing about my possibly winning the American League's Most Valuable Player award for the 1977 baseball season. It was early November. The announcement was scheduled to be made in a few days. The Associated Press wanted to come out to our house to take a picture of the family, just in case I won. The *Minneapolis Tribune* wanted an interview concerning the award. Tom Mee, the Twins' public relations director, had organized a press conference. Just in case.

"How can they do this to somebody?" Marilynn asked. "If you don't win, then they've set you up for a big crash."

"Marilynn," I said, "it's not all that serious. Those guys are just doing their job. And besides, I'm not gearing myself up for the award." What I meant—and she knew it—was that I was *trying* not to gear myself up for the award.

Look, the MVP is the most prestigious award in my profession. It means that of the 350 or so ballplayers in your league, you have been voted the best by the baseball writers who cover the games. I had never won it, though there were seasons in which I thought I should have. Like the 1977 season. But if I didn't get it, I told Marilynn, no big deal. It couldn't in any way detract from the season I'd had.

I had never come close to winning the MVP. I'm not sure

why that is. One guess is I've never played on a pennant winner. Another is that I play in Minnesota, far from the influential press and television centers of New York and Los Angeles. Another is that I've never been a big, flashy power guy: my game is to hit to spots, bunt, steal bases.

A lot of people now were telling me that this year was different. It had been. I had received more publicity this year than in my previous ten combined. And winning my sixth batting title meant that only Ty Cobb, Honus Wagner, Rogers Hornsby and Stan Musial had won more. I thought that that was pretty fair consolation for not reaching .400. Also, my 239 hits for the season was the best total in the majors in forty-seven years, and I had scored more runs—128—than anyone in the league since 1961.

Even with all that, I still didn't think I'd win the MVP. Other guys had had good seasons too. Al Cowens and Ken Singleton and Jim Rice, for example; and Reggie Jackson had come on strong at the end of the year. Also, I played on a fourth-place club. Reggie said that the award ought to go to a member of a pennant winner. (Which I guess meant Reggie, since the Yankees won.) But I disagree strongly with Reggie's concept, though I know it's one shared by many. My view is, the best should be honored as the best, regardless of how his team does in the standings.

I tried not to think about the MVP. I went through my typical off season: To stay in shape I ran a couple of miles a few times a week at an indoor track at the University of Minnesota,and I played some tennis, and I bowled once a week with a team in a St. Paul league (my average is about 180). I read. Lately, I've enjoyed science fiction like *Close Encounters of the Third Kind* and novels such as *The Boys from Brazil,* about the capture of Nazi war criminals. I also involved myself with charities, such as Multiple Sclerosis, the March of Dimes, the Association for the Blind and state mental hospitals. I feel it's important that I do work like this. I've been blessed, and I imagine my charitable activi-ties are a kind of repayment for that blessing. I do know that when I leave a hospital where I've been with kids who are in wheelchairs, and who can't talk or even feed themselves, I feel good, not depressed. For one thing, I say to myself, Man, you've got no problems—all that salary stuff, or MVP concern, ain't nothin'. But also, many of the people I see in the hospitals inspire me in the way they struggle with their handicap.

Like Kenny. He's a teen-ager, and a palsy victim. He's confined to a wheelchair. But he rarely misses a Twins game. Even in freezing temperatures, he's out there in his Twins cap and Twins jacket. He's often alongside the runway between the clubhouse and the dugout, and most of the players stop and talk to him. He'll say something like "You'll get two hits today, and we'll beat 'em." I think he truly encourages the players.

Well, on Monday afternoon, November 14, Tom Mee called and said he had just spoken to Jack Lang in New York—Lang is the secretary of the Baseball Writers Association of America, the organization that votes for the MVP—and asked him if he had any information yet. Lang said he hadn't, but would count the ballots on Tuesday and call me at home at 10 that night to let me know the results.

That Tuesday night I went out to dinner with a few friends. Then we stopped downtown for a drink. It was starting to get late, and I told the guys that I had to be home by 10. I hurried back and came through the door at 10:03. On the dot.

"You just missed a phone call," Marilynn said.

"Jack Lang?" I asked.

"Uh-huh."

"What did he say?"

"He just asked for you. I told him you'd be home any minute. He said he'd call right back. He sounded kind of abrupt."

I was wondering what that meant when the phone rang again. I picked it up.

"Hello."

"Rod?"

"Yes."

"Congratulations."

That was all I had to hear. I had a pack of chewing to-bacco in my hand and I threw it into the air.


OUR THIRD CHILD, and third daughter, was born on No-vember 21, two days after the MVP announcement. Like the other two girls, she was born in the Golden Valley Medical Center. It's a small hospital, and everybody came around to see the new baby. Nurses, doctors, secretaries—even other patients—would come down to see the new baby. When I first saw Michelle, I said to myself, God, she's gorgeous. She had a little round face and a dimple on her left cheek.

I've thought about having a boy. But I'm glad that it didn't happen. Maybe the pressure to follow in my foot-steps would have been too great for him. It's happened to sons of other athletes and people in the public eye.

Michelle Ciarra was named for my late father-in-law, Morris Sheldon Levy. I wished that he could have been there when she was born, and also to share the MVP with us.

When he was dying in the hospital, we'd go up and visit him, and one day Marilynn asked me to take pictures of him with Charryse. This might be one of the last times we'd see him alive. He said, "You don't think I know why you're doing this? You think you're trying to fool me?"

We always got along. He accepted me from the first. He had never been to a baseball game until he met me; then he went several times with Marilynn. I think what he enjoyed most was the excitement of the crowd and the people cheer-ing for his son-in-law.

In the hospital, he gave me a "Chai" as a gift. It's the Jewish symbol for a good and healthy life. I wear it around my neck. I never take it off.

Marilynn's father was always easy to talk to, and he didn't point a finger and say, "You shouldn't do this." He'd say, "Be careful. Know what you're doing."

When he died, he made sure that he left no bills unpaid. No one was going to say that Morrie Levy died owing anybody anything.

MY GREATEST pleasure is having had my mom see me accomplish what I once told her I would. I have always respected her so much. I can never repay her enough for how she sacrificed for me and the rest of the kids and how she protected the kids against our father.

She lives in the Bushwick section of Brooklyn, in a house with my Uncle Clyde and his family and my sister Sugar and her family. My brother and two other sisters live nearby. Mom works as a receptionist at St. Luke's Hospital. I've suggested that she stop working. I told her I could handle all of her financial worries. She said no, that she is a working woman, has been all her life.

She still worries about us. She has always warned me not to eat at banquets or at places where I don't know how the food was prepared. When I get to New York she doesn't want me to come out to visit her because she's afraid I'll get mugged on the subway. She doesn't even want me to take a cab. She worries about each of the kids, but perhaps me most of all because I had always been sickly.

One day my brother, who has a good job with a business-machines company, was saying to her, "Mom, we're adults now; you've got to cut us loose from your apron strings." She said, "I know, I know; one day I will."

I don't even think about my father. Or try not to. I just wanted to get away from him and have him get away from me.

My mother told me that once years ago he stood up at Yankee Stadium with his chest out and told people, "Good boy . . . good hitter . . . that's my son." Maybe he is proud of me. But never in his life was he able to express warm feelings toward me.

None of the kids see him much now. My mother hasn't seen him in many years. The last we heard, he was working in a bar somewhere in the Bronx.

My mother called one day in the winter and said her mother had died in Panama. She was going back and asked if I would go with her. I try to avoid funerals, but I felt my mom needed my help, and of course I had loved my grandmother. I arranged the trip, as well as the particulars of the funeral.

On the plane, my cousin Eugene Madeam and my brother and I were playing a card game called blitz, which is like gin rummy. It's a game we played as kids.

I noticed Eugene looking at me kind of funny. I said, "What are you thinking about?"

"Just nothing," he said.

"What is it?" I said.

He said, "There's supposed to be a lot of reporters there when we land, Rod. Do you want me to interpret for you?"

"Interpret what?"

"Spanish."

"Hey," I said, "I grew up speaking Spanish. You know that because I grew up with you."

He said, "Yeah, but you speak English so good it seems like you'd forget Spanish."

When we got off the plane and met the photographers and reporters, I started rattling Spanish off like there was no tomorrow. Eugene was at the edge of the crowd and listening to everything. I caught his eye and winked. He cracked up.

There were bodyguards for me, and they went everywhere I went. I wanted to go back to Gamboa, where I grew up. I felt I was home, that this is where home is. It's where I started and grew up and learned how to play baseball and listened to those games on the radio and dreamed about one day playing before all those crowds of people.

On the way to Gamboa, we drove past the tree I used to run away to. I saw kids riding their bicycles and the men still sitting on the sidewalk playing dominoes.

A lot of people didn't recognize me at first. There were a lot of new people in the neighborhood. But as soon as they found out who I was, the kids came up and wanted to talk and take pictures with me and take me into their homes. I went in to say hello to their families.

A man named "Painter" was playing dominoes. He had been a friend of my father's and was a painter like my father.

He said, "It's been a long time, Carew."

I said, "Yeah. How you been, Painter?"

"Hey," he said, "you remembered my name!"

He asked me to play a round of dominoes. So I sat down and he offered me a drink. He and his friends were drinking rum and Coke. I said I'd just have a Coke. I played a hand of dominoes and lost.

I ran into other people I knew as well. They asked me how it was going and said they were proud of me and happy to see that I was doing well and that I hadn't forgotten about the town that I grew up in. I remembered a number of the people who were there when I was a boy, and I remembered their names. Even after fifteen or sixteen years, you can see a person and his name comes immediately to mind.

Something had changed, though. When I was growing up, neighbors would wander into and out of one another's homes. But the new families that had moved in, seemed to be off to themselves more, and their doors were closed.

I saw the field where I had played, with the hill in the outfield. It looked so small now. I remembered how I had had that burning desire to be a baseball player. I used to take the bat and glove and ball to bed with me. I'd dream of playing in the major leagues. I thought how great it would be to go to America and do it, like Jackie Robinson.

I looked at the kids now and I saw myself when I was

their age. I thought how determined I had been to make something of myself. I think I'm someone who means a lot to these kids in Panama. I can tell that by the way they look at me. They know that I came from the same small country and I didn't have anything. When we talked, I told them I thought it was possible to make something of yourself no matter who you were, or where you lived, and in any field. Mine happened to be baseball. Another kid's could be medicine. Or carpentry. But you must have the desire and the talent. And luck. God, I was lucky. I told them that. I was lucky to have people all along the way who helped me, who cared for me. I was fortunate that I didn't let other people destroy me who could have destroyed me.

My mother said to me, "I see all the little kids in Panama and you ask them their name and they say, 'Rod Carew.' I say, 'Gee, so much Rod Carew here in Panama.' " I have to shake my head. Sometimes I wonder if I'm not dreaming all this, and that I'll wake up in the morning with my bat in my bed and hear the striking clock in the living room, and know it's time to get up and get myself ready for school.

# Afterword

As the 1978 season began, I felt that my days with the Minnesota Twins under Calvin Griffith were definitely numbered. I wanted to go, even though Minnesota is my home and I've spent many of the happiest days of my life there. But I felt I could no longer work for a man like Calvin Griffith.

Calvin is a hardheaded guy who has not admitted to himself that times do actually change. He continues to live in the Stone Age of baseball, when there were reserve clauses and no free agents, and the owner was lord and master and the player a grubby peasant.

Because of his attitude, the Twins have sunk in the standings and suffered at the gate. We didn't keep pace with other clubs in buying quality ballplayers. Calvin was cutting off his nose to spite his face; most teams that have spent

225

money to obtain and keep top talent have improved on the field and on the accounting books.

Every proud ballplayer wishes to play in a World Series. I've dreamed of it ever since I heard those first games over the radio in the Dust Bowl in Gatun. I've always thought how sad that some great players such as Ernie Banks and Billy Williams never had the opportunity to play in a World Series. So it's not startling that Calvin's position frustrated me. It appeared we were going nowhere but down.

The Twins in spring training of 1978 were without two of their best players from the season before. Larry Hisle, the classy power hitter, had signed a $3.5-million contract for five years with Milwaukee, and Lyman Bostock, a high-average hitter, went from $20,000 a year with Minnesota to $500,000 a year with California. Calvin made only a feeble attempt to keep either player; and although we had some good young players coming up from the farm system and some decent trades had been made, we were considerably weakened from 1977.

I knew that my job at the plate would be tougher without big bats behind me; pitchers would "pitch around me"— that is, throw me careful pitches and not mind walking me. They would prefer taking their chances with the next batter.

All right, I thought, I'll just make the best of an uncertain situation. I had one more year to go on my three-year contract (with the added obligation of playing my option year with Minnesota in 1979). My hope was to talk to Calvin about a long-term contract of $3 million for eight years, so that I would never have to hassle over a contract again. It would also put my mind at rest as far as security for my family was concerned.

Many people have said that even at $170,000 a year, I was paid unfairly in light of my achievements. According to *Sports Illustrated*, I was the most underpaid player in the major leagues. Red Smith, the *New York Times* sports columnist, wrote that in comparison with current standards, my proposed terms for a new contract were "eminently reasonable, if not beggarly."

I had never complained about my salary. No one had forced me to sign that contract. And I wasn't attempting now to renegotiate. I wanted to discuss a contract to follow the present one.

On March 26—Easter Sunday—my lawyer, Jerry Simon, flew into Orlando, Florida, from St. Paul, after Calvin had agreed on the phone to speak with him about my future contract. The three of us sat down in Calvin's office. After a few moments Calvin said, "All these f——— owners don't realize they're ruinin' the f——— game by giving out all that f——— money. Pretty soon they're gonna find their asses up a pole. I'm not gonna ruin my f——— organization like that."

Before we could even put forward our proposals, Calvin ended the meeting.

Oh, he did say something else at the brief meeting. He said, "I know Rod has been underpaid for a long time." And he left it at that.

I was appalled by his language in this meeting and was mad as hell at his high-handed treatment of us. I mean, not only had I just come off that terrific season, and not only did I think I should have been treated with more consideration, but the man representing me had flown a thousand miles only to be insulted.

My respect for Calvin had been diminishing for some time. He has denounced players, including me, in public instead of calling us into his office and explaining what it was that displeased him. I believe he has turned his back on some players who were loyal to the organization for many years, such as Harmon Killebrew.

I have no respect left for Calvin. This is not to say that I don't appreciate what Calvin did for me early in my career. He supported and encouraged me when many others did not.

I demonstrated my appreciation and loyalty. On the field

I gave all I could, of course; that's my job. But off the field I'd do a lot of promotional work for the club. Without pay I'd conduct clinics and give talks; at Calvin's request I'd go to the office of a big season-ticket holder on the verge of cancelling and take pictures with him and sign autographs. In most cases, the season tickets were kept.

I thought I owed all that to Calvin. I don't anymore.

The season begins, and we're in the cellar right from the start. In May we have a chance to sign Mike Marshall, a onetime Cy Young Award winner who is still effective. We're desperate for a relief pitcher like Marshall. We have the worst record in baseball. So Calvin refuses to sign Marshall. I was steaming. I told the press it was demoralizing for all the players and that I'd never sign with this team again. Gene Mauch, I imagine, appealed to Calvin too, and Marshall was signed.

Although I was hitting .377 at the time, I could feel my competitive juices ebbing amid all this turmoil. There was a lot of talk about my being traded to another team. The pressure was on Calvin to either pay me what I wanted or trade me before I became a free agent. He didn't want to make the same mistake with me that he had made with Larry and Lyman. They became free agents and the Twins were never compensated in a deal for them.

Since I'm a ten-year veteran with at least the last five years on the same club, I could veto any deal involving me. I told Calvin that if I were traded I'd go only to a contender. I gave him a list of five teams I'd consider: New York, Kansas City, Texas, California and Boston.

I began to think about other clubs, and what it would be like living and playing in other towns. The best park for me probably would be Yankee Stadium. It is so spacious, and the power alleys in left center and right center are so deep, that it gives a spray hitter like me a lot of room. But I've lived in New York, and I really don't like that big a city. I prefer a gentler kind of life than what the Big Apple offers.

Royals Stadium in Kansas City has that hard artificial turf, and I think I could eventually get used to it. I could learn to hit those mile-high bouncers that don't come down until you're safely on first; also, because the infield is so hard, balls zip through there faster than on natural grass. I think they have a good-looking park, and I like the people. They really support the club—enthusiastic in the way Milwaukee and Boston fans are.

The main attraction of the Texas Rangers is the ball club. The owner, Brad Corbett, seems intent on building the best team he can, and is spending a lot of money to do it. The negative point there is the field. It's one of the worst in baseball. The infield is rocky, and I'd have to learn to play first base with a chest protector and shin guards.

Possibly the best-looking of all the modern ball parks is where the California Angels play. I think it also has the best lights. I don't like the smog that sometimes settles around there, but then, playing with instead of against pitchers like Nolan Ryan and Frank Tanana would ease the pain considerably. The Anaheim area might also be the finest place for my kids to go to school—in case we'd think of moving our home. (Needless to say, these thoughts would come to have tremendous importance for me less than a year later.)

I've always liked Fenway Park in Boston, and have hit well there. With my inside-out swing, I could hit that huge close left-field wall all day. I'm partial to the old-time feeling of Fenway Park (which was built in 1915), and of Boston itself. I often go on picture-taking excursions among the historic buildings there. I also love the seafood restaurants with those big, juicy lobsters.

It's funny, but Metropolitan Stadium, my home park for twelve years, has been one of the more difficult for me to hit in. The lights are good, and the dimensions of the park are spacious, but during day games and for the first few innings of night games there is a hard glare from the sun hitting the bleacher seats. And it's hard for me to pick out pitches, especially when a right-hander is throwing. The ball seems to come right out of that blaze of sun. At first base, the glare makes it hard to see throws from the left side of the infield.

My least-favorite park is in Baltimore. It's got a cold, undistinctive atmosphere. Totally unlike the fans, though, whom I really appreciate, and who have been very kind to me over the years.

It was getting close to the June 15 trading deadline, and I was a mess. I had heard that Calvin was talking with several clubs; and one minute I'd hear he was close to a deal, and the next minute I'd hear it was off and he was involved in another deal. I didn't know if I was coming or going—literally.

Although I was still leading the league in hitting, my play was affected by all this. For the first time in my career, I wasn't concentrating on the ball at the plate; I was thinking of all those other things. I was losing my taste for the game. It was no longer fun, but a job—a grind. There were even times when, amazingly to me, I didn't even look forward to going up to hit.

At home, Marilynn tried to bring some perspective. "Rod," she'd say, "if worse comes to worst and you stay with the Twins, you'll still be able to sign a contract for a minimum of two million dollars." There *are* other people in the world with problems a bit more severe than that. I read someplace that the per capita income of Panama is $1,150 a year. And I thought that if I had stayed in Panama my big worry would be to get $2,000, not $2,000,000. Yet the whole thing shook me up.

I continued to stay in shape. I ran a mile every day at the ball park, did wind sprints and stretching exercises, and took my usual amount of batting practice. Calvin, meanwhile, was turning down offers for me from several clubs. By midnight of June 15, the trading deadline, I was still a Minnesota Twin—which was good: I could finish the season and not have to worry until the winter about my future.

The All-Star game was a treat for me. I made the team for the twelfth straight year, starting at first base. I opened the game in San Diego with a triple to center field, and followed that with a triple my next time up. I was delighted to raise my skimpy All-Star average; but once again the National League came back to win.

The Twins continued to founder as a team, and as I had anticipated in spring training, I was getting very few decent pitches to hit. One July night in Boston, for example, I was walked four times. But Danny Ford, the next batter, foiled the Red Sox. He had two hits and a fielder's choice, to drive in three runs in a 5–2 Twins victory.

A pleasant surprise for the Twins was Mike Marshall. Mike was an outstanding clutch relief pitcher for us. He's a strong, well-built guy who wears a bushy moustache and is perhaps the smartest baseball player in the game. In the off season he has been a professor of kinesiology at Michigan State University. He's a veteran who will talk all day with an interested young player—or older one, like me.

He teased me about striving to become a Gold Glove winner. He drew a line several feet away from first base. "Never go past this line," he said. "If you reach for a hard chance and don't get it, the official scorer might call it an error. Don't risk it." He told me that when I scooped up a ground ball I should hold the ball high and show it off to the crowd—as if no one else could ever have made a play like that.

He was more serious when I developed tendinitis in my right elbow. Mike encouraged me to continue soaking it in hot packs before the game to loosen it up, and soak it in ice after the game to keep the elbow from swelling. He also urged me to keep wearing the elbow brace on the field. There were times late in the season when I could hardly lift my arm because of the tendinitis. And when I swung and missed, I'd have to wait a few moments until the ache subsided before stepping back into the batter's box.

I wasn't hitting the ball particularly hard, and I wasn't as aggressive at bat as in previous years, yet my average stayed pretty high, around .340. But it began to drop, and on August 7 it hit a low point. For the only time that season, someone passed me in average: Al Oliver of Texas went to .323, a fraction ahead of me. But the following two nights I felt the adrenaline flowing again; I went 7-for-10 and had my lead back for good. I finished the season at .333, to Oliver's .324 second-place finish.

After all that had occurred during the season, this was definitely the toughest of my seven batting titles. But all of that seemed insignificant after a phone call I received in late September. Sid Hartman, a sports columnist for the *Minneapolis Tribune*, called and said, "Rod, did you hear what happened?"

By the sound of his voice I could tell it was something bad.

"No," I said.

"Lyman was shot and killed."

It was unbelievable. "Are you sure they've identified the right guy?"

"It's Lyman," said Sid.

Lyman Bostock was my teammate on the Twins for three years. I knew he was very close to an uncle who lived in Gary, Indiana, just outside Chicago. Lyman often visited him after games against the White Sox. On this night they were with three other people, including two women, and were driving to dinner. Another man allegedly pulled up beside their car, raised a rifle and shot, hitting Lyman in the head.

How senseless. How horrible. I still can't believe it happened. Everyone really liked Lyman. I remember how he loved to argue about anything—no matter what. And he'd always come out a winner, because he'd argue until you gave in. He loved to fish and actually told big whopper tales, about all those tremendous fish that he *nearly* caught.

Lyman was a poor black kid who came out of Alabama. His dad had been a Negro League player and had just missed the time when blacks entered the big leagues. I can imagine how proud his father was of Lyman.

Early in the season Lyman was hitting poorly for California and obviously felt guilty about his $500,000-a-year salary. He spoke about returning the money or giving it to charity until he improved. That was pure Lyman, all right, but it upset me. I didn't think he had anything to be ashamed of—he was trying, and that's all anyone can ask of anyone else.

When we played the Angels, he sent the batboy over to me with a newspaper photograph of himself wearing sunglasses with dollar signs on the lenses. Above the picture Lyman had written, *Rod, I need help.* His average was around .200. So I watched him in the game. I noticed he was lunging at pitches. He was too anxious. His swing wasn't smooth, as it normally is. I told him I thought he was trying to hit the ball into "holes" between fielders instead of swinging with the pitch. No one can manipulate a bat so well that he can consistently hit the ball into holes. I don't know if I helped or not, but Lyman picked up and was batting .296 when he died, at age 27.

The season couldn't have ended soon enough for me. In many ways it was a nightmare, especially coming immediately after that dream year of 1977.

On the day of our final game, Calvin Griffith was in the headlines. He had made a speech at a Lions luncheon in the small Minnesota town of Waseca in which he said, among other things:

• "I'll tell you why we came to Minnesota in 1961 [transferring the Washington Senators to the Twin Cities]. It was when I found out you [Minnesota] only had fifteen thousand blacks here. Black people don't go to ball games, but they'll fill up a rassling ring and put up such a chant it'll scare you to death. . . . We came here because you've got good, hardworking white people here.''

• He called me ''a damn fool'' for signing a contract for what he thought was less than I was worth.

• He said Butch Wynegar's performance had suffered because he got married, and that he would have been better off indulging in free love.

There was more yet. He offended and antagonized everyone. Soon he was apologizing, saying he had only been joking after having a few drinks. I don't think it was an excuse; it was an alibi.

I was quoted in the papers accurately as saying, ''The days of Kunta Kinte are over,'' in reference to the main character in *Roots*. I added, ''I refuse to be a slave on his plantation and play for a bigot.'' I reiterated that I would never sign with him again. Commissioner of Baseball Bowie Kuhn made a rapid statement to the press disassociating the baseball community from Calvin's remarks. The Twin Cities' newspapers called for Calvin to sell the club.

Calvin was in Kansas City for the American League play-offs when the reaction hit. He kept calling my house. But I refused to speak with him. Finally I did get on the phone. He tried to explain his remarks, but it didn't change my views.

Thinking back on the season, I was determined I would never again allow myself to be put through the kind of emotional wringer I was in in 1978. I love baseball too much not to give it every ounce of energy I have, mentally and physically.

The winter was filled with rumors about impending deals for me. Finally Calvin traded me to San Francisco. After much thought I turned it down, mainly because I wanted to stay in the American League. Learning a whole new set of pitchers at this stage of my career was not appealing, and I also would miss the familiarity of the A.L. cities.

The Angels called. I went down to Anaheim with my lawyer and in fifteen minutes we had made a deal—$4.4 million to be paid in full over five years. Well, Calvin turned *that* down, because he wasn't completely happy with the players the Angels offered in trade. The Yankees bid. But they eventually dropped out after a month of negotiations. So Calvin went back and accepted the Angels' deal. I was delighted. They had been my first preference all along. The Angels are on the upswing and the owner, Gene Autry, has spent lavishly for talent in recent years, getting such players as Joe Rudi, Bobby Grich and Don Baylor. I'm genuinely looking forward to contributing to a championship team in Anaheim.

When I look back on the 1978 season, the moments I want to remember are the pleasant ones. There were three in particular that I'll savor for a long time.

In Baltimore on July 14 I received a standing ovation when the public-address announcer told the crowd that I needed just one more hit for a career total of 2,000. I didn't get the hit that night, but I did the following evening, in Boston. I sent a crisp single to right field off Bill Lee. When the crowd was informed of the milestone, the full house of 32,861 stood up and cheered. Here I was an opposing player in Baltimore and Boston and the fans expressed their appreciation like that. I was thrilled.

I may have been even more moved a week later in Minnesota. Carl Yastrzemski of the Red Sox singled to knock in the 1,500th run of his eighteen-year career, putting him up there in an RBI class with Mantle, DiMaggio and Tris Speaker. Now it was the Twins fans who gave a rival player a rousing standing ovation.

Yaz was on first base and I congratulated him, and then someone was hollering to get the ball to him as a trophy. I stepped away while all this was going on and looked at Yaz. His cap, as always, was yanked low on his face, creating a shadow on his dark, intense profile. Yaz is close to 40 years

old and still an amazing player—a consistent clutch per-
former on a winning team. And he plays with the same
vigor as when I first saw him and admired him in 1967, my
rookie year.

Only a handful of great hitters in our time have played
into their 40s: Willie Mays, Henry Aaron, Stan Musial and
Ted Williams come to mind. They all were durable, kept
themselves in top shape and, what is so important, main-
tained their enthusiasm—that boy's love for the game. I
hope I can be like that when I'm 40, and getting my 3,000th
hit for a pennant contender.

So when I heard that warm applause from the crowd—it
wasn't just to honor a milestone, but to honor a long and
distinguished career that *still* has a few years left—and I
saw the umpire's hand outstretched and Yaz accepting the
ball, I felt a tingle run up my spine. I pictured myself in that
situation and I thought, What a great way to wind it all
down; what a great way to go.

# Appendix

Courtesy of the *Baseball Register* and the *Minnesota Twins Yearbook*

## RODNEY CLINE CAREW
### (Rod)

Born October 1, 1945, at Gatun, Panama.
Height, 6.00. Weight, 175.
Throws right- and bats left-handed.

| Year—Club | League | Pos | G | AB | R | H | 2B | 3B | HR | RBI | BB | SO | SB | BA | PO | A | E | FA |
|---|---|---|---|---|---|---|---|---|---|---|---|---|---|---|---|---|---|---|
| 1964—Melb'rne Twins.. | Coc. Rk. | 2B | 37 | 123 | 17 | 40 | 5 | 3 | 0 | 21 | 14 | 22 | 14 | .325 | 86 | 48 | 7 | .950 |
| 1965—Orlando ......... | Fla. St. | 2B | 125 | 439 | 57 | 133 | 20 | 8 | 1 | 52 | 73 | 74 | 52 | .303 | 290 | 328 | 28 | .954 |
| 1966—Wilson ......... | Carol. | 2B | 112 | 383 | 64 | 112 | 19 | 3 | 1 | 30 | 50 | 79 | 28 | .292 | 248 | 275 | 21 | .961 |
| 1967—Minnesota* ...... | Amer. | 2B | 137 | 514 | 66 | 150 | 22 | 7 | 8 | 51 | 37 | 91 | 5 | .292 | 289 | 314 | 15 | .976 |
| 1968—Minnesota† ...... | Amer. | 2B-SS | 127 | 461 | 46 | 126 | 27 | 2 | 1 | 42 | 26 | 71 | 12 | .273 | 266 | 285 | 18 | .968 |
| 1969—Minnesota‡ ...... | Amer. | 2B | 123 | 458 | 79 | 152 | 30 | 4 | 8 | 56 | 37 | 72 | 19 | .332 | 244 | 302 | 17 | .970 |
| 1970—Minnesota§ ...... | Amer. | 2B-1B | 51 | 191 | 27 | 70 | 12 | 3 | 4 | 28 | 11 | 28 | 4 | .366 | 79 | 122 | 8 | .962 |
| 1971—Minnesota ....... | Amer. | 2B-3B | 147 | 577 | 88 | 177 | 16 | 10 | 2 | 48 | 45 | 81 | 6 | .307 | 324 | 331 | 16 | .976 |
| 1972—Minnesota ....... | Amer. | 2B | 142 | 535 | 61 | 170 | 21 | 6 | 0 | 51 | 43 | 60 | 12 | .318 | 331 | 378 | 16 | .978 |
| 1973—Minnesota ....... | Amer. | 2B | 149 | 580 | 98 | 203 | 30 | 11 | 6 | 62 | 62 | 55 | 41 | .350 | 383 | 413 | 13 | .984 |
| 1974—Minnesota ....... | Amer. | 2B | 153 | 599 | 86 | 218 | 30 | 5 | 3 | 55 | 74 | 49 | 38 | .364 | 375 | 416 | 33 | .960 |
| 1975—Minnesota ....... | Amer. | 2B-1B | 143 | 535 | 89 | 192 | 24 | 4 | 14 | 80 | 64 | 40 | 35 | .359 | 408 | 377 | 21 | .974 |
| 1976—Minnesota ....... | Amer. | 1B-2B | 156 | 605 | 97 | 200 | 29 | 12 | 9 | 90 | 67 | 52 | 49 | .331 | 1398 | 110 | 16 | .990 |
| 1977—Minnesota ....... | Amer. | 1B-2B | 155 | 616 | 128 | 239 | 38 | 16 | 14 | 100 | 69 | 55 | 23 | .388 | 1463 | 124 | 10 | .994 |
| 1978—Minnesota ....... | Amer. | 1B | 152 | 564 | 85 | 188 | 26 | 10 | 5 | 70 | 78 | 62 | 27 | .333 | 1362 | 105 | 16 | .989 |
| Major League Totals ........... | | | 1635 | 6235 | 950 | 2085 | 305 | 90 | 74 | 733 | 603 | 716 | 271 | .334 | 6922 | 3277 | 199 | .981 |

* On military list, August 5 through August 21, 1967.
† On military list, June 8 through June 24, 1968.
‡ On military list, August 17 through September 1, 1969.
§ On disabled list, June 24 through September 1, 1970.

## CHAMPIONSHIP SERIES RECORD

| Year Club | League | Pos | G | AB | R | H | 2B | 3B | HR | RBI | BB | SO | SB | BA | PO | A | E | FA |
|---|---|---|---|---|---|---|---|---|---|---|---|---|---|---|---|---|---|---|
| 1969—Minnesota | Amer. | 2B | 3 | 14 | 0 | 1 | 0 | 0 | 0 | 0 | 1 | 4 | 0 | .071 | 6 | 3 | 1 | .900 |
| 1970—Minnesota | Amer. | PH | 2 | 2 | 0 | 0 | 0 | 0 | 0 | 0 | 0 | 1 | 0 | .000 | 0 | 0 | 0 | .000 |
| Championship Series Totals ... | | | 5 | 16 | 0 | 1 | 0 | 0 | 0 | 0 | 1 | 5 | 0 | .063 | 6 | 3 | 1 | .900 |

## ALL-STAR GAME RECORD

| Year League | Pos | AB | R | H | 2B | 3B | HR | RBI | BB | SO | SB | BA | PO | A | E | FA |
|---|---|---|---|---|---|---|---|---|---|---|---|---|---|---|---|---|---|
| 1967—American | 2B | 3 | 0 | 0 | 0 | 0 | 0 | 0 | 0 | 1 | 0 | .000 | 2 | 3 | 0 | 1.000 |
| 1968—American | 2B | 3 | 0 | 0 | 0 | 0 | 0 | 0 | 0 | 0 | 0 | .000 | 2 | 2 | 0 | 1.000 |
| 1969—American | 2B | 3 | 0 | 0 | 0 | 0 | 0 | 0 | 0 | 0 | 0 | .000 | 0 | 2 | 0 | 1.000 |
| 1971—American | 2B | 1 | 1 | 0 | 0 | 0 | 0 | 0 | 2 | 0 | 0 | .000 | 1 | 2 | 0 | 1.000 |
| 1972—American | 2B | 2 | 0 | 1 | 0 | 0 | 0 | 1 | 1 | 0 | 0 | .500 | 2 | 3 | 0 | 1.000 |
| 1973—American | 2B | 3 | 0 | 0 | 0 | 0 | 0 | 0 | 0 | 0 | 0 | .000 | 5 | 1 | 0 | 1.000 |
| 1974—American | 2B | 1 | 1 | 0 | 0 | 0 | 0 | 0 | 1 | 0 | 1 | .000 | 0 | 1 | 0 | 1.000 |
| 1975—American | 2B | 5 | 0 | 1 | 0 | 0 | 0 | 0 | 0 | 1 | 0 | .200 | 3 | 1 | 0 | 1.000 |
| 1976—American | 1B | 3 | 0 | 0 | 0 | 0 | 0 | 0 | 0 | 1 | 1 | .000 | 9 | 2 | 0 | 1.000 |
| 1977—American | 1B | 3 | 1 | 1 | 0 | 0 | 0 | 0 | 0 | 0 | 0 | .333 | 7 | 0 | 0 | 1.000 |
| 1978—American | 1B | 4 | 2 | 2 | 0 | 2 | 0 | 0 | 0 | 0 | 0 | .500 | 6 | 1 | 0 | 1.000 |
| All-Star Game Totals ... | | 31 | 5 | 5 | 0 | 2 | 0 | 1 | 5 | 2 | 2 | .161 | 37 | 18 | 0 | 1.000 |

Named to American League All-Star Team in 1970; replaced because of injury.

# Index

243

# About the Authors

ROD CAREW, a native of Panama, has proven himself to be one of the best hitters in the history of baseball. During an outstanding career that has spanned more than a decade, he has won innumerable accolades. In 1967 he was named American League Rookie of the Year and in 1977 was the league's Most Valuable Player. Named to the American League All-Star Team each year of his career, he has won an amazing seven league batting titles. Carew is married and has three children.

IRA BERKOW was born and raised in Chicago and now lives in New York City. He won a Front Page award when with the Minneapolis Tribune and has been a syndicated feature columnist for Newspaper Enterprise Association. He is the author of MAXWELL STREET, BEYOND THE DREAM and THE DUSABLE PANTHERS, and co-author with Walt Frazier of ROCKIN' STEADY.